Victorian furniture

STUDIES IN
DESIGN
AND
MATERIAL
CULTURE

general editor
Paul Greenhalgh

Victorian furniture
Technology and design

Clive D. Edwards

MANCHESTER UNIVERSITY PRESS
Manchester and New York

distributed exclusively in the USA and Canada by St. Martin's Press

Copyright © Clive D. Edwards 1993

Published by Manchester University Press
Oxford Road, Manchester M13 9PL, UK
and Room 400, 175 Fifth Avenue, New York, NY 10010, USA

Distributed exclusively in the USA and Canada
by St. Martin's Press, Inc., 175 Fifth Avenue, New York,
NY 10010, USA

British Library Cataloguing-in-Publication Data
A catalogue record for this book is available from the British
Library

Library of Congress cataloging in publication data
    p. cm. — (Studies in design and material culture)
    Includes bibliographical references and index.
    ISBN 0–7190–3782–4
    1. Furniture industry and trade—England. 2. Furniture,
Victoria—England. 3. Furniture industry and trade—United States.
4. Furniture, Victorian—United States. I. Title. II. Series.
TS810.G7E39 1993
684.1'0942'09034—dc20   93–16089

ISBN 0 7190 3782 4 *hardback*
ISBN 0 7190 3783 2 *paperback*

Typeset in Times
by Graphicraft Typesetters Ltd., Hong Kong
Printed in Great Britain
by Redwood Books, Trowbridge

To the memory of my parents

Contents

Contents

Figures

Figures

Acknowledgements

The research for this work was largely carried out during my tenure as a Research Fellow in the Furniture and Woodwork Collection at the Victoria and Albert Museum. I would like to thank all the colleagues in that department, especially Frances Collard and Clive Wainwright for their encouragement and support.

Gillian Naylor, of the Royal College of Art, and Charles Saumarez-Smith of the Victoria and Albert Museum, have been staunch allies and friendly critics, and I am grateful to both for their guidance.

To the committee of the Hagley/Winterthur Fellowships in Arts and Industries, I record my gratitude for the financial award which enabled me to pursue my researches in the United States.

Librarians and archivists have been helpful and considerate: I owe special thanks to Eleanor McD. Thompson of the Winterthur Library, as well as the staffs of the Hagley Library, British Library, and the National Art Library.

Of the many people who have helped me at different times and in various ways, I would particularly like to thank Judy Attfield, Edward S. Cooke Jr, William Voss Elder III, Graham Hood, Pat Kirkham, Bill Massil, Jerome Phillips, Rodris Roth, Carolyn Sargentson, and Suzette Worden, as well as the many furniture companies that answered my enquiries. Finally I extend my thanks to Lynne Green, without whose continual encouragement, advice, and assistance this work would not have been completed.

C.D.E.

General editor's foreword

Amongst the various histories which we have constructed for ourselves over the course of the past three centuries, the History of Design has been one of the more ambivalent. At various points in time, it was the most important discipline within the humanities. It held this status in many countries, for example, at the turn of this century. After this flourish, it virtually disappeared from view. Over the past twenty years, it has returned and rapidly grown in significance. It is the aim of this series to aid and consolidate this growth.

In essence, the History of Design is the history of objects. It is the study of the way we make things, the way we consume them, and the myriad of meanings they have for us. The range of functions which objects have, in the daily existence of all peoples, makes the History of Design inevitably into an inter-disciplinary subject. It must range through economic, political, aesthetic, psychological, and social discourses in order to fully expose its subject-matter.

These books will largely be concerned with the major genres of architectural ornament, ceramics, furniture, glass, graphics, jewelry, metal-working, textiles, product and interior design, and will cover painting and sculpture to provide a context for these other genres.

The Victorian furniture industry is principally interesting for the way it exposes the mythology of production systems during that period. There was no 'mass-produced' furniture, in the strictest sense of that term, made in England during Victoria's reign. Rather, Clive Edwards's narrative describes a complex infra-structure of small workshops and retailing outlets, using a mixture of new and established modes of practice. The taking on of new materials and techniques resembled less an industrial revolution, than a pragmatic and rather piecemeal process of adoption. Likewise styles, shapes, and colours. There was a demand for furniture, which the manufacturers were answerable to. As the demand fluctuated and varied, so too did the techniques and materials.

1   Introduction

In recent years furniture historians have begun to investigate the conditions of furniture production and the nature of the technology and materials used by the trade in the nineteenth century.[1] This has been partly in reaction to the art historical bias of furniture studies that have been concerned with provenance and stylistic attributes to ensure an accurate assessment of the object, while often giving only lip-service to the materials and techniques used. Such an approach has also been encouraged by the development of social and design-history disciplines, which take a greater interest in technology and its associated products. As Ettema has pointed out, 'much of the confusion about the way technology was employed in furniture manufacture stems from the persistent desire to view furniture as a decorative art.'[2] This confusion can be diminished by acknowledging that the majority of the products of the nineteenth century furniture trade were for the popular market, and the decorative art objects represent a small section of the total output.

Concurrent with this thinking has been an interest from furniture historians in the conditions of furniture production, the organisation of the trade, and the importance of distribution and consumption. The impact of this 'new history', which is more interested in the life of people, the production and consumption of products, and the interest in material culture, combined with the influence of the social sciences, has led to a complete re-evaluation of Victorian culture.[3] It is in this context that my investigations into the materials and manufacturing techniques of Victorian furniture have been undertaken.

This re-examination of the familiar principally looks at the nature of the materials and technology that were used and available to furniture-makers during the nineteenth century. The somewhat arbitrary period of 1800–1900 can be taken only as a guide, but it is

1

argued that innovations and improvements occurred to a greater extent in this period than in any other except the twentieth century. Indeed, many innovations founded in the nineteenth century were the bases of even greater changes wrought in the twentieth. Although there were pockets of time during the century which seem to have had a greater preponderance of changes taking place within them, it has been necessary to cover the whole time-scale to illustrate the nature and degree of progression.

In addition to this wide chronological remit, the geographical focus is not limited to Britain. Although the study concentrates on achievements in Britain (especially England), references are often made to experiences in Europe and the United States. This is particularly necessary as the finished-goods trade was international, as was the machine-tool business in which the United States and France were leaders. Secondly, research into the nature of manufacture in the United States has led to a greater understanding of the position of the trade in the United Kingdom. By drawing comparisons and contrasts between the two, a greater illumination of both occurs.

It should be apparent that the focus of this work is towards two main areas: technology and materials. The chapter on technology is based on an analysis of changes in manufacturing, along with a series of case studies that take certain aspects of furniture-making and trace changes within them. The materials chapter is centred around a number of case studies that examine the changing role of a variety of furniture-making materials.

The nature and role of patents are studied in Chapter 4. The importance of the patent system and the impact it had on furniture-making and design is discussed, with the aim of identifying the role of innovation and invention within nineteenth century furniture-making.

The debate about design is examined in Chapter 6. The central issue of industrialisation as a destroyer of handwork, and its consequent effect on design, is a theme running throughout the century.

Consideration had been given to the inclusion of other important aspects of nineteenth century furniture history, e.g. 'the battle of the styles', the exhibitions, and the growth of the trade press; but these were rejected in favour of a concentration on the main themes of material and technique.

The overall question I am addressing relates to how technology and materials were used to alter, improve, or otherwise change furniture design and manufacture in the nineteenth century. The term 'design' in this context relates to the process of planning the creation of a product, thereby covering a variety of elements or categories. These include concepts, economics, ergonomics and comfort, and style (two others, technology and materials, are discussed in separate chapters), and all these elements have acted as guide-lines for the methodology in this work.[4]

Concepts are crucial as a basis for new or continuing designs. The furniture business has perhaps suffered from having a long tradition of types, shapes, and forms that have become recognised as the norm. It takes an enormous effort to break free from preconceived conceptions, and the public reaction is always unpredictable. This question of tradition is one aspect that will keep recurring in this work and I have labelled it 'the enduring nature'. The label applies equally to techniques, materials, designs, workshop practice, and the attitudes to all of these from makers, critics, and consumers alike.

Economic objectives are always in a 'tug-of-war' situation as an element in manufacture. On the one hand, the consumer demands value for money and makes cross-market comparisons; on the other hand, other non-furniture markets make demands on a limited consumer budget, and the manufacturer has to show a profit. The introduction of technological solutions have some influence here, but cost control and the re-shaping of the manufacturing and distribution systems had an equally great effect on the economics of the trade during the century. It is one of the tempting arguments of technological determinism that efficiency, alias profitability, becomes the only norm for progress and change.[5] The idea that new technologies and techniques tended to subsume existing practices is incorrect. What happened in the furniture trade was a coexistence of traditional methods alongside the new advances, thus giving the maker an increased repertoire of skills, materials, and techniques. The impact of the new was therefore not necessarily a dramatic one, but was rather an assimilation, from a wider choice, of what each maker or factory required for their particular product and market.[6]

Ergonomics, and its associated notion of comfort, is my third element of design. As a science it was hardly considered by nineteenth century furniture-makers, but the intriguing possibility that consumers were sitting differently and consequently needed different

3

supporting systems was proposed by Giedion in the 1940s.[7] Forty has argued more recently that it seems implausible that the nineteenth century should have devised a new way of sitting.[8] However, it may be possible to imagine a demand for greater comfort brought about by more of the population living in homes separated from the workplace, and by the increasing demand for facilities to enable relaxation in private. This is the distinction between acceptable and unacceptable social behaviour which may have encouraged new shapes of furniture and new techniques of production to make them.[9]

In addition to comfort, cost, and suitability, consumers demanded other attributes from an object that would convey particular images and connotations to themselves and to others. Furniture and furnishings are a classic case of unspoken communication. They reflect the times and conditions that have made them, but at the same time express the aspirations and values of the owner. It was one purpose of technology and materials science to respond to these elements of design, by enabling makers to meet these unseen public demands. The point is demonstrated by K. Grier: 'chairs are most expressive in a context of use, where they are part of a communicative unit including the sitter, the dress of the occupant and his or her deportment.'[10]

Industry and machine

It used to be a truism that much nineteenth century furniture was cheap and nasty, and that it was invariably made by machine. Early twentieth century commentators exaggerated the power of the machine in relation to furniture manufacture, and this discouraged any serious study of the popular furniture of the nineteenth century for a long while. Although this aspect of nineteenth century furniture studies has since changed, accounts of the supposedly adverse influence of machines and mass production on design and production may still be found.[11] The continuing confusion about the impact of factory modernisation and mechanisation on design is well illustrated in a quote from a general study of furniture (Grant 1976): 'technological processes were directly responsible for radically changing the appearance of furniture.'[12]

One of the purposes of this work is to evaluate the substance of such statements. John Oliver was among the first to respond to these traditional approaches towards the history of the furniture trade.[13] He suggested that the period 1870–1919 may be regarded as the *dawn of the machine age*. This date range, which is considerably later than once thought, was qualified by the crucial point that the dawn was one of machine-assisted craft, and any change was a very slow transition from the craft orientated workshops to factories. In a study of the High Wycombe furniture trade, I was able to confirm this by showing that the changes from the craft to machine-based production only really occurred after World War I, encouraged by wartime aircraft production and its associated demands.[14]

On a broader note, Samuel (1977) remarked that the process of mechanisation in Britain in general was slowed for reasons such as the relative abundance of labour, better use of hand technology, the division of labour, and the specific profitability coming from small economic organisations.[15] The furniture industry is a good case study to support this theory, as it was for these same reasons that the impact of the machine age on the furniture business was slowed.

Some furniture scholars have taken a fresh look at the nineteenth century trade. Edward Joy (1977) has shown that the trade organisation of the nineteenth century was established in the eighteenth century. For much of the nineteenth century it was based on workshops set up in urban areas to supply local needs, or in the case of London (the centre of the trade), to supply a local, national, and international market.[16] During the century, the trade began to divide into the larger manufacturers who were able to produce a complete range of furniture, the specialist manufacturers who limited their range, and the small producers who produced cheap furniture for wholesalers and drapers (see Chapter 2, Industrial organisation). Kirkham (1988) has identified the 'comprehensive manufacturing firm': organisations which were notable for bringing all the main crafts under one roof.[17] This form of organisation was generally limited to the quality trade and based on the principle of complete house furnishing, rather than the production of furniture for resale to a third party. The majority of this category of firm's output would have been special orders for private customers, and would therefore have been individually produced.[18]

The bulk of the trade was also divided between the so-called honourable and dishonourable sections. The honourable section, generally located in the West End of London, employed unionised

Victorian furniture

labour, paid regular wages, and demanded a high standard of work. The dishonourable side revolved around the sweated labour of garret masters who produced goods 'on spec', and generally limited themselves to a particular specialism. These enterprises were geographically based in the East End of London, but it is worth noting that both these trade types also existed in the larger towns and cities of Britain. This division between the honourable and dishonourable trade helps shed some light on the myths of mass production and machine-made innovations. The organisation of the honourable section of the trade was based on quality production of a wide variety of objects. It may seem to be a paradox that when machinery was introduced into the trade, it was these larger businesses, producing the higher quality objects, that exploited its advantages.

Contrary to this, in the dishonourable trade, the maker was confined to producing the same type of object. Such narrow organisation was not conducive to any sort of investment in machinery, and resulted in an increasing division of labour and a consequent reduction of wages. This end of the trade also grew to service the rising demand from retail outlets who were not producers, which in turn ensured the maintenance of the status quo by encouraging more operatives to set up on their own to produce their specialism, thus continuing the sweating system.

With few exceptions, much of the technology and 'new' materials that were introduced in the period under review, were directed at reproducing whichever of the fashionable styles was prevalent at any particular time, and producing it as cheaply and efficiently as possible. For example, R. C. Smith, an American historian, has suggested that:

The success of the style [Rococo Revival] coincided with the application of new mechanical techniques that led to mass production methods in the cutting of scrolls and irregular frames and the carving of ornament.[19]

In other words, rather than leading style changes, technology was most often used to meet the growing demand for an existing style.

All the evidence points to the fact that most of the machines applied to woodworking processes in the nineteenth century were used in the prime conversion of raw materials and the preparation of parts. Although machines could make decoration for furniture, the assembly was always a hand operation. In other words, there was only a gradual change in the nature of making furniture.

David Pye's ideas on the nature of risk and certainty in workmanship are helpful in analysing the process.[20] Pye suggests that when the result of operations can be determined solely by the skill of the workman, there is an amount of risk in the result. As processes began to use machines that acted in a predetermined or programmed way, and were outside the operator's control, the resultant work would have a higher degree of certainty. The implications of this are that greater quantities of usable furniture might be made to a particular standard with the introduction of machines. This was increasingly so during the latter part of the nineteenth century, due to the undoubted growth in the use of machines, but it does not explain the apparently paradoxical growth in the workforce which occurred during the period 1850–1900 (see Table 1), especially when received opinion often suggests that the machine displaced labour. It would appear that the increase in labour indicates the very specialist nature of machine use across the trade which was supplementary to the growing semi-skilled labour force. Often mechanical processes were only viable in large economic units that were able to keep the machines fully operational, and therefore their introduction by much of the furniture trade was limited.

As late as 1919, a government committee could remark that 'the economic unit in furniture manufacturing still remains the small master, who in his turn has to compete with the independent worker, producing on his own account in the backyard or back room of his dwelling.'[21] This approach to business organisation may be seen to be the ideal response to the differentiated demands of the period that required a wide assortment of objects to satisfy localised markets and the ability to respond to changes in fashion as they occurred. It was also responsible for the iniquitous sweating system, whereby retail and wholesale outlets would take advantage of the independent maker. Being without capital, an independent had to rely on the sale of one item to be able to produce another, so this was exploited by some retailers, who pressurised the craftsman for the cheapest price, thus increasing their own profit.

Some critics have acknowledged that large-scale furniture manufacture, powered by machinery, was not a major feature of the nineteenth century trade: they have, however, sometimes assumed that

Victorian furniture

Table 1 *Number of workers involved in the wood, furniture and carriage trades, 1841–1881*

Year	1841	1851	1861	1871	1881

270,000

260,000

250,000

240,000

230,000

220,000

210,000

200,000

190,000

180,000

170,000

160,000

150,000

	1841	1851	1861	1871	1881
Males	166,700	202,700	226,000	238,000	248,500
Females	4,900	9,200	15,400	21,500	20,800

Source: G. Routh, *Occupations of the People of Great Britain 1801–1981*, London, 1987.

technical innovations led to increased furniture production at lower prices.[22] This has privileged the power of technology in the furniture trade with too great an influence.[23] It is important to remember that the furniture trade was first and foremost a business, subject to all the economic forces that affected other trades. Any changes, including the development of new products and investment in machinery, would only be brought about if there was an economic advantage to be gained. However, there were a number of these developments and I have made a detailed study of some technological initiatives that did have an influence on furniture-making and design. These include wood-bending and laminating, changes in carcase construction techniques, veneering, machine carving, and upholstery springs. Many of these processes and operations were subject to patent protection.

Patents and innovation

There is little doubt that one of the major features of the nineteenth century was innovation of all kinds. As innovation is spurred by economic benefit, it is not surprising to find that variation in demand was one of the main instruments of change. These changes are both consumer and producer led. Typical consumer demands are portability, the combination of functions, particular or unique solutions for seating or sleeping, and high-style objects at the cheapest prices. Producer demands include the use of new materials to reduce costs or increase market share; the introduction of new manufacturing techniques for similar reasons; labour-saving machinery; and novelty of design. To cut costs and achieve higher sales it might seem that the interface between technology and the two types of demand might have found some common ground.

The patent records can give some insight into what processes and techniques were being invented, although it is less easy to quantify how many of these ideas were taken up and used in the trade generally. Any successful technology was responding to a need, and was sometimes directly responsible for creating a demand.

The introduction or revival of a wide choice of materials such as bamboo, cast-iron, wicker, papier mâché, or gutta percha, enabled manufacturers to offer a range of goods and finishes which gave choice and had the all-important ingredient of novelty value. Not only are these natural materials interesting *per se*, but throughout the century, processes were developed which gradually altered the nature of the material in a wide variety of ways. Although unaltered natural materials were most popular, there was an acceptance of transformed materials, and indeed materials that bore no relation to their natural state, as long as they satisfied other criteria. Examples of materials that created an illusion were finishes imitating more expensive processes, and added decoration that was intended to appear integral.

The case studies relating to the invention of materials often show that the initiatives came from outside the traditional trade. The furniture business, always a craft-based operation, never considered itself a leader in the use of innovatory materials or production techniques. It accepted new ideas only when they were economically viable, but otherwise saw no need for change. The 'industrial revolution' in the furniture trade had to wait until the twentieth century.

Notes

1 See, for example, Kirkham, 'London furniture trade'; J. Porter *et al.*, *Furnishing the World*, exhibition catalogue, Geffrye Museum, 1988; E. S. Cooke, 'The study of American furniture from the perspective of the maker', in *Perspectives on American Furniture*, 1988.
2 Ettema, 'Technological innovation and design economics', p. 196.
3 See, for example, the *Winterthur Portfolio* series: Forty, *Objects of Desire*; Fraser, *The Coming of the Mass Market*; Miller, *Material Culture and Mass Production*.
4 Edward Cooke has usefully described design as composition; in that composition is the process by which craftsmen draw from experience and observation a structural, technical and decorative solution to the question of creation. The craftsman makes the decisions, derived from choices of alternatives that suit the physical and social environment, and his own expectations and needs: Cooke, 'Study of American Furniture', p. 122.
5 See Chapter 2 for a further discussion of technological determinism.
6 I am indebted to Edward Cooke for discussions about this subject.
7 Giedion, *Mechanisation Takes Command*, p. 396. See also 'The scientific principles of easy chairs', *Furniture Gazette*, 9 November 1878.
8 Forty, *Objects of Desire*, p. 92.
9 Scientific principles of sitting encouraged designs that raised the feet such as chaise-longues, kangaroo chairs, etc. In the twentieth century, Le Corbusier argued that there were three ways of sitting: upright and formal for work situations; casual lounging for conversation; and complete relaxation with the feet level with the head: see C. Benton, 'Le Corbusier, furniture and the interior', *Journal of Design History*, III, 1990, p. 113.
10 Grier, *Culture and Comfort*, p. 108.
11 For example, see A. Blunt, *Phaidon Guide to Furniture*, 1978, pp. 204–6.
12 Grant, 'The machine age', p. 191.
13 Oliver, *Development and Structure of the Furniture Industry*, p. 81. (John Oliver worked in a geographical discipline.)
14 C. Edwards, *Stimulus and response. An investigation into changes in the furniture industry 1880–1920*, unpublished MA thesis, Royal College of Art, 1988; see Case Study on High Wycombe.
15 Samuel, 'Workshop of the world', pp. 6–72.

16 Joy, *English Furniture.*

17 Kirkham, 'London furniture trade'.

18 The remaining records of the Gillow company testify to this. An inspection of the 'estimate sketch books' reveals the singular nature of each order.

19 R. C. Smith, 'Rococo Revival furniture 1850–1870', *Antiques*, May 1959, p. 471.

20 Pye, *Nature and Art of Workmanship.*

21 *Profiteering Acts 1919–1920. Report of the Sub-Committee on Investigation into Prices in the Furniture Trade.*

22 See Earl, 'Craftsmen and machines'.

23 Although see Wright, *Thirteenth Annual Report of the Commission of Labor.*

2   Technology and technique

Introduction

The distinction between technology and technique, two similar words whose meanings are often confused, is cogently summarised by Ingold:

> technique is embedded in the experience of the particular shaping of particular things: technology is a body of objective generalized knowledge embodied in the structure of the machine and manifested in its performance. Technique places the subject at the centre of making activity, whereas technology affirms the independence of production from human subjectivity.[1]

This summary makes a clear distinction between technique as individual process and technology as a general structure of knowledge: it is clear that the nineteenth century furniture industry saw the partial and gradual change from the application of technique to the use of technology. Some further de-construction of the notion of technology will help to understand these changes more easily.

Mitcham (1978) has identified four components that are part of an explanation of technology: purpose, knowledge, activity, and artifacts.[2] The first part, purpose, relates to the degree of purposive activity or volition that instigates production. The distinction becomes apparent when used to compare a craftsman's personal involvement in a product and a machinist's impersonal activity. In terms of furniture-making, this refers to the very gradual change from joiner to cabinet-maker to machine-minder and assembler. Of course this simplifies the situation, but relates to an individual's degree of involvement in the production of a furniture item, resulting in a product that reflects that involvement.

The next part, knowledge, refers to the distinction between skill and intelligence or 'know-how'. Skill is simply manual dexterity or the manual techniques of a practitioner, whereas 'know-how' enables a person to envisage forms in advance. Ingold notes that 'the priority of technology as "know-how" over technique as skill marks a crucial threshold in the evolution of human constructive abilities, making possible the deliberate design of new forms'.[3] Again this distinguishes an operator from a craftsman.

The third aspect, activity, pertains to processes of making and using, which are differentiated by degrees of skill or technique. The difference between the activities of a joiner and a cabinet-maker are marked by the difference in skilled processes. For example, a certain amount of knowledge is required to cut joints; a greater amount is required to make a veneered commode.

Lastly, technology as artifacts. Here the whole range of fabricated items are part of technology, but a distinction is to be drawn between artifacts and instruments (or tools). Artifacts are complete in themselves; instruments are artifacts as well as part of the process of making.

It will be useful to continue this analysis and draw distinctions between machines and tools. The process of change from hand-tools via human-powered tool or machine-tools to automatic machines will be discussed later, but some general definitions can be proposed here. Hand-tools allow the operator to supply power and to control the operation, while machine-tools supply external power but remain under the operator's skilled control. Man-powered machines give no control, simply power. Automatic machines remove both power and control from the maker. These distinctions relate to the degree of involvement of man and machine in the final product.

By applying Mitcham's components to the methods and processes of furniture-making since the eighteenth century, it can be seen that technology has, in varying degrees, gradually superseded technique in many aspects of production. This moves the human from the centre to the edges of the productive process, and this change has often been associated with the alleged relentless advance of the machine.

Publications about the development of technology relating to furniture-making and design have usually followed a diachronic path based on a progression from the medieval carpenter via the joiner, to the cabinet-maker and finally to the machinist. In this journey, the techniques of construction, decoration, and finishing are related to the degree of sophistication achieved by the various craftsmen. This process of sequential development can be identified as 'technological determinism'. The theory suggests that there is an inevitable path of technical development along which societies will travel. This argument is reinforced by three ideas identified by Heilbronner.[4]

First is the concept of simultaneous inventions. This refers to situations where societies at roughly the same level of development in a sphere of endeavour, will devise a new or improved method within a few years of each other; an example of this process might be the development of the rotary veneer-cutter. It was introduced in Russia, France, the United States, and England between 1817 and 1847, by completely independent individuals with no obvious contact, but they all perceived the benefits of the new process within a few years of each other (see Veneering, below). Some developments tend to reinforce the idea that evolving societies of similar standing reach similar points of advancement at a particular time. There are, however, other plausible reasons, such as the copying of technology and the transferral of knowledge via journals and exhibitions.

The second point Heilbronner suggests, is that technological innovations seem to develop by a process of incremental advances rather than by sudden leaps. The development of springs might serve as an example, whereby the gradual development of a type, slowly became more advanced and suitable for a growing list of applications. Third, the argument continues, technologically determined advances in science appear to be intrinsically predictable. By linking advances in science to developments in technology, which are themselves linked to improvements in expertise and skill, a predictable and fixed sequence can be mapped out.

So far this argument has suggested that science and technology lead the search for knowledge, and by definition create progress and change. These assumptions ignore three important points. Firstly, the distinctions between various technologies are ignored by referring to technology in the singular. Developments in cabinet-making moved at a far faster pace than those of upholstery, for example. Secondly, the assumption that all technological change encourages progress is questionable. There are many who would disagree with this statement, particularly considering that with every advancement comes a whole series of disadvantages. Thirdly, the social perspective which relates the question of design and making to the end use of the product, must take into account the nature of the market. In other words, the theory of technologically determined design ignores the influence of the consumer.

The changing organisation of a craft into an industry was allegedly based on changes in techniques; advocates of technological determinism would view this as a progression from hand production, through batch manufacture, to mass production. Certainly in the instance of the furniture industry this simplistic explanation was never applicable. It is evident then, that technological determinism, with its one-way and autonomous cultural impact, is an unsatisfactory explanation of the relation between technology and design in a society.

A more realistic model proposed by Staudenmaier (1985) is a concept he has labelled as a 'momentum model'.[5] It is based on the idea that changes in technology are ineffectual unless they are part of a set of cultural values relating to institutions or individuals. This model replaces the abstract notion of progress, and substitutes the idea that cultures prioritise given technologies which then become the agents of dynamic change. A classic example from the woodworking industry might be Bentham's inventions relating to machinery for the preparation of wood (see below). The impact at the time was limited to the specific needs of the naval departments, related to ship-building, and it had no influence on the furniture industry for fifty years. It was only when social and cultural developments espoused the need for machinery that its full impact was felt.

The reasons for the usefulness of the 'momentum model' are not hard to find. The model takes the idea of the 'enduring nature' of aspects of society which affect its relations with technology, and gives an attractive reason for technological change based on need rather than notional progress. The furniture industry is an especially good example of this. The enduring nature of existing technical concepts, a continuation of the old ways, was frequently ingrained in furniture-makers. Specific methods that had become the dominant process tended to perpetuate themselves and hinder any radical innovations, because they worked satisfactorily.

Apart from this perpetuation of traditional methods, there were economic considerations that slowed the impact of technology on the furniture trade. The reluctance to re-invest or improve existing facilities was partly due to the fragmentary nature of a trade that was based on the activities of a multitude of small traders, and which inhibited attempts to amalgamate, diversify, and grow. The impact on design as a result of these drawbacks should not go unnoticed. When an item was made by a craftsman, the design repertoire was limited only by his own capabilities; when factories produced batches of furniture using jigs, or moulds, etc., the designs were limited to the predetermined components available, and variety was only achieved by mixing parts and adding various accessories. The enduring nature of styles or models is often seen in pattern books which might be as much as fifty years apart but still illustrate the same article. Among a number of examples the trade price books are the best. However, these production methods should not be seen as too much of a brake on variety, as the expansion of supply of pre-prepared parts was an ever-growing business.

Even the nineteenth century's abiding enthusiasm for technology, which often resulted in solutions looking for problems, had relatively little effect on furniture due to the cultural values of the persons involved. It must be remembered that the aims of business were to achieve an optimum level of profitability. If this could be achieved without investment in plant and machinery then there was little reason to introduce it. Technology was often only seen as a response to other innovations, or as a method of 'beating the competition'. Using the 'momentum model' as a basis for the analysis of furniture-making techniques, I shall show how traditional methods of construction, decoration, and finishing continued right through the century. I will also demonstrate how, in some parts of the trade, some of these processes underwent significant changes as cultural and economic demands made amendments necessary. In addition to these two ideas, the model helps to show how changes in design are more related to social conditions than mechanical ones. Nevertheless, there were developments in technique that were important to the trade and I will examine them to identify what they were and what influence they had on design and production. These developments can be classified under two headings: innovative in themselves, or improvements on existing processes. Case studies of innovative techniques and processes that I will study in depth include bentwood, machine-carving, construction, finishing, mechanical decoration, and veneering. Existing processes that were improved include sawing, veneer-cutting, and, most important in the long term, the mechanisation of basic processes that would either allow a craftsman more time to devote to his real skills or encourage the growth of batch production systems using semi-skilled labour.

Manufacturing and the use of machines

> The timber is cut to the requisite shape by means of handsaw, lathe, planing machine and other admirable but somewhat terrible inventions which deal with a log as though it were so much soft cheese.[6]

The development of the furniture industry has been a continual process, but change has been gradual rather than radical. Like many other trades that had to adapt to a new set of circumstances in the nineteenth century, its problem was its traditions. Unlike many other trades, the industry did not take much advantage of the new possibilities that were then made available to it. Society prioritised certain technologies such as transport and communications, weapons production, materials science, etc., but, if it did not ignore other industries such as furniture, it certainly did not push them. During the period of the 'classic' industrial revolution, the furniture-makers did not industrialise in the same way as the engineering or cotton industry did. The trade's response was to react to changed circumstances in the nineteenth century rather than to spearhead innovation. It could be said that the era was to make demands upon a trade that appeared ill-equipped to handle them. However, the position of the trade did improve. An increasing turnover encouraged a growth in employment and this confirms that the machine did not cause unemployment, although it did redistribute job types. The industrial organisation of the trade and the nature of machine use are an integral part of the history of the influence of technology on the furniture trade of the nineteenth century.

Industrial organisation

The English furniture industry at the beginning of the nineteenth century was similar in many respects to the previous century's trade. The eighteenth century industry could be roughly divided into four divisions: independent working masters, craftsmen shopkeepers, businesses combining manufacturing and retailing, and retailers. There was a centre of trade based in London; and the various crafts were divided and sub-divided so as to provide groups of specialists in any particular production field.[7] In the provinces it was often a different matter: the local carpenter might have to double as a furniture-maker, undertaker and so on, although some towns and cities developed considerable furniture-making businesses. Such features in the trade organisation continued well into the nineteenth century.

In one of the great contemporary studies of nineteenth century industry, George Dodd (1843), described the furniture business:

> The tables, the chairs, [etc.] all are made to a vast extent in London, but not generally in large factories: they are the production of tradesmen, each of whom can carry on a tolerably extensive business without great extent of room, or a large number of workmen.[8]

This extract illustrates the point that there was no wave of factory building, and by implication mechanisation, commonly associated with nineteenth century furniture production.

Contemporary critics of the Victorian industry also noticed the lack of mechanisation due to the availability of labour at the lower end of the trade. Booth's survey in London (1888) noted that:

> machinery for these [cabinet-making] processes is rarely set up in a market in which workers are so numerous and labour so cheap as in the East End of London. There the small system prevails, and there are no signs that it will not continue to hold its own against the large system that would have to take its place if all the processes were ordinarily done by machinery.[9]

The individual worker gradually became limited in his repertoire and was capable of producing only a small range of designs, so it is not surprising to find that a majority of basic furniture designs, especially those published for trade use, remained similar over long periods of time, with only minor decorative changes.

A noticeable feature of the trade was that until after World War I, there was a lack of integration and amalgamation (similar to that which had occurred in other industries), with a consequent lack of capital expenditure on plant and machinery. One of the reasons for this was that furniture-makers constantly had to juggle with the problem of balancing the factors of costs and style.

Economies of scale could not be made when such a volatile demand for merchandise was being encouraged by the retail outlets. A continually changing demand for a choice of styles meant that any continuity of process or decoration could not be exploited. Even for those manufacturers who wished to develop, increased output could only be achieved by adding more men or machines, and even then actual productivity would not be much greater than from a smaller unit.[10] The craft of furniture-making was for the most part not susceptible to rationalisation.

As I have already pointed out, there were other variables that restricted or, conversely, encouraged changes in the nineteenth century trade. The economics of the furniture trade had much to do with its haphazard and piecemeal growth. However, it was not only the manufacturing end of the cycle that posed problems. Indeed the nature of the consumption of furniture was integral to the equation. The ownership of furniture, above the very barest essentials, has often been considered something of a luxury. The market was therefore very volatile. During boom times there was an enthusiastic market, but during slumps one of the first trades to feel the effects was the furniture trade. Under these trading conditions it can be no surprise that technical progress was relatively slow and was limited to the necessities of meeting demands or adapting methods to save money and improve profitability. It is interesting to speculate that it was perhaps only in the twentieth century that the two World Wars produced sufficient incentives to develop new materials and methods in woodworking and manipulation of materials that could be used later in furniture-making.

Machine use

Confusion about the role of machines can be reduced by attempting to ascertain whether they democratised the production of well-made furniture.

Therefore, the question to be addressed in this section concerns mechanical methods in manufacturing: did these allow for the production of vastly increased amounts of goods, with the added bonus of reproducing cheaply and easily the decoration that had previously only been available to the few? The implicit assumptions have usually been that new materials and technologies introduced in the nineteenth century altered the balance between cost factors and design factors. They were apparently altered in favour of allowing

1 Ransome and Co.'s irregular moulding and shaping machine, complete with examples of finished work

makers to produce high-style products at low prices. The main assumption within this perceived trend, was that the use of machines made these design changes possible.

The evidence so far has indicated a very piecemeal approach to the use of machinery in England. The enduring nature of techniques already mentioned, applied to tools and machines as well. The circumstances of the English trade were such that the impact of changes in this area were at best uneven.

John Richards, author of a treatise on woodworking machinery (1872), referred to Furness and Co. and their importation of American woodworking machines in the 1840s. He noted that 'the ruling idea in these machines was economy in cost, and rapid performance in the hands of skilled men, neither of which elements fitted them for the English market at the time'.[11] In other words, labour costs were not a major consideration for British manufacturers, while skilled machine operators were at a premium in the 1840s. Richards also suggested that the real savings using machinery were quite small:

as a rough estimate, the labour and the materials in common household furniture is about equal in value and the saving effect due to machine work must be estimated on the labour alone. Now to go to facts we shall find in England and North America that the general saving effected by the use of machinery does not exceed fifteen percent, as an average; it is even so little that in some instances we yet find hand labour competing in the manufacture of chairs, tables, &c., and were it not for the division of labour, carried out by the exclusive operations of the manufactories where machinery is employed, the difference would be still less.[12]

Nevertheless there was a belief that machinery ought to reduce prices. Pollen (1877) pointed out that the hoped-for cheapness resulting from the employment of machines was not forthcoming, but rather the use of machines brought a greater profit for the manufacturer:

Neat furniture, unornamented by hand work, ought to be turned out of the engine room, the perfection of lightness, convenience and strength. And here the buyer will look for the advantage of cheapness. We do not find that our large makers supply well-made furniture cheap. As a broad rule, prices seem to be calculated on what a man would do and work done in the machine is priced as if a man had made it by hand. In point of fact, five or six men's work is done in the same time, and the cost of wages charged in articles so made, will leave a disproportionate profit, notwithstanding the expense of setting up and maintaining the steam plant.[13]

However resistant the furniture-makers were to machinery, a growing demand, a declining level of skill in the workforce, and economic pressures led gradually to a wider acceptance of the need for some mechanisation. One solution was found in a mix of labour and machines. The labour components of this mix were semi-skilled men who had to be directed towards a 'workmanship of certainty', using specialised machines to perform particular tasks in the production sequence. The results of this were then assembled, fitted and finished by the balance of the workforce.

I have already suggested that in England machine technology was employed only when necessary, and was not deliberately used to dispel handwork unless this course was economically viable. This reluctant attitude to change was noticed in respect of the continued use of the pole lathe in High Wycombe chair-making districts. The *Furniture Gazette* (1877) told its readers that

it seems almost incredible that in this, the last quarter of the nineteenth century, any intelligent man can be found who will go on day after day with arrangements that were old when their grandfathers were born, instead of adopting the improvements which have been introduced in the construction of the lathe.[14]

Nevertheless, it was presumably worthwhile to continue with these traditional methods, albeit in ever decreasing amounts, while an economic advantage existed. The pole lathe, already cited, continued to be used by chair bodgers well into the twentieth century, and is a perfect example of the enduring nature of trade practice. In contrast, another contemporary critic suggested that machinery had all but taken over in furniture-making. Mateaux (1883) described a furniture factory in eulogistic terms:

> Everywhere machinery is busy with the simplest and most complicated forms and things it has to do. Man seems merely its servant to attend upon and put together properly the parts and pieces of timber it has planed, sawed, cut and carved or turned, ready for his hands.[15]

When machines were introduced they were often designed to break bottlenecks in the production system or alternatively to assist handwork. For example, delays occurred when timber and veneers were sawn by hand, so the first part of furniture-making to be mechanised was the conversion of wood. An important incident in furniture-making labour history also gives a clear impression of some of the 'bottlenecking' problems connected with machine production when it was associated with hand methods. In November 1874, the workforce (who were members of the Alliance Cabinet-Makers' Association) of Jackson and Graham withdrew their labour. According to the union report, the men

> complained to the firm that they were compelled to lose much time waiting for the machinery in a machine-assisted hand production situation. If the machinists had not got the next work roughed out or converted, the men had to wait until they did so, but without receiving any payment for this waiting time.[16]

This was the result of using an unbalanced combination of part machine and part hand labour. Bottlenecks therefore inevitably occurred, and to some extent the history of the development of machines in furniture-making is linked, in part, to attempts to remove these obstacles in the production run. This becomes a continual process because as soon as a machine is introduced to unblock a bottleneck it creates another one at a further stage.

Whatever the problems caused by the use of machines, there was a growing acceptance of their role alongside handwork. Discussing machine-carving, a *Scientific American* reporter wrote:

the simplest [carvings] are at present made by ingenious mechanical processes, for it is now well recognised in industry that certain things are best done by machinery whilst others are better executed by the hands of man.[17]

The craftsmen saw some obvious benefits when machines were applied to cabinet-making. C. Hooper, one of the artisans sent out by the Society of Arts to report on the 1867 Paris Exhibition, noted that much of the drudgery of preparation had been removed: 'In shape work, the wood is cut by machinery as well as by hand, and very close and fine, so in cleaning of it only requires the scraper and glass paper to finish'.[18] The important point shown by these details is that even when machines were used they only assisted production – no machine in the nineteenth century ever made furniture.

Nevertheless there were some commentators who thought that that time was not far away. Mateaux envisaged amazing results from the machine:

By the time we have seen half the wonders it [the machine] can produce out of wood, we should not be so very astonished to see a plank placed in one end of some iron monster, come out a finished chest of drawers or a neat armchair at the other.[19]

This illustrates the great gap between the culturally acceptable concepts of mechanisation and the actual capability and practice of the trade.

There is still much confusion between producing furniture with machines, and the machine preparation of timber parts for use by furniture-makers. This confusion is compounded by the idea that the machine is often closely associated with mass production, which allegedly results in a subsequent lowering of quality, and a standardisation of design. The development of the process of making interchangeable parts that could be assembled in a particular order may be seen to hail the beginning of mass production in the few industries that took it up. The furniture trade rarely did. However, this was not necessarily because the technology was not available. Copying-lathes were able to produce quantities of similar parts to an original: timber could be cut to fixed sizes and shapes, using jigs; parts could be prepared and jointed ready for assembly; and decoration could be produced in a number of artificial materials for speedy and consistent supply. Why did the trade not take advantage of

23

these sorts of innovations to develop their industry, enabling production of large quantities of high-style objects at cheaper prices?
Perhaps one major reason was due to the costs involved in setting-
up steam-powered works. In 1850 Henry Mayhew reported that there
were sixty-eight steam mills in London. The cost of two steam
engines of ten horsepower each would be between £650 and £800. In
addition to this capital charge, there was the wage of the engineer
to supervise the machine and the cost of the one ton of coal that
each machine consumed in every twelve-hour period.[20] It is not
surprising then that it was only the large comprehensive firms that
could afford such investment.

Another more plausible reason might be that mass production
requires a developing and continual market with an inelastic demand for the same item. Any standardisation in the nineteenth
century woodwork was best exemplified by the manufacture of
gunstocks and sewing-machine cases,[21] which were the antithesis of
the furniture business because they were produced in large numbers
using repetitive designs, and were based on a simple shape formula.
The underpinning of the furniture business was founded on design
differentiation, which relied on a wide selection and a great variety
of choice in design, finish, and fabrics. This rendered 'mass production' an inappropriate form of organisation.

Machines

To fully locate the development and use of machines in furniture-
making it will be useful to distinguish three major machine categories which equate to the main processes of furniture-making.
Firstly, machines for preparing, shaping, and joint-cutting of timber,
which include circular saws, planers, mortisers, borers, dovetail
cutters, and veneer-cutters. Secondly, machines for processing and
shaping parts, which include band-saws, scroll or fretsaws, and lathes.
Thirdly, machines for decorating independently, which include
routers, moulders, embossers, and carving machines.

These machines can also be categorised into other divisions.
Some machines were owned and operated by entrepreneurs outside
the industry who operated either a bulk service for cutting and
preparing timber or let space in their workshops for individual
users. Secondly, processing machines were often of a size or price

that enabled a small workshop to employ them and were able to be operated by either human or non-human power. Finally, machined parts for decoration were often produced by separate companies who specialised in various patent processes; legs, balusters, seats, carvings, mouldings, and decorative shaped parts, were all ready for application to a carcase or frame (see Mechanical decoration, below).

Whichever breakdown of machine types one uses, the sequence of machine preparation, hand assembly, and final application of ready-made decorative parts can be seen as the basis of the trade's production system which persisted into the twentieth century. The gradual introduction of tools and machines allowed the industry to develop towards a factory system, at the same time maintaining a workshop system.[22] This meant that the development of hand tool processes into mechanised ones, still operated by human power, was the first stage of machine development, and the application of independent power to create self-acting machines followed. The history of woodworking machinery has been dealt with by a number of authors[23] but an outline here is necessary to illustrate and describe the machinery that was introduced and developed during the period.

Saws

Although sawmills had been established in the seventeenth century, these early efforts were based on attempts to replicate the reciprocal motion of the human arm through the handsaw. In 1777 Samuel Miller of Southampton patented the important concept that made the first circular saw possible.[24] Development was rapid from then on. In 1781 it was recorded that William Taylor was using circular saws[25] and in 1791 Samuel Bentham developed the principle of saw segments mounted on a disc (see also Veneering, below). In 1805 Marc Brunel took out a patent for a large circular saw[26] particularly associated with veneer-cutting, and in 1807 developed the saw further in association with block-making machinery.[27] The importance of large powered saws for converting timber has been recognised in the development of the timber, joinery, and furniture trades. However, one of the most important developments was not on this scale at all. The small circular saw of up to 7 in. diameter, often operated by a treadle, was one of the keys to the success of small-scale furniture-makers. It allowed makers of inexpensive furniture

25

to square up, mitre, and rabbet cleanly and accurately. Bitmead noted that 'The cheap furniture-makers could not work at the price they do if they did not use this saw'.[28]

According to Bitmead, in cheap carcase work the frame was not dovetailed together, rather the ends were simply rebated and nailed. This method of construction, using a circular saw, was particularly useful for drawer-making which was traditionally a place for using dovetail joints. The advantage of this cheap method was that a dozen drawers could be made in the time it took to dovetail-join just one, and it obviously had great advantages when such objects as Davenports and chests were being made.

Planing

Planing machines had been developed in a similar way to saws, and in 1776 the first machine was invented by Leonard Hatton.[29] Bentham improved upon this patent, first with a reciprocating plane and then with one based on the rotary principle. In 1827 Malcolm Muir of Glasgow patented a planing machine[30] and in 1851 William Furness of Liverpool exhibited a planing machine at the Great Exhibition. All subsequent planing machines were then based on the rotary-knife principle.

Joint-cutting

A variety of machines were introduced which enabled makers to machine-cut joints. The mortiser and tenon shaper were early developments in Britain, and the dovetail-cutter was developed in America. In particular, the Knapp dovetail-cutting machine was an important innovation, producing its own peculiar joint that was obviously not cut by hand[31] (see Chapter 5, Machinery section).

Band-saws

The development of band-saws originated with the invention of W. Newberry in 1808. However, it was not until the success of M. Perin of Paris in producing a band-saw blade which lasted reasonably well, that the machine was really viable and operated satisfactorily. Even in 1862 Clark could say that the band-saw was a 'comparatively novel class of machine'.[32] The fretsaw, also known as the jig or scroll saw, developed from the simple marquetry-cutters saw which was one of the simplest and most useful tools for the cabinet-maker.

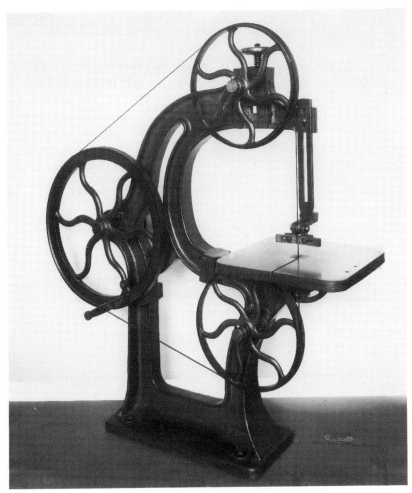

2 Band-saw. Although invented as early as 1808, it was only
commercially successful from the middle of the century

Often treadle-operated with a single blade, it could cut out intricate
shapes and satisfy the demand for the most elaborate decoration.

Ornamenting machines

The third category of machines includes two different divisions.
Firstly, the patent processes run by companies producing such items

Table 2 *Factory report figures related to the quantity of factories connected with the cabinet and furniture trades in England and Wales*

County	Factories	Steam power	Persons		Total no. of persons
			Male	Female	
Buckinghamshire	10	14	630	190	820
Cheshire	1	8	74	13	87
Devon	1	40 (water)	91	–	91
Gloucestershire	1	25	80	2	82
Hampshire	2	4	174	49	223
Lancashire	10	33	575	70	645
Middlesex	12	127	2177	281	2458
Northumberland	1	18	96	12	108
Surrey	2	10	105	27	132
Sussex	2	–	28	30	58
Warwickshire	3	6	145	117	262
Yorkshire	6	22	347	73	420
Total	51	307	4522	864	5386

Source: *Kelly's Post Office Directory of the Cabinet, Furniture and Upholstery Trades,* 1877.

as carvings, mouldings, and embossed ornament for sale to cabinet-makers (see below), and secondly, the machines that allowed a cabinet-maker to produce the decoration for his own work. The most important of this second group would seem to be the spindle moulder or toupie.

Bitmead (1873) commented that the rotary moulding cutter or toupie was quite new to English manufacturers, although it had been used for some time on the continent. He said it was particularly useful for Gothic or medieval work 'as more chamfering can be done by it in one hour than could be done by handwork in a day'.[33]

The machine in industry

By the second half of the century there was evidence of a growth in the use of machinery in factories, belonging to companies producing high-quality objects. It has already been pointed out that the high-class firms were among the first to embrace machinery and steam power. It is clear that high-quality 'hand production' businesses combined powered machines for basic operations such as sawing, veneer-cutting, and planing, with hand-assembly, decoration, and finishing. In these instances the machine became an enabling mechanism that re-distributed the nature of work, allowing some craftsmen more time to attend to the art of cabinet-making and to be relieved of the repetitive aspects of the job. Examples of this group include firms such as Holland's, Jackson and Graham, and Seddon and Co., who equipped their works with steam-powered saws, veneer-cutters and other machines during the mid-century.[34]

It was at Jackson and Graham's that Wyatt noticed that 'A steam engine, and machinery for various purposes connected with cabinet-making, have recently been erected and put into operation'.[35] The company were advertising themselves ten years later in 1866 as having an 'extensive manufactory adjoining, with machines worked by steam power [which] is filled with all means and appliances to ensure superiority and economise costs'.[36] This claim is interesting, as according to Arkell and Duckworth, the West End work 'is always supposed to be entirely by hand, but the influence of the more rapid methods of machinery begins to make itself felt.'[37]

Apparently the stigma of machines was not a problem in these instances. Thomas Scott, a Dublin cabinet-maker, stated the advantages of machines in his evidence to the *Royal Commission on Technical Instruction*, in 1884:

> these machines are no drawback to cabinet manufacture. They do all the hard work and still a good cabinet-maker is more essential than ever. The hard work is performed by the machine but still the work for a good tradesman is left.[38]

These points were also noted in London. Edwards and Co., who started a business renovating antiques, went on to develop a trade in the fine reproduction of marquetry pieces. It was noted by the trade press that in 1883 they employed a wide range of machines for all the preliminary processes of furniture-making,[39] and this clearly shows how machines assisted the preparatory and final decorative stages of some furniture-making at the 'better end' of the trade.

Apart from their use of machines for the preliminary processes, other aspects of these firms' practices were influential. Although their exhibits at International Exhibitions showed off their products, the factory methods were also admired. Wyatt, in his report on the 1855 Paris Exhibition, noted that Holland and Son's workshops were apparently used as examples by at least one French firm:

> so excellent, and so well arranged with every known appliance for good and cheap production, that the great cabinet-maker, Jeanselme of Paris continually and voluntarily refers to the fact that he took his ideas and models from their establishment.[40]

Another more pragmatic reason for using machines appears to have been the greater control over the workforce. The firm of Gardner and Son of Jamaica Street, Glasgow, were reported as using 'extensive machinery' which has 'rendered them free from the control of trade union lists and combinations',[41] which perhaps gives an indication of the impact of machines on the value of labour.

The use of machinery, though, is easy to exaggerate, as throughout the latter part of the century there was a very uneven development pattern. In 1877 the *Furniture Gazette* published an article about the supposed invasion of the British furniture markets by foreign competition, suggesting that

> if only English manufacturers in general will once overcome the unreasonable prejudice they seem to entertain against the use of woodworking machines, there will be no fear they will be able to hold their own against all comers.[42]

A year later, Paterson made the following observations on the reasons for a slow acceptance of machinery in the furniture trade:

> The application of machinery in the ordinary sense to cabinet work is not at present very extensive. The harder and more difficult materials which are used, and the greater variety of the work, have hitherto prevented any wide use of the machines which are used in joiners work.[43]

These examples confirm the enduring nature of attitudes in the trade, but the contrary point was made in a report on the cabinet and chair works of Messrs Morrison and Austin, who commenced business as wholesalers and then took up the opportunities that investment in steam machines would give. According to a trade press report they employed machines for every process of manufacture, and in addition took in some trade work for machining.[44]

However, only a year earlier the same journal had a telling description of the business of Walker and Sons of Bunhill Row, London, which gave the following reasons for their not using much machinery:

> They do not consider that the extensive employment of machinery gives the opportunity for changes of moulding and pattern that are so essential in the manufacture of real art furniture. Thus it is that, apart from the preparatory stages, they rely on the ancient methods of fabrication which are dear to old cabinet-makers.[45]

All these examples reinforce the notion of a fragmentary and uneven use of machines in the industry, and also illustrate a variety of attitudes to machine use. Nevertheless, comments about the impact of machines during the last thirty years of the century often seem to have anticipated change, albeit not always for the better. Reporting on the 1878 Paris Exhibition, Paterson wrote:

> There is no doubt a considerable advance in the substitution of machinery for hand work, one firm indeed showing some pieces of furniture made almost wholly by machinery; and this increased use of machinery can also be traced in a more complete mechanical accuracy in the finish of some portions of the work which is not however, always an improvement.[46]

In the same report, another example of the lack of initiative in the general furniture trade is given:

> still one would have expected that the great advance made in the last eleven years in the application of science to the arts and manufactures, would have shown itself more decidedly in our furniture trades.[47]

By this time no one suggested that a serious cabinet-making business could do without machinery in some form or another. On the other hand, some unmechanised, rather tedious tasks such as polishing, caning seats, and wrapping and packing finished goods, were reserved for women.[48]

It seems that the classic view that efficiency or progress would inevitably be achieved through specialisation (division of labour combined with the increased use of machines) was at least, in the

British furniture trades, delayed until the twentieth century. In fact it is evident that productivity growth in low-tech industries such as furniture-making relied upon alternatives to machines, in particular the use of skilled and semi-skilled labour; new hand tools, batch production systems, and labour-saving methods as much, if not more, than machines themselves.

Veneering

Origins and attitudes

The art of decorating furniture with a slice of highly-prized wood placed on to a carcase of less precious timber has its origins in ancient furniture-making. The Egyptians, Greeks, and Romans were all masters of the art of veneering. Pliny's *Natural History* has a chapter on it, not only describing the use of timber as a veneer but also horn, ivory, and tortoiseshell.[49] Even at this early stage, prized veneers were cut from roots and burrs and the value of rare timber was evident in Pliny's remark that 'In order to make a single tree sell many times over, laminae of veneer have been devised'.[50] It was not until the relative peace and prosperity of the Renaissance that the ancient arts were revived. The popularity of intarsia in Italy, marquetry in France, and inlay in England, is evidence of the renewal of the art of decorating wood.[51]

Veneering, as opposed to inlay, was a limited practice before the Restoration in England, but in 1664 John Evelyn made one of the earliest references to the process. In *Sylva*, in a passage urging a greater use of cedar-wood, he wrote: 'it might be done with moderate expense, especially in some small proportions and in Faneering [sic] as they term it'.[52] Veneering practice developed rapidly through the remainder of the seventeenth century, and reached a peak in the late eighteenth century. Much has already been written about the cabinet-makers' mastery over veneering processes and the results of their work. I intend to develop the discussion into the nineteenth century to investigate veneering practice, as it is a fine example of the machine being used in conjunction with hand-work processes.

Although many of the finest seventeenth and eighteenth century cabinets were produced using veneer, during the nineteenth century the word 'veneer' acquired an unpleasant connotation: it was often assumed that the veneer was to cover up 'cheap and nasty' work underneath. The literary use of the word, to denote a specious covering, also became common during the mid-nineteenth century. Dickens, in *Our Mutual Friend*, immortalised the Veneerings family, the 'bran-new people in a bran-new house in a bran-new quarter of London'.[53] In addition to Dickens, there were at least two other novels that used the idea of veneers as a camouflage of respectability which suggested the superficial and the pretentious.[54]

In an onslaught on the values of mid-Victorian Britain, W. Maclerie wrote 'Veneer' (1876),[55] an article in which he used the two meanings of the word to lambast society. Although he starts off his piece by declaring that 'Veneer is both useful and ornamental and in itself perfectly unexceptionable, so long as it is honestly acknowledged to be veneer', Maclerie continues to criticise the desire to 'live with deception' and goes on to illustrate many deceptions that he saw around him. He ends with an amazing plea for the excision of the 'veneers in society' to encourage a more wholesome populace. This balance between illusion and reality continued as a feature in much nineteenth century furniture, and the whole concept is discussed elsewhere in this work.

The cabinet-making trade was well aware of the dual nature of the reputation of veneer. Sheraton (1803), did not praise either veneered or solid work: he simply pointed out that 'sometimes the object of veneering is cheapness and sometimes appearance. In most cases however the ground, glue and extra time are equivalent to the expense of solid work'.[56] The onslaught on veneering as part of furniture construction was also linked to questions of honesty in making and design. Some considered veneer a sham compared to the true nature of solid wood. For example, in a revealing passage in *Where do we get it and how is it made?*, Dodd (1858), links the idea of 'cheap and nasty' veneer with illusion: 'The employment of such veneers is a mask or deception; for the wood which does not meet the eye is cheap and inferior, but like many other masks, it has grown to be a custom of our age.' Even the trade magazine, *Furniture Gazette*, in an article dealing with veneering, written in 1873, had the following to say on the matter: 'Obviously, the first intent in veneering is to deceive – to represent as solid substance what is only surface'.[57] Although they do go on to say that the veneering process was often the only practicable way of using expensive and exotic woods, it does indicate how ingrained was the image of the falsity of veneers.

Eastlake (1868) strongly advocated the benefits of solid wood, but interestingly did not use the argument that veneer was a deception. He pointed out that it was no more a deception than marble lining a wall or silver-plating a base metal: rather, it was the technique that was faulty. 'To cover inferior wood completely in this fashion, thin and fragile joints must be used, which every cabinet-maker knows are incompatible with perfect construction.'[58] He then makes a similar point to Sheraton's remark: 'It is never worthwhile to buy furniture veneered with mahogany, for a little additional cost may procure the same articles in solid wood.'[59]

Despite Eastlake's exhortations, the decorative aspects of veneer versus solid wood were subject to the vagaries of fashion. The *Cabinet Maker* could comment in 1883 that, until recently, 'Every purchase seemed imbued with the doctrine that art must be solid'. The article continued by noting a move away from solidity brought about by a Georgian revival:

> This desertion of uncovered solidity is no matter of surprise, if we consider the hundreds of old specimens of eighteenth century inlaid work which has been sought out and brought into the market during the last few years. Such veteran articles have given the lie to anti-veneerists and become the progenitors, so to speak, of hundreds of beautiful copies.[60]

The rehabilitation of veneered furniture was achieved through a successful marketing approach by relating it to a historical pedigree.

Manufacturing processes and patents

It is often the case that technical processes have a long gestation period before they come into common usage. Veneer production by machine is one such example. The first patent that related to the production of veneers was for an 'Engine for cutting timber into thin scales, for making band boxes, scabbards for swords and the like.' This patent was taken out in October 1635 by Sara Jerom and William Webb.[61] Three years later, in 1638, Sara Jerom took out another patent with the same description.[62]

These early patents were isolated ones, and the period between 1700 and 1830 was the heyday of the hand sawyer and hand veneer-cutter. The hand veneer-cutter worked in a similar way to a pit

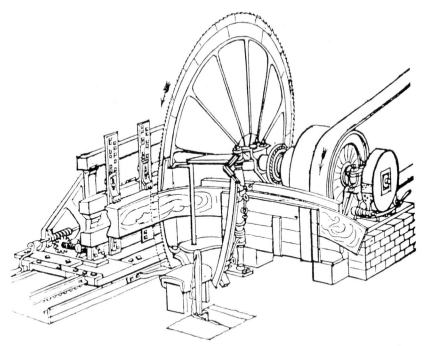

3 Brunel's veneer saw (*c*. 1811) was the first satisfactory machine for the
mechanised cutting of veneers

sawyer but was able to cut five to six veneers to the inch by using
a vice to clamp the timber piece upright. For finer work using smaller
baulks of timber, a cabinet-maker could cut seven or eight veneers
from a piece of timber. In 1806, over 150 years after these first
patents, Marc Isambard Brunel obtained a patent for machine-
cutting veneers and thin boards.[63] Soon after this, Brunel, with partners, set up a veneer and saw mill in Battersea.[64]

The principle that Brunel first used was based on a horizontal
knife to slice veneers from a log. The basis of the process was that
the knives would be held in line and they would extend beyond the
block to be cut. The knife would then reciprocate as the log was
brought forward to the blades. The machine, according to Holtzapffel,

answered moderately well with straight grained and pliant woods, such
as Honduras mahogany, but there were serious objections to its use for
woods of irregular, harsh and brittle grain such as rosewood.[65]

He goes on to point out that this was a shame 'as the splitting machine converted the whole of the wood into veneer without waste, whereas the veneer saw on average cuts one third of the wood into saw dust.'[66]

Brunel's next attempt, after abandoning the knife-cutting process, was the application of the circular saw. His initial experiments were again unsatisfactory due to the friction of the saw that made it buckle and twist. To overcome this, Brunel nicked the saw-blades to avoid buckling, and eventually developed this idea so that his final saws were made up of segments of saw blade attached to a circular casting which could be of variable size. The uses of the saws were described by a visitor to the mill:

> in a small building on the left, I was attracted by the action of a steam engine of 16 horse power and was ushered into a room where it turned, by means of banding, four wheels fringed with fine saws. I beheld planks of mahogany and rosewood sawed into veneers sixteenth of an inch thick, with a precision and grandeur of action that was really sublime ... A large sheet of veneer 10 feet long by 2 feet broad was separated in ten minutes, so even and so uniform that it appeared more like a perfect work of nature than one of human art![67]

The incredibly long-running success of Brunel's saw system was noted by the *House Decorator* (1881): 'the soundness of this conclusion [Brunel's segment blade device] has been proved for half-a-century, as nothing in the way of substantial improvement has been added to the machine.'[68] In the full development of this mill 'eleven machines were at work on the ground, the diameter of the saws being from 7 ft to 17 ft the largest of the saw teeth being of the gauge of five to the inch.'[69] The report noted that veneer was cut at the rate of about 1 ft in four seconds, a great improvement in speed, even if the sawing principle remained the same:

> Saws for veneers are built of a circular cast-iron wheel upon which are fixed segments of soft steel. Upon the soft steel are fixed hardened steel serrated blades which are the cutting edge of the saw. This saw is capable of handling up to 24 feet long and 5A feet wide timber. The number of veneers usually cut varies between 15 with a six inch wide plank and eight with a sixty inch wide plank.[70]

The application of steam to veneer-cutting and the centralisation of the process was a natural development, as was the combination of sawmill, timber, and veneer supplier in one company. Henry Mayhew, writing in 1850 about the application of machinery to the carpentry and joinery trade, confirmed that veneers were 'now exclusively made by means of steam machinery'.[71] He noted that the veneer mill he visited in London was the largest in the world, having six acres of ground next to a canal. He described the saw room as 120 ft long and 90 ft wide containing eight circular saws, varying between 7 ft and 17 ft in diameter. It is quite likely that Edward Esdaile, a patentee of a machine for 'cutting leaves of wood', was also the proprietor of the sawmill visited by Mayhew. Holtzapffel, in *Turning and Mechanical Manipulation*, noted that the same company, Esdaile and Margrave of the City Sawmills, owned eleven veneer saws ranging from 5 ft to 17.5 ft in diameter, and also nearly every kind of machine saw and shaping engine for wood.

Apart from the application of steam engines, the veneer-sawing process was further developed in the mid century. The horizontal saw frame was introduced to do finer cutting work than the circular saw was capable of. This was achieved by the use of fine-ground saws, and resulted in the production of one or two more veneers per inch. The disadvantages of saw cutting, i.e. limited veneer sheet size, slow speeds, and waste through sawdust, were overcome by the development of the knife-cutting process, essentially either a slicing or a peeling operation.

The rotary knife-cutting or peeling process was important not only for veneers but also for the development of plywood. The early history of the process is difficult to unravel. A number of conflicting claims from Russia, Germany, and the United States do not help. In a report published in 1817 it was said that a Russian piano-maker in St Petersburg was producing 'sheets of veneer of about a hundred feet in length, and four, five or even more in width'.[72] This claim was countered by the allegation that cabinet-makers in Furth (Germany) had been producing peeled veneer for a long time prior to 1817. However, in 1822, a prototype of a peeling machine was made by the Vienna Polytechnic Institute.[73] A short time later the process was developed as the 'Improved Patent Rotary Veneer Cutter pro-pelled by steam power' which was supplied by Richardson and Co. of Philadelphia in 1825.[74] Greeley (1872), writing about the United States, reported on the success of rotary veneer cutting in that coun-try. He pointed out that the principle was based on a turning lathe and that the machine could be used for cutting bone and ivory as well as wood.[75] The first rotary veneer-cutting machine to be patented in the United States was designed by John Dresser of Stockbridge, Massachusetts, in 1840.[76] It is noteworthy that it could be either hand or power operated, and the machine design was based on the common turning lathe.[77]

Whatever the merits of each claim were, they illustrate how technological changes may occur simultaneously in various economies.

The rotary process was not without its problems. Holtzapffel made an interesting comment on a Russian machine for spiral-cutting or rotary-cutting a whole log. He suggested that it seemed to be open to the same objections as those raised against the knife-cutting process, namely that irregular or brittle-grained woods would curl or split, and it also failed to expose the ornamental grain.[78] In the case of non-wood materials, this did not matter so much, as is shown by H. Pape of Paris, who spirally cut ivory, and advertised his ability to supply sheets 30 by 150 inches, and one-thirtieth of an inch thick. Pape's speciality was piano veneering, and examples of his process were on display at the 1849 Polytechnic Exhibition in Regent Street, London.[79]

The first British patent for continuous rotary veneer-cutting machinery was registered by Mr Fontainmoreau in May 1847.[80] His main claim was that the log of timber could be cut, whatever its width. It did not need to be cross-cut to fit the jaws of the machine and therefore it yielded larger slices of veneer. Fontainmoreau also patented a veneer-joining machine which used the principle of rotary cutting, combined with a method of gluing the veneers to a thin canvas backing.[81] The invention of English patent machinery to cut veneers from a log in a rotary motion was also claimed by Messrs Taylor and Goater of Nottingham and Finsbury. The company specialised in the production of scaleboard for box-makers and it was their researches to find a more even and regular cutting method that developed the rotary principle. Their machine was designed so that it could cut veneers of the order of eighty, sixty, forty, and twenty to the inch. Contrary to Holtzapffel's objections about the lack of ornamental grain (see above), it was pointed out in the *Mechanics Magazine* (1849) that 'In many instances figures are obtained even in bay mahogany, which cannot be cut in any other way: therefore, these veneers must prove a great boon to the cabinet-maker and workers in fancy woods.'[82]

This important point had been noted by the *Mechanics Magazine* in 1848 when it referred to a veneering machine that was able to cut a roll of bird's-eye-maple veneer 300 ft long and 3 ft wide from a log 3 ft long and 20 in. in diameter.[83]

Perhaps this demonstrates the conjunction of the machine and new design potential, for without this rotary cutting the particular grain would not be exposed. The new possibilities increased the repertoire of the designer's choice of finish, but despite them, much of the trade used the familiar processes. Dodd (1860) pointed out the different methods used in Britain and on the continent:

> the English usually adopt the method described, [Brunel's vertical cutting saw] but on the Continent a singular mode is practised of cutting a continuous veneer in a spiral form. The English plan wastes a little more wood, but yields stronger veneers than the foreign.[84]

This is yet another example of the enduring nature of the trade's attitude, and shows that techniques continued to be used if they produced a satisfactory product even in the face of new and improved inventions. The trade press continued to report on the rotary system as if it were new, and as late as 1881 the *House Decorator*, in an article on veneering, reported that

> a new and highly successful machine is the rotary, on the principle of the knife – a system highly favourable to wood in the round and to figure, as in the case of bird's-eye-maple, found only on the face of logs. The number of veneers in this case is greatly increased as there is nothing lost by the saw or with the rib or set of the same marking the face of the veneer.[85]

According to this article the veneers were so thin that it was not practicable to use inlay or banding for further decoration. Whatever the problems or merits of the rotary system, it had shown that the application of knives in veneer-cutting was successful.

It was the French who then revived Brunel's original but unsuccessful idea of knife slicing. The benefits of the process were extolled in the *Practical Magazine* in 1875, when it reviewed the products of the French machinery company, Arbey.[86] It was reported that their knife-cutting process could not only cut 100–150 veneers per inch, but could also leave the surface so even that it was ready for use straight from the cutters. It is also interesting to see

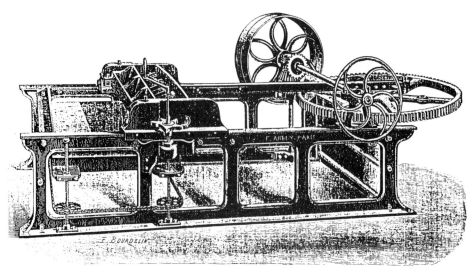

4 Veneer-cutting machine by Arbey, *c.* 1850. Introduced in France in the middle of the century, this machine could slice veneers without waste

that Arbey offered a choice of steam-powered or hand-operated machines.[87] It was only two years later that the well-known City saw-millers and timber suppliers, Esdaile's, were advertising the new process: 'Veneers can now be cut by the new knife-cutting process whereby all waste is avoided and a product is given of from twenty-eight to one hundred veneers to the inch'.[88]

By 1878 a report on the workmanship of modern furniture in the *Furniture Gazette* could claim that 'knife cut veneers will soon be universally used [as opposed to saw cut], even though the saw cut takes polish better and is more solid'.[89] These changing techniques of veneer-cutting follow the demands of the trade. With a need for more and cheaper veneers, the benefits of the knife-slicing machine, which produced up to twelve times the number of veneers obtainable from the same log, was obvious.

With the development of rotary cutting, the plywood industry became established. The process allowed a regular-sized sheet of veneer to be made into panels, usually using cheaper non-decorative timbers for the inner plies. As an example of the 'momentum model' (in which parts of society prioritise certain technologies for their own benefit), changes in veneer-cutting illustrate an economic imperative which had an impact on design. The improvements contributed to a cost reduction through central processing and a better use of raw materials, which resulted in the availability of fashionable furniture for a broader market range.

Veneering processes

The basic process of applying veneers to surfaces involves a few simple tools and the requisite materials. There are two traditional methods of hand-laying veneers: by the hammer or by the caul. The hammer method was used for simple flat work with pliable and mild veneers. The process involved the warming of both the veneer and the base, followed by the spreading of glue on to both surfaces. The veneer was then rubbed down on to the base and the hammer was applied to the surface, thus removing all the air to obtain a good adhesion. The caul method was based on applying heat and pressure to the veneer in relation to the shape, dimension and form of the base. Sometimes the cauls would be made of sandbags and were especially suitable for round or hollow work, otherwise they would be specially constructed, often out of pinewood, to fit the pieces to be veneered.[90]

These practices, which had endured since the seventeenth century, were beginning to be inadequate for the larger volume of furniture being made during the nineteenth century. As with machine tools, large manufactories used steam power to heat the cauls which were made up from iron boxes with screws and clamps. Shops without steam power used a thick iron plate heated with gas jets in the same way.[91] In contrast, the manual method also continued in use; it involved the prepared panels being put in a press, and then held down by planks and poles which abutted against the beams of the workshop.[92]

By the 1860s there were attempts to mechanise the veneering process, either to speed it up or to make it more reliable. Again, the basic processes of the twentieth century industry were devised in the nineteenth. The tower press and the vacuum press were two of the most important methods. In 1861 the cabinet-maker Charles Board patented the tower press. His invention used the idea of a stack of presses that were heated and cooled alternately so as to melt the glue and then set it rapidly.[93] In addition to the benefits of speed, the multiple processing of panels was a major advance.

The invention and patenting of a caul operated by electromagnets was devised by A. McIvor, a chemist from Edinburgh University.[94] This, in essence, used the force of the electromagnet to force down the caul on to the surface of the veneer, thus pressing it against its baseboard. McIvor also devised a version of the vacuum-bag method of veneering which used a flexible diaphragm and a steam exhauster to create a vacuum over the work to be veneered, thus creating adhesion. Both these methods obviated the need for the craftsman to apply his own energy.

In addition to the improvements in basic veneering methods, there were other attempts at developing greater decorative possibilities within the veneering process. Many of these were aimed at achieving effects that could not be made with the traditional methods. For example, Amies invented the method of veneering in relief, which was intended to represent carved surfaces. It was a process that involved using two moulds (as in the cameo and intaglio process). These moulds were heated and a sheet of veneer was placed between them. The hollow part was filled with a plastic substance and the veneer pasted with paper and then glue. The sandwich was heated again and pressurised, allowing the veneer to take the shape of the mould, thus producing an imitation of a carved surface. When dry, these veneered shapes could be used in any decorative design.[95]

Yet another attempt was the process of 'patent veneering' described by Mateaux (1883):

Here the thin slices of wood are glued fast to board, and on it is placed a piece of zinc in which has been punched a scroll or other design. This metal plate is somewhat thicker than the sheet of wood. The whole board is then submitted to a roller which forces the metal into the surface of the veneer, which is then planed until the zinc itself is reached. This is of course, forming a pattern which has been fairly squeezed into the surface of the solid wood.[96]

In 1849 John Meadows patented a process which allowed veneer to be continuously carried without a break or joint over all forms of curved surfaces or angles.[97] The method was based on a series of cauls hinged together, and screw pressure applied to each part of the gadget. The *Cabinet-Maker's Assistant* noted that 'several excellent examples of its efficiency were displayed in the Great Exhibition of 1851.'[98] However, it did also point out that

> This invention seems best adapted for veneering surfaces (of mouldings or other) of such frequent use, and determined form and dimension, as would warrant the preparation of a fixed series of cauls adapted to them.[99]

This may explain why many seemingly good ideas were never commercially adopted: the wide range of products and styles produced in limited quantities inhibited the introduction of 'long-run' processes. However, ideas continued. In 1871, a Birmingham cabinet-maker, J. E. Tysall, patented a method of inlaying by cutting inlay into a carcase, then veneering over the top, finally carving out the pattern again to reveal the inlay underneath.[100] Inlaid marquetry was a similar process, patented in 1875 by two cabinet-makers from Camden Town, J. Thornton and J. Thallon. The process used relief-cut rollers that impressed the pattern on to the surface, which was then planed level to reveal a marquetry-like design.[101] All these variants on the basic process of veneering illustrate attempts to either copy more expensive processes or achieve effects that would otherwise be unobtainable. As in other cases, the result was to broaden the repertoire of available processes and to further encourage a narrowing of differentials between the real and the illusory. Yet again, however, the evidence does not indicate a great deal of interest from the bulk of the trade, for most of these processes remained specialised and limited.

Construction

It might be inferred from the few manuals or instruction books involving the technique of furniture construction, that trade publishers assumed that most makers had served an apprenticeship and learnt the trade from the bench. In the later nineteenth century, a number of manuals were published for the use of amateurs and the technical schools, but the trade seems to have relied on the passing-down process of instruction rather than any serious textbook learning. This might indicate that construction methods (as opposed to decorating and finishing and, of course, machining) tended to remain the same as eighteenth century techniques. This is a reasonable assumption because when working with traditional materials and similar shapes, the accepted craft operations will remain the same. This also relates to the idea of the enduring nature of the trade that I have already established. An amazing example of this continuity is *The Complete Cabinet Maker and Upholsterer's Guide*, first published in London in 1829. Its printing history ran into at least five editions, and was reprinted as *The Cabinet-Maker and Upholsterer's Companion*; the last edition in 1906 was the same as the one in 1829, save for the addition of a small appendix to bring the book up-to-date!

However, there are examples of publications introducing new or improved processes of construction. For example, Kelly (1826) discussed a device that prevented warping in made-up panels:

> In preparing a surface of considerable width without the appearance of framing, and where warping is to be prevented, it was recommended that holes should be bored through the panels and strong iron wires inserted at intervals across the piece. Thus acting as clamps to prevent warping but not being affected by shrinkage in the width.[102]

Whatever inventions or improvements were suggested, the economic imperative remained. The growing number of masters who set up small businesses to make furniture on their own account, soon found out that they were unable to make a living by using traditional methods, so they had to skimp. It was often done by using poor-quality materials, but the construction suffered as well. An early example was the practice of bending drawer and table rails by kerfing. The process involved making a number of regular saw cuts into the underside of the rail and removing slivers of wood: sometimes, in the case of cheap work, after this was done, a piece of canvas was glued on to the inside. To make curves correctly, according to Martin (1816), pieces of shaped wood should be built up like brickwork to the required thickness.[103] The reuse of second-hand timber was another cost-cutting exercise. Table-makers would purchase old teak taken from ship-breakers to build up the bulk of the pillars for, e.g. centre tables and loo-tables; turned, artificially stained, and veneered, these apparently passed as walnut.[104]

By the middle of the century though, there were a number of opportunities for the English trade to see the benefits offered by changes in workmanship. The forums were the Great Exhibitions that took place from 1851 onwards in London, Paris, and New York.

The opportunity to compare English workmanship with its continental counterparts led to many commentators having their suspicions confirmed. Much of English craftsmanship, as well as design, was found wanting. There were exceptions of course, but throughout much of the century, furniture-making, even if of fine quality, had developed a reputation for being pedestrian.

One major example of these criticisms came from Wyatt. In his review of the English furniture at the 1855 Paris Exhibition, he suggested that the English cabinet-maker was uninspired by the choice of materials and processes that were available to him:

> although granting that English cabinet-making is generally creditable for the use of excellent materials and perfect workmanship so far as it goes, they neglect materials such as ebony, ivory, tortoiseshell, bronze, brass fittings, mother of pearl and Colonial woods.[105]

The workmanship, according to Wyatt was

> for the most part confined to good joinery, gluing up and mitring, smooth plain veneering and clean but not intricate carving. All the more elaborate technical processes of fine carving; incrusting in mosaic, marquetry, buhl, etched metal and engraved ivory, uniting work carved in the solid with veneered fascias, veneering on swept and circular surfaces, applying chased and gilt brass-work, elaborate fret cutting, engine turning, and gadrooning, hardwood mouldings etc ... and many more varieties of cabinet-makers' work taxing skilled labour to the utmost, seem to be excluded almost in toto from the catalogue of English capabilities.[106]

Wyatt censoriously suggested that this was caused by a narrow-minded public, masters with little pride in the technicalities of the trade, and workers uninterested in the intellectual aspect of the craft. In contrast, Wyatt applauded the French and German governments, who encouraged the trades and arts in the form of libraries, museums, free schools, and technical institutes, and considered that they played a major part in establishing design superiority over England. Wyatt also assessed the responsibility of the trade unions: he suggested that the stifling effect of the *London Cabinet-Makers' Union Book of Prices* inhibited innovation, and that it was responsible for many of the constraints on English furniture design. In its place he suggested a system of arbitration to render the book obsolete and its constraints unnecessary. Wyatt thought that this new initiative would then achieve some positive results:

a better division of labour would at once ensue; the men would be kept each one at the particular process of which he was the most thorough master; many more processes would be introduced; furniture would be made both better and cheaper; and there is no possible reason why with improved mechanical appliances we should not make cabinet work a very much more important article of commerce than it now is amongst us.[107]

The restrictive trade practices (that according to Wyatt were caused by the use of the union book of prices), lasted from 1793 to at least 1866. There is some evidence that the price books remained a stable guide during a period of unsettled prices, but there is little doubt that from both a design and a constructional point of view, they inhibited parts of the trade.

Over twenty years later a different criticism was levelled by H. R. Paul, one of the furniture-making artisans invited to report on the 1878 Paris Exhibition. Rather than complaining about the lack of enthusiasm for adopting continental techniques of decoration as Wyatt had done, this complaint referred to the English practice of exposing joints and devising ways of showing construction. Paul criticised the English use of (allegedly honest) exposed joints and massive solid timbers. Referring to a cabinet designed by Norman Shaw:

> This cabinet looks very much like a horse manger, supported on a wretchedly ugly stool and is made uglier by the construction being shown by the tenons going completely through and being then pinned.[108]

Paul continued by pointing out that 'a tenon would be no better for being pinned, nor would it improve a badly made tenon', and complained that the reason for its use was that 'it is continually recommended for the sake of its truth to sound art; and this by some who should know better'.[109] Paul singled out Christopher Dresser as an advocate of exposed construction and as a deprecator of veneer, cross-grain wood, and excessive carving in furniture-making. Dresser explicitly stated that 'an obvious and true structure is always pleasant. Let then the tenon and the mortise pass through the various members and let the parts be pinned together by obvious pins'.

Design critics took the nature of construction very seriously as an important component of design. Eastlake (1868) took the trouble to point out 'how many practical mistakes [in construction] are blindly perpetuated by cabinet-makers of the present day who have widely departed from the principles of old joinery.'[110] He singled out the use of mouldings, which he considered were originally intended to form part of the outer framework, and should therefore be made from solid timber framing:

> instead of this [solid framing] they are detached slips of wood, glued into their places after the door has actually been put together. To such an absurdity is the system carried, that these applied mouldings are often allowed to project beyond the surface of the door frame and not infrequently are repeated in the centre of the panel itself.[111]

Of course this was an example of the growing availability of ready-made parts that allowed a furniture-maker to build up his construction from prepared panels and mouldings. Eastlake's one-sided view does not take into account the economic imperatives of these constructional forms. This concern for a return to correct cabinet-making or more properly, joinery, was also expressed by Talbert (1873). He suggested that one bad process led to another: 'It is to the use of glue that we are indebted for the false construction modern work indulges in: the glue leads to veneering and veneering to polish.'[112]

Not content with deprecating glue and veneer, he continued to criticise other cabinet-making processes:

> the indiscriminate employment of veneer, glue, sandpaper and polish and the cutting of straight grained wood into wanton curves [was] opposed to common sense as well as the spirit of all Gothic work.[113]

The practical cabinet-makers seem to have ignored the design reformers and continued to produce furniture in their own way, ignoring calls for reform or invitations to look to European models. The Irish artisan, John Fraser, reporting on cabinet-making in the 1878 Paris Exhibition, noted an important difference in construction that exemplified the traditional English approach to cabinet-making. The English makers constructed carcases to be rigid and fixed, by using glued dovetail and mortise and tenon joints. In contrast, Fraser remarked that the French makers produced carcases in several parts which were 'put together with thumbscrews'.[114] Bitmead (1873) described a similar process to this. He suggested that the continental systems of carcase construction 'offer some very good examples of quickness and quantity, but not quality'.[115]

5 Mid-nineteenth-century chair in 'knock-down' format

These differing methods would also affect the look of any object. With woodworking joints the solidity and process were represented equally. With knock-down construction using thumbscrews, the objects might appear flimsier than in reality they were, as they appear to have had a generally lighter, more delicate look. Bitmead went on to describe the making of 'French cabinets', known to the trade as 'steamers'. The process described did not allow any joints in the framework of the carcase; it was made in machined pieces that were then nailed and dowelled together. He remarked that

6 Same knock-down dining chair assembled

Carcases are seldom dovetailed together; the ends are merely rabbeted with the saw, and French nailed together. In the French cabinets there are neither mortises, tenons, nor dovetails used; the circular saw does the whole.[116]

The most important part of this section of Bitmead's Guide are the remarks regarding the use of particular tools and their impact on British construction techniques. Bitmead singled out the circular saw as the prime aid to the makers of low-cost furniture. He suggested, not unnaturally, that this device assisted them in mitring, parallel and tapered work, so the value to the 'slop makers' was enormous. Bitmead thought that 'The cheap furniture-makers could not work at the price they do if they did not use this saw.' (It is important to remember that these saws were very often worked by foot treadle and did not necessarily imply factory conditions.) Bitmead then identified the fretsaw as the next most useful tool for cabinet-makers. This again was operated by a treadle and was essential for curved and fancy work. The third tool he mentioned was the toupie, or 'Improved rotary moulding cutter': operated like a spindle moulder, it was a quick and simple tool to incise designs into panels or 'carve' shapes in sections of timber. Bitmead identified the particular benefit of this tool: 'For Gothic or medieval work it is invaluable, as more chamfering can be done by it in one hour than could be done by hand-work in a day.'[117] As if reflecting the disinclination of British cabinet-makers to use modern methods, he noted that although these moulding machines had been in use on the continent for some time they were quite new to English makers.

Although it may appear that the trade may have been complacent in matters of construction and quality, they were not altogether uninterested in the state of English cabinet-making. The subject was discussed by a report in the *Furniture Gazette*, published in 1878.[118] In 'The workmanship of modern furniture', the editor reproduced the essence of an article that had recently appeared in the *Builder* magazine. The *Builder* complained of the alleged corrupt construction practices of the trade. They were particularly vehement about the attempts to delude the public as to what was being purchased. Examples of the deceits they uncovered included joints giving way to screws or nails; top chair rails screwed to backs and then buttons of wood inserted to hide the fact; chair seats with the framework halved into the back stile instead of being mortised and tenoned; and the assumption of solidity created by adding thick mouldings to edges of flat-topped tables. The *Furniture Gazette* took the stance that things were not as bad as the writer implied, but it would welcome correspondence on the matter. In a follow-up article in December 1878, the *Builder* gave a response to the angry reception of its article.[119] It continued to expose bad practice and gave a further example of the abuses it had found, involving the dissection of a sitting-room suite: it was apparently found that the alleged walnut

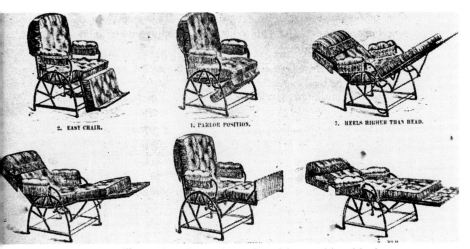

2. EASY CHAIR.   1. PARLOR POSITION.   7. HEELS HIGHER THAN HEAD.

7 A broadsheet illustrating the variety of positions achievable from a multi-purpose recliner chair

wood was stained beech, the mouldings were nailed on, the side rails were dowelled into rails less than an inch thick, and the alleged hair stuffing comprised flock, alva-marina, hay and some amounts of rubbish! As if in partly unwitting confirmation of at least one of these bad practices, the *Cabinet Maker* (1880), in a 'Technical Chapter' on 'How to make easy chairs' mentioned that 'in a cheap class of work it is customary to dowel many parts together that we have shown mortised and tenoned.'[120]

Although the trend was towards cost reduction in construction methods, there were examples of extreme care in the making of furniture. The work of Charles Wadman, a cabinet-maker in Bath, is revealing:

> Wadman's great round tables would be made up and stored, the large tops being placed in racks. After storage for about three months, they would be taken out in succession, carefully inspected and polished, re-placed in storage and later again re-polished. This process continued in three-monthly intervals and rarely less than a twelvemonth would be allowed before sales took place. This prevented shrinkage in the joints or sinkage in the veneers.[121]

Surely this was very rare, even in a high-quality firm, as the commercial considerations must eventually rule. The evidence demonstrated by construction methods has shown two things. Firstly, it has confirmed the enduring nature of trade processes, and secondly, it has shown that if large and varied quantities of stylish goods were to be produced for a price-conscious market, traditional methods of construction were inadequate.

Mechanical decoration

> The question really is not whether a process is mechanical but whether the result is mechanical.[122]

If there was one area in which the machine and its use in furniture-making was of interest in an otherwise reactionary trade, it was in the production of mechanical decoration. The need to produce larger amounts of goods, suitably decorated but sold as inexpensively as possible, encouraged developments in the field. In addition to this demand, the diminishing amount of skilled labour also furthered the development of mechanical decoration.

The trade press, usually a supporter of innovation, often pointed out the benefits that accrued from the sensible use of machines in producing decoration. In 1873, the *Furniture Gazette*, discussing carving, made the realistic point that man and machine were perhaps the best combination:

> The simplest [carvings] are at present made by ingenious mechanical processes, for it is now well recognised in industry that certain things are best done by machinery, whilst others are better executed by the hand of man.[123]

This distinction between handwork and machine use, realistic as far as it goes, ignores the increasing demand for inexpensive ornamental furniture, the production of which was hampered by a shortage of skilled labour. During the nineteenth century a number of inventors, who devised an amazing variety of methods for mechanically decorating furniture, attempted to respond to the demands.

Many of the processes were designed to reproduce more expensive methods. Others were unique and represented a new method of decoration in their own right; these were often patented, and can be divided into completely new and innovative processes, and adaptations of existing methods. The earliest patent that purported to ornament furniture dates from 1638. William Billingsley patented a method of printing furniture etc. with liquid gold and silver.[124] Over a century later, in 1774, Joseph Jacob patented a method of using tin foil, lead, or pewter, beaten or rolled into sheets for applying to cabinets and other articles.[125] In 1786 a glass cutter named Thomas Rogers patented a process of using coloured, stained, and clear glass to produce decorations for furniture, looking-glasses, etc.[126] In the same year, John Skidmore devised and patented a process for ornamenting furniture with 'foil stones, Bristol stones, paste and all sorts of pinched glass, and every other stone glass and composition used in or applicable to the jewellery trade.'[127] The early nineteenth century patentees generally concentrated on patents for bedsteads, castors, and furniture types. There was a patent taken out in 1818 to protect an invention related to the manufacture of ornamented wooden furniture by machinery.[128]

The prospect of a flood of machine-made decoration caused some voices to be raised against the possibility of decoration being so easily available. The fears of some critics regarding the excesses that might be perpetrated in the name of ornament were again eluci- dated by Dr Christopher Dresser. At a presentation at the Society of Arts, he was asked his opinion of a particular mechanical process of decoration. He thought that because ornament was a good thing, some considered that they cannot have too much of it and its excess was only checked by its cost: remove that restraint, he said, and too much elaboration was bound to follow with a consequent loss of effect.[129]

Of course, this criticism of unrestrained ornament has been level- led at Victorian furniture ever since, but was simply a reflection of the desire to display objects which were apparently full of 'work'. Whether design pundits liked it or not, methods of mechanical dec- oration were yet another manifestation of the attempts by furniture- makers to meet the demand by using new or revived techniques, often in imitation of the original. These include boulle revivals, marquetry, imitation carving, fretwork, and turning.

Boulle revival

The revival of interest in French designs in the early nineteenth cen- tury stimulated a demand for boulle work. (Boulle work is a highly decorative form of marquetry using tortoiseshell and metals, and requires particular cabinet-making skills.) A number of well-known

53

makers established themselves about this time. In 1816 Louis Le Gaingneur set up a 'buhl manufactory' in Edgware Road, and by 1817, Thomas Parker of Air Street was advertising himself as a Cabinet and Buhl Manufacturer. George Bullock was using techniques similar to boulle, using native woods, in the early part of the century.

As with most techniques, there were attempts to mechanise the boulle process because there was an increasing interest in making these styles available to a wider market. In 1830 the *Mechanics Magazine* carried a report on an invention for 'buhl-cutting':[130] made by Mr McDuff, a member of the London Mechanics Institution, it won a prize of £10 for the best machine invented in the year 1829. McDuff was a working turner who devised an arrangement that allowed a frame with a reciprocating saw to be mounted on to an existing wheel-operated lathe. It had the benefit of freeing both hands and of having the work surface flat. This method still used a saw process similar to the original 'donkey' method, but reduced the time and improved the efficiency.

The cutting-out process was speeded up by the use of stamping techniques for the metal (usually brass) sections of the work. Prior to 1818, George Bullock had a stamping press with an iron vice and dies, which can reasonably be assumed to have been used to cut out the brass-strip decoration that he used as inlay.[131] Interest in mechanical boulle work continued into the middle of the century. Ure (1839) described boulle decoration, in which he mentioned the use of punches to cut out the shapes required,[132] and Wyatt (1855) noted that 'stamps or punches are sometimes used in buhl work of brass or wood, but only to a limited extent.'[133] Initially the techniques were used to revive old designs rather than create new ones. Wyatt commented on the practice of makers using the techniques to doctor old furniture instead of designing new models:

> It is a great pity that much of the ingenuity and dexterity which are now brought to bear in doing-up old foreign work, should not be devoted to the improvement of our contemporary productions.[134]

But as the century progressed, other processes were introduced into boulle work. A note in the *London Cabinet-Makers' Book of Prices* (1863) that 'Buhl borders stamped into veneer tops are charged at half the price of banding', seems to indicate that decorative borders were punched straight into the wood veneer surface to create a boulle-like effect at a reduced cost. Other methods of obtaining boulle effects without great cost included substitutions of materials. Siddons (1830) suggested using a mixture of tin and quicksilver mixed with size as an alternative to the more costly silver inlay.[135] Another process, devised by Mr Cremer, involved a method of applying a mix of japan and copper to a base frame to create an effect that resembled boulle, but was made for between a tenth and a twentieth of the cost. The process involved engraving a copper plate, then taking an impression of this in gutta percha on to which was deposited a film of copper. The whole surface was then painted with strong japan colour and this was built up and stoved between each layer. When it was as thick as the excised parts, it was rubbed down to the copper surface leaving the japan colour in the excised parts of the pattern.[136] Naturally, this process required a substantial demand for it to be an economic proposition.

An indication of the decline in the fashion for boulle work can be found in Williams (1881). In a guide to finding work in various trades, boulle-cutters were recommended to 'apply to the old furniture and curio dealers who want repairers, inlayers and workers'.[137] Even so, the commercial use of boulle continued, but it seems as if the quality of the workmanship had deteriorated badly. In 1890, *Furniture and Decoration* noted that 'The modern manufacturers saw out simultaneously ten or twenty sheets and the whole result is so rough and paltry that to call it Boulle is a calumny on the name.'[138] This would appear to be the triumph of economy over craftsmanship.

Marquetry

The process of building up decorative patterns cut and inlaid into veneer, the whole of which was then applied as a sheet to a cabinet surface, would seem to be a difficult process to mechanise. However, machine-made marquetry was produced in an attempt to speed up what was essentially a hand process. The problems attached to such a process were well described by Paul in one of the reports on the 1878 Paris Universal Exhibition. He noted that a wardrobe by Howard and Sons had 'some machine made marquetrie [sic], which is simply an abomination', and he goes on to describe how the abomination was created:

It is made by cutting the pattern with a stamp, placing it on the veneer that is to form the ground, and squeezing the one into the other by machine pressure . . . Anyone may imagine the ragged edges left by such a process. In fact the wood must become pulp before it can do what is intended.[139]

The report ends with a sombre announcement: 'So long as wood is wood, and until a machine can be invented to deal with it as wood, marquetrie will have to be made by hand.'

Perhaps this was the crux of the problem: using machines to attempt to re-create handmade work such as marquetry, rather than using the machine for what its capabilities were designed for. Nevertheless, at least one manufacturer was happy to declare his use of the imitative process. Maddox (c. 1865), in his catalogue of bedroom furniture, declared that his suites 'were made of polished deal with the additions of ornamental borders, centres etc. of imitative marquetrie [sic] having all the appearance of being really inlaid and being equal in every respect to satinwood and marquetrie.'[140]

Apart from true marquetry, there were a number of attempts made to improve or vary the process. A decorative process described as mid-way between artistic marquetry and Tunbridge ware (see below) was invented by M. Marcelin, a French marqueteur who exhibited mosaic veneering at both the 1851 and 1855 exhibitions. It was made by gluing together pieces of wood to make a mosaic pattern, then this was cut at precise angles. These blocks were then sliced into as many thicknesses as required and laid down as a mosaic veneer.[141] In 1863, G. Colomb patented a process that mixed wood shavings with glue and 'other material', which was then compressed into blocks ready to be sliced into veneers.[142]

Another noteworthy patent that attempted to reproduce very fine marquetry or parquetry effects is the mosaic veneer process. This patent was taken out in 1867 by the American Mosaic Veneering Company of New York, and used a 'plastic' material, not wood parts. The process involved forcing the material through a metal plate with the appropriate design upon it, then drawing the resulting rods together and gluing and hardening them. Finally, the bundles were sliced into veneers ready for application.[143]

All these were in fact variations on the theme of Tunbridge ware, in which spills of wood of various colours are glued together following a pattern. These blocks can then be sliced through to reveal a decorative veneer. Boulle, marquetry, and parquetry, along with their variations, were all designed to decorate flat surfaces. For shaped surfaces the mechanical production of imitation carving was important.

Imitation carving

The public demand for evidence of 'work' in their furniture proved the necessity for substitute or imitation carvings. This was noticed by the *Cabinet Maker* in 1890: 'With a public insisting upon a great show for little money, the maker must either smother his work with bad carving ... or he must employ an inexpensive substitute.'[144]

The problem, however, was evident at the beginning of the nine-teenth century. As early as 1816, Smith noted the difficulty in getting good carvers, particularly away from major towns.[145] In response to this problem, he suggested a method of producing a wood substitute that could be moulded to create a carved effect, using raspings of wood or sawdust and Flanders glue. Even at this early date he noted that the art was not absolutely new.

Apart from the problems of available skilled labour, cost factors were equally important. In addressing this matter during the 1870s, the *Practical Magazine* discussed substitutes for wood-carving and concluded that imitation and real carving could exist side by side. Discussing the bois-repoussé process of pressure carving (see below) it said:

> In truth hand work, from its costliness, never can obtain a general de-mand and from that very circumstance it is evident that this discovery opens a new chapter in the history of taste as applied to the ornament of dwellings without interfering with the venerable art of the artificer in wood.[146]

But it also warned of poor quality reproductions:

> the popularisation of art, which has been characteristic of society during the last thirty years has induced many attempts to imitate the sculptured handwork of the artificer ... but public taste and the voice of authority has condemned them on the grounds of their unreal nature.[147]

The main imitation carving method was reported in the *Civil Engineer and Architect's Journal* in July 1841, although it had actually been patented in 1840. It was not carving in the true sense of the word, but was a sophisticated embossing technique, based on burning

8 Cabinet by the Burntwood Carving Company, displayed at the 1851 Great Exhibition to demonstrate the technique of carving by hot brands out a pattern into the wood with an iron mould pressed on to a dampened surface. The process involved using pressure of between ten and thirty tons, and it was apparently possible to obtain up to 250 impressions before the mould needed to be re-chased. After approximately 500 impressions the mould had to be renewed.[148] The company who used this method was the Patent Decorative Carving and Sculpture Works, Ranelagh Road, Thames Bank, Pimlico. The process is best described by a contemporary article writer, one Philotechnicos:

> An iron mould is first cast from a plaster or wood model. The iron mould is heated to a red heat, and applied to a piece of wood, previously damped, with great force, and repeated until the wood is burned to the required form. The char is then cleaned off, and any undercutting that may be required done by hand; when the operation is finished it has the appearance of old oak.[149]

The 'old oak' finish was thought to be particularly appealing in so far as an image of antiquity was produced. Some results of other pyrotechnic processes were displayed at the Manchester Exposition of British Industrial Art held in 1846. The *Art Union* (January 1846) illustrated a chair produced by the Patent Wood-Carving Company which was 'highly carved' in the late seventeenth century manner, and recorded that it was sold for the sum of thirty shillings.

Further experiments abounded. The Guattari process used heated moulds to burn or char away parts that were not required, using variably controlled heat and pressure. It was noted at the time that hardwoods were best suited to this process, but softer woods could be hardened by the removal of gums and sap and replaced with a glue to harden the wood.[150]

A cruder method of producing carved parts for application to furniture carcases was by the so-called steel carving method, perfected by the Ornamental Wood Co. of Bridgeport, USA. Their method was to apply a steel cutting die to the end grain of timber under pressure.[151] In a similar vein was bois-repoussé, invented by M. Ley. This process involved applying up to 1500 tons of pressure on to cut steel dies to produce relief carvings to a depth of 1 in. It was used for panels, friezes, medallions, borders, etc.[152] Importantly, it carved into the wood horizontally with the grain so it could not be reproached for being such a false principle as the American 'end-grain' method. The *Practical Magazine* declared that this process was not a sham, and therefore has a claim for durability and solidity which has never been possessed by any previous discovery; and moreover, the grain of the wood being horizontal, in contra-distinction to an American device which could only give the pattern on the end grain of the wood – an obviously false principle – gives the work exactly the same appearance as if produced by the wood carver.[153]

The attempts to reproduce carving involving some form of artificial wood that could be moulded into shapes continued. The most well known was bois-durci. Invented by Charles Le Page under a provisional patent,[154] it was subsequently produced by Latry of Paris. The method used was to take rosewood sawdust, reduce it to a fine powder and then moisten it with a mixture of animal blood and water. This mix was then put into dies and subjected to heat and pressure which caused a chemical reaction and created an ebony-like material that was used to make medallions, rosettes, paterae, etc.[155] Pinto (1970) describes it as a precursor of plastic-like materials,[156] and indeed the reduction of wood to cellulose can perhaps be considered as part of the history of plastics. Yet another method of producing artificial wood was devised by Harrass of Thuringia. In 1883, a report on this process mentioned the recipe as including sawdust, animal blood, ground wood and glutinous flour. This mixture was placed into metal moulds to produce the requisite shapes. It was different from bois-durci in that it had pasteboard applied to its underside to give a regular base for fixing. It was also possible to veneer the face of the object.[157]

There were other strange attempts at imitation carving. Hydrographic carving, invented by Cowan and Stuart of Liverpool, was one such process. It involved pressing cut dies into wood to a predetermined depth. The surface was then planed level, after which the material was 'relaxed' by water or steam and this apparently enabled the pattern to rise and stand out in relief. Alternatively, the level surface could be left with the compressed material standing out as a different shade or density. Another version of this process was to inlay veneers by pressing the pattern through the sheet of veneer into the wood below, and the surrounding wood was then planed down.[158]

The nature of these materials and the intentions of the makers are obvious in a rider to the trade catalogue of O. A. Nathusisus of New York, a producer of patented artificial wood ornaments: 'No provision is made for screws, as they (the ornaments) are designed more especially for a cheaper class of work and are intended to be attached in the simplest manner by glue and brads.'[159]

All the preceding examples illustrate attempts to substitute varying types of decoration for original handwork. In all cases there was no attempt at making an original contribution to design: they were simply reducing costs or speeding up processes by devising substitutes. However, there was one machine process that did have an influence on the design of furniture.

Fretwork

The *Cabinet Maker* commented in 1882 that 'among the somewhat numerous attempts which have been made of late to hit the popular taste in the matter of furniture, nothing probably has hit with more conspicuous success than fret-cut work.'[160] The development of the frctsaw to a state of reliability, and the fact that the power source could be human, steam or, later, electrical, stimulated its speedy adoption. Although the fret-cutters tried to maintain a 'mystery' around their trade, the importation of cheap and simple fret machines from America in the 1880s encouraged manufacturers large and small to use them. The demand for fretted designs grew to a point where there developed a separate trade of fret-cutter who produced fretted parts for furniture and piano-makers. They also made small items which they sold themselves.[161] The fret machine's success in relation to other machines was noted by Paterson (1878) in writing about the state of the trade:

> The application of machinery in the ordinary sense to cabinet works is not at present very extensive. The harder and more difficult materials which are used, and the greater variety of work, have hitherto prevented any wide use of the machines which are used in joiners' work. Still there are some excellent fret-cutting machines which have in great measure superseded hand-cutting in this branch and provide a very cheap and effective means of decoration.[162]

The further possibilities of the fret machine as an aid to stylistic development were also described by J. H. Pollen. He discussed the problems of machines and design and the difficulties associated with trying to shape wood against fixed cutters like the toupie moulder: 'it is nevertheless in the turnery and the fret-cutting machinery that a furniture artist must find the elements of style.'[163] This is revealing

61

because it implies that the designer needs to take into account the capabilities of the machine when considering how to produce an object.

The relationship between technique, machine, and design can also be noted in the use of materials. There is an interesting connection between laminated or plywood and fret-cutting designs. The inherent stability of the laminated material made it ideal for the relatively delicate process of cutting frets in wood. In any case, more elaborate designs could be achieved by the use of plywood because there was less likelihood of breakage. The experience of Belter in producing chair frames had already shown this.

The conjunction between plywood and frets was best seen in the front panels of pianos. A report on a pianoforte manufactory in Grays Inn (London) noted that the decorative fretwork panels for piano fronts were 'formed of three separate veneers joined into one thickness in such a manner that the crossing of the grain in each veneer imparts an extraordinary degree of strength.'[164] In a report on the Broadwood piano factory, the operation of the fretsaw was discussed, which showed the processes involved: a vice, opened by the foot, gripped the work, and the workman used a fretsaw blade to follow the chalk design.[165]

Fret-cutting was used in the search for improvements in design. In 1885, W. Robertson, a cabinet-maker from Alnwick, patented a method of decoration[166] involving a process of temporarily joining thick and thin bars of wood, and then fret-cutting designs through them. The thinner piece was then inserted into the thicker one and attached to a carcase. It was alleged this would ensure that the piece appeared integral rather than applied. Turning was another traditional technique that was improved in a similar way to fret-cutting.

Turning

This was possibly the earliest process of mechanical shaping. The lathe allowed either a basic or a complex decoration to be made using simple tools, while simultaneously shaping the member. The origins of the process can be traced back to Graeco-Roman times, when lathes were well known. The efficiency of the simple traditional methods is illustrated by the continued use of the pole lathe in various forms, by furniture-makers ever since. Turning is a decorative process whereby the operation completes the design and

9 Chair with polychromatic turning. The combination of inlay and turning produced polychromatic turning, which enabled multi-coloured decorative designs to be produced directly on the lathe

decoration in one sequence, and it is tempting to think that the lathe creates the design. Again, it is only a tool which, when used in conjunction with other tools, is able to create a variety of designs. In some cases, these can be very complicated, double barley-sugar twists being an example. In other cases, turning can be used to create a design that is more than a reflection of the mechanism. Polychromatic turning was one such process.[167] The term related to a process of inlay that was combined with turning. In its simplest format, it comprised a turned part that then had similarly turned studs inlaid into it in the manner of a band. A more complex process was the lamination of blocks of varying coloured woods that were glued together, then turned, and possibly studded, revealing their colours. Finally, the lathe was used for creating geometric inlay: a circular disc of an appropriate size was inlaid with other coloured circular discs of varying sizes; the whole was then finally fitted into pieces of furniture.

Carving machines

Mr Burley (Merchant): 'I have seen first rate carving done by machine'. Mr Mantley (Clergyman): 'All machine carving that I have seen loses its charm at the second glance. There is no life in the work, no expression'. The Artist: 'You might as well try to paint by machine'.[168]

The reasons for investigating machine carving are a way of evaluating Victorian attitudes to the machine, work, and design in the furniture trade. Machine carving is a fascinating and relatively unknown area of furniture history, but is also important in its own right because it has sometimes been held responsible for the mass production of ornamented furniture in the latter part of the nineteenth century. Many historians do not understand how machine processes were used in the nineteenth century furniture industry, and have seen them as immensely powerful tools which turned the industry from a hand to a machine operation.[169] The carving machine, like other machinery that was applied in the later nineteenth century furniture trade, needs to be put into its proper perspective.

Development

Recent historians who have studied machinery, and in particular machine carving, have started their work with the mechanism invented and produced by Thomas Jordan.[170] However, it is evident that the history of the attempt to achieve machine carving goes back further than 1845 when Jordan patented his machine: indeed Jordan acknowledges this himself.[171] According to an article in the *Art Union* in 1848,[172] one of the first machines to achieve true carving was invented by James Watt in the latter part of the eighteenth century.

Attempts to produce successful carving machines continued, and in 1822 John Buckle of Mark Lane, a merchant in the City of London, obtained the patent rights to a carving machine invented by J. P. Boyd of Boston.[173] Buckle's machine operated by inserting a model into the machine and cutting copies from blocks set parallel to the original model. However, he gives no details of its application to making furniture parts, and it would appear that this machine was a multiple turning operation rather than a proper carving machine. This seems to follow on the work of Thomas Blanchard in the United States, who was responsible for setting up the processes and machinery for gunstock-making on a semi-automatic basis for the Springfield Armoury.[174] Another more noteworthy attempt was perhaps the patent taken out by Joseph Gibbs in November 1829.[175] Gibbs's patent machine was based on having the model to copy set on a platform with the tracer, and below it on another platform the drill acting on the copy block. The operation of the machine was based on the swing frame which had the tracer and drill connected and mounted upon it so it could move both vertically and horizontally and forward and back. Although this machine was apparently successful in cutting letters for shop fronts, it appears that the duplicated swing frame construction was prone to vibration which caused distortion. Attempts were subsequently made to produce a machine that would avoid this problem, but it could not be fully overcome until the framing for the machines was made from iron rather than wood.

Interest in mechanical carving, especially in relation to sculpture, was continued by Mr Cheverton who developed a machine that could be used to produce copies of sculpted works. This machine was based on the pantograph principle with the ability to enlarge or reduce the original. Although it was essentially like Watt's version, Cheverton was able to patent his machine in 1844. The results of his work were publicly displayed as examples of mechanical (sculptural) carving.[176]

In 1845 George Myers patented a method of carving wood or

10 The American 'improved wood-carving machine' demonstrated the pantograph principle that was successfully used in a number of versions of carving machine

stone.[177] According to the specification, this machine would cut 'any circular forms with great expedition and perfect accuracy'. It is perhaps no coincidence that Myers, who was a builder, was associated with A. W. N. Pugin in producing buildings and furnishings in the Gothic revival style.[178]

The first patent that directly relates to machine carving in its specification title, is William Irving's, taken out in 1843.[179] This patent, with the brief title of 'Machinery and apparatus for cutting or carving substances to be applied for inlaying and for other purposes', was important in the early history of machine carving: it was the first to be a proper carving operation, and was the basis of the more successful Jordan machine improvements.

His ingenuity was apparently greater than his business acumen as it transpired that the commercial exploitation of his invention lay in his partnership (?) with Samuel Pratt of New Bond Street. Within a few months of Irving having his patent granted, Pratt became involved. They appeared to have moved with great speed to start promoting the invention, as in 1843 Pratt founded the Patent Carving Company. It seems that Pratt took over the marketing and sales operation; he was a good publicist, and took every opportunity to promote both himself and Irving's machine, to the extent that Irving gets no mention in many references in the press to Pratt's carving machine. Pratt himself is perhaps more well known as part of the family of patent camp-équipage and upholstery makers based in Bond Street.[180] However, his own interest in patent processes is obvious. He had six patents granted to him over a period of twenty-one years varying from wardrobe-trunks to beds to combat sea-sickness, as well as the most well known – the spiral upholstery spring. He also holds an important place in the history of carving machines.

One of the first mentions of Pratt and Irving's machinery was in a report about the King Street competitive exhibition of the decorative works to be selected for the new Houses of Parliament in 1844. Success was not assured though. In its review, the *Art Union* dismissed Pratt's work made on Irving's machine:

> The specimens by S. Pratt jun. are we suppose examples of machinery work; at least the marking of a tool, and the unfinished appearance of the geometric tracery, give the notion of work left as delivered by the senseless machine.[181]

The *Builder* was only slightly less derogatory. Reviewing the same exhibition, it commented that Pratt's design was 'a rich design, but too much in the French flamboyant style; over done with ornament; the carved specimen of which is not sufficiently finished.'[182] These two criticisms perhaps illustrate the need for the refining of an invention before it can be put into practice. (The problem of finish seems to have been overcome, because later in the same year the *Builder* reported on the Royal Society's conversazione in which some examples of Pratt's carved Gothic tracery were shown. These were apparently well received and comments were made about the remarkable finish.) Even so, the most favourable remarks were reserved for the fact that with Pratt's (Irving's) process, better carving for a tenth of the usual expense would be obtained, with the bonus of saving labour and time. Although mention was made of the possibility of supplying anyone with carved artifacts for their homes, the only example given was work for Camberwell's new church.[183] The democratising dream of machine carving and its possibilities had to wait another thirty years to be realised.

Contemporary with the rise of Pratt and Irving, was a development that has become more well known: Jordan's Patent Carving Machine. Jordan's invention, patented in 1845 as a 'machine and apparatus for cutting, carving and engraving', was a new departure in machine construction but (as he admitted) it was not a new invention in its own right. He and his partners claimed that the introduction of machinery was able to assist in the production of every class of carving whatever it might be. With the arrival of Jordan's machine there were then three distinct methods of producing carving or carved effects competing with each other.

The essential difference between Jordan's machine and its predecessors was that his machine worked on the principle that the solid material to be carved had movement given to it, while the tools remained virtually stationary. This enabled the operator to trace the model to be copied and also to produce up to eight copies simultaneously. The main rival machine was Irving's: the material to be carved was fixed on a table which turned on a centre. Guided by a cast-iron template, the tool drilled out the pattern according to its depth and shape. However, it was only capable of copying one object at a time. The third competing method was the pyrographical or imitative carving which relied on heated iron moulds to burn away the excess wood and char the surface to the required pattern (see further below).

Although Jordan's patent was registered in 1845, he was obviously promoting his machine beforehand. His contact with Charles Barry, the architect of the new Palace of Westminster, dates to before 1845 when Jordan's machine was recommended for use on the works. Apparently, the carving machines were a great success in producing the carved woodwork, and Jordan was able to trade on the publicity from the contract. Indeed, Irving and Pratt were not the only people to promote their machine with the aid of influential people. Jordan did as well. In addition to Barry, the advocates of Jordan's machine included Sir John Rennie. In 1846 Rennie held a conversazione at his residence in Whitehall Place, where, amongst other interesting objects, specimens of machine woodcarving by Taylor, Williams,

11 Sideboard, *c.* 1848–50, with Jordan's machine-carved decoration on the lion monopodia

and Jordan were on view.[184] Jordan also had a review in the *Patent Journal and Inventors Magazine* as the first in a series of Sketches of the Principal Manufactories of the Metropolis.[185] Perhaps it was because of the particular interests of the magazine, but the choice of Jordan as the first in the series again illustrates the degree of curiosity.

The enlightened understanding of the sensible use of the machine was commented on by Dodd (1854):

> There is something like a legitimate union of powers at work upon the new Parliament house, where Jordan's machine produces carvings too extensive for Rogers [see below] fingers, and Rogers hand and eye produce results too tasteful for Jordan's machine.[186]

Developments in machine carving after the Great Exhibition were apparently influenced by the demands of both the church and government building works in London (especially the new Palace of Westminster) and a little later by the requirements of the army during the Crimean War. The *Art Journal*, in a review of wood carving by machinery in 1856, noted that 'the art element has been clouded by the commercial one'.[187] It suggested that this was caused by the demand for wooden gunstocks consequent upon the War. It went on to extol the virtues of the Wood Carving Company and tell how a Mr Rogers, 'the well known wood carver', had been appointed Art Director of the company in an effort to return to art-reproduction. In 1855 the *Builder* made a brief reference to the announcement of the sale of the stock-in-trade and plant of Jordan's machine carving works.[188] It seems that Jordan left the business at this point, although up to 1859 the trade directories list the carving and moulding works (with various managers) as using Jordan's patent mechanism.

Two entries in the catalogue of the Patents Museum (1863) list items which may indicate the end of the initial reign of the machine carving ideal. The first item is a machine for carving wood and other materials by T. B. Jordan, and the second is a selection of wood-carving by machine that had been contributed to the exhibition by Cox and Son.[189] Although these items were in the museum for the benefit of other potential patentees, by 1863 the wider vogue for carved furniture had diminished and perhaps a museum show-case was a form of epitaph for these early initiatives. Even so, the *Illustrated Builders Journal* in 1865 again reviewed both patent woodcarving and carving machines. The reviews mentioned Braithwaite, Jordan, and Irving and discussed their processes; it would appear that the processes were still current at the time.[190]

Despite some new initiatives, such as Cunningham's patent carving machine,[191] many commentators considered the carving machine unnecessary. Richards wrote of it:

> As to the history of carving machines thus far, leaving out special cases and taking the results generally, it has been an even race against hand labour, to say the best, and gives no great promise of gain in the future. In this assumption we are guided by the only fact that is reliable in the matter, which is that carving in both England and America, as well as on the continent is mainly done by hand.[192]

As late as 1880 the *Scientific American*, in reporting on the manufacture of parlour furniture, pointed out:

> it is found more economical in practice to do a large proportion of the carving by hand, rather than fit up the knives and patterns for the machine for all the new and elaborate designs in carving which are always being introduced.[193]

This difficulty of wasted time is confirmed by a comment from Powis Bale on the history of Jordan's machine: 'it was extremely ingenious and novel in many of its working details, but being somewhat complex, has never come into extended use.'[194]

The contrary argument of the use of carving machines and their products was made in the 1870s by W. J. Loftie. He commented on the ability of the machine to respond to changes in design. Talking about an imaginary neighbour's house he wrote:

> Take the chairs as an example. Say they cost Brown £2 10s. each. They are carved by machinery, and are of the latest pattern. But since he bought them, a newer and still more attractive pattern has come out, and so their value as being in the fashion is gone; and their carving too, is rather a drawback, for the carvers have invented a new way of doing such work, and can turn it out so cheaply, that chairs twice as fine as Brown's are to be had for 25s.[195]

Eastlake (1878) also complained that 'as a general rule . . . wherever wood carving is introduced in the design of second-rate furniture it is egregiously and utterly bad.'[196] One of the reasons for this, he suggested, was that the 'ordinary furniture carver has long since degenerated into a machine'. He continued: 'The fact is that a great

71

deal of his work is literally done by machinery. There are shops where enriched wood-mouldings may be bought by the yard, leaf-brackets by the dozen, and scroll work, no doubt by the pound.'[197] Of course he was right in pointing out that designs could easily be made up from machine-made parts, but again he misses the point that the commercial market wanted lots of 'work' for a little price.

The reaction of the wood-carving trade to the machines was also very negative. J. Curran, a working woodcarver, acknowledged in his report on the 1889 Paris Exhibition, that carving machines might be useful for cutting tracery and Gothic work, but as far as general use was concerned, he considered them a very poor investment indeed.[198] Curran warned against investing in carving machines because he alleged that 'in every case there has been a screw loose that nothing could tighten it, or save these instruments from falling into decay'.[199] Despite these warnings and discouragement, there was to be a serious revival of interest in the last quarter of the nineteenth century, especially in the furniture trade.

Revival of interest

An indicator of interest in any particular aspect of the industry can be found in the volume of articles that appear in the trade press at any one period. Machine carving is no exception. The original interest in the early 1840s was based on the new inventions and the hoped-for possibilities that may have resulted from its use. The year 1860 was another vintage year with the developments of Cox and Son which were widely reported in a variety of journals. Again, interest revived in the early 1890s with a number of articles about the different machines available to the furniture-maker. For example, in the space of just over a year the Wood Carving Company of Birmingham had three reviews that extolled the virtues of their products.[200] The most revealing of these was in the *Cabinet Maker* in December 1890. Commenting on the capabilities of the Wood Carving Company, it noted the demand from the public for carved furniture. 'With a public insisting upon having a great show for little money, the maker must either smother his work with bad carving ... or he must employ an inexpensive substitute.' It continued by saying that 'good reproductions of carving are much preferable to the dreadful scratching which has to pass muster in the cheaper class of goods now in the market.'[201]

12 A group of Moores carving machines in operation in the factory of
Harris Lebus of London *c*. 1899

In other words the trade accepted machine-made carvings that
were of a high standard of finish in preference to feeble hand carving. The *Cabinet Maker*, in an obituary for Harris Lebus in 1907,
recorded that he was the first to 'press the wonderful carving machinery into the service of woodworking'.[202] He started business in the
1870s and it is evident that the machine referred to in the obituary
is the 'Universal' carving machine which had an extensive write-up
in the *Cabinet Maker*, (1 September 1891). In this article, reference
was made to the fact that the machine could be seen in the factories
of Mr Lebus, or in the offices of the Universal Wood-carving Machine Company in Lombard Street. A few years earlier, in 1889, the
same journal had suggested that an American model, the Moore
carving machine, could be operated by a boy and therefore 'no
manufacturer who employs carvers and has any quantity of duplicate carvings to make, can afford to be without a machine, as it will
save its cost in three months'.[203]
    These multiple carvers were based on Jordan's idea, but they also
suffered from problems of cost-effectiveness associated with the

13 A bank of hand carvers employed in finishing machine-carved parts as well as full hand carving

multitude of adjustments required to achieve a pattern. Embossing machines were also used to produce 'carved' ornament, but as the dies were expensive to make, the process was only cost-effective when applied to large batches of objects.[204]

American carving machines were operational in advanced factories like Harris Lebus in London and William Birch in High Wycombe. Indeed, the use of American machines in conjunction with hand carving was noted by a report in 1894 on the Birch factory:

> on the framing floor are to be found two of Moore's Universal carving machines which are kept busy carving backs for the oak chairs which have long been a speciality of the firm. In addition twenty carvers are also employed in finishing and carving the more delicate work.[205]

Perhaps the most interesting part of the quote is the detail about the employment of carvers for finishing and delicate work. The aim of the carving machine to democratise carving by avoiding expensive hand labour was never completely fulfilled. It was not until the establishment of applied carving manufacturers, producing relief mouldings and routed designs with the 'new' carving machines, that the demand for carved-style furniture could be met. But still the need for a conjunction between hand, eye, and machine was deemed necessary to achieve artistic results. Goss (1906), an observer of the American industry, remarked that:

> the automatic carving machines supplanted the laborious process of re-moving by hand superfluous wood, preparatory to the final artistic touch of the hand tool, which infuses life into each upturned leaf as guided by the skilled carver.[206]

Finishing processes

As well as material, construction, and decoration, the finish of fur-niture was an important communicating device. In fact even if the furniture was badly made but looked well finished, it would pass many a consumer's test of appropriateness. Because finishes were more than just protective, and, in some cases, a complete façade, I have divided them into three broad groups which encompass the decorative and illusory treatments as well as purely functional ones. The first group of finishes are those used with the intention of either enhancing or protecting the natural grain of the timber by providing a defensive coat of a matt or gloss finish. These would include oil, varnish and polished finishes. The second group relates to ideas of disguising the quality of the timber or imitating another type of timber or material, by altering the colour, grain, or texture. This group includes staining, graining and dyeing. The third group are the decorative finishes that are applied to furniture, to ornament them without attempting to imitate wood-grains, but possibly to imitate other materials. These include japanning, painting, stencil-ling, marbling, and other painting techniques.

Historically, the question of finishes has always been important. One of the earliest treatises on the subject is *A Treatise of Japanning and Varnishing* by John Stalker and George Parker, published in 1688. By the eighteenth century the state of the art was well estab-lished, and in the nineteenth century there were many publications on the subjects of varnishing, painting and finishing.[207] These works were aimed at the two distinct crafts of japanning and varnishing on the one hand, and furniture painting on the other. Both crafts were well established in the eighteenth century and survived various changes in taste, remaining as separate trades into the twentieth century.

Along with the traditional methods of furniture finishing, the possibilities offered by the discoveries and inventions of science and their application to the furniture trade did not go unnoticed. In 1829 a furniture-maker's guide thought that

> The researches of the chemist are daily adding to a stock of information valuable to every department of the arts and sciences; among these the cabinet-maker and upholsterer will find many peculiarly serviceable – witness the modern improvements in cements, varnishes, gilding, polishing and every other part of ornamental decoration.[208]

This explosion of information was made available in the wealth of practical volumes on the subject of furniture finishing, as well as many articles in magazines and dictionaries published throughout the nineteenth century. Although these works are useful in discovering recipes and techniques, very little seems to have been recorded about the introduction and early history of some of the new methods, their relative success and popularity.

Enhancing and protecting the surface

The degree of shine or the obvious 'newness' was at times very important to the consumer, so this was often a major consideration in the development of varnishes. The benefits of French polish in this respect were one of the reasons for its immense popular appeal. The example of Ruskin's comments on the 'fatal newness' of furniture in Holman Hunt's painting *The Awakening Conscience* is not only a condemnation of the taste of certain sections of society, it is also a moral judgement on the tastes of society.

Friction varnishing or French-polishing was the most important furniture-finishing innovation in the nineteenth century. It replaced the laborious methods of waxing and oiling that had been standard practice for many years previously. It also created a highly polished and smooth finish which was a great selling point. It is claimed that French practitioners of the art were established in London as early as 1808,[209] but writers in the second decade of the century were still asserting its novelty. Gill (1818) found French-polishing to be 'nearly new' in furniture-making. He pointed out that hitherto it had been used for lathe-turned work, especially musical instruments.[210] In 1823 the *Mechanics Magazine* ran a report extolling the virtues of the new process:

> The Parisians have now introduced an entirely new mode of polishing which is called plaque, and is to wood precisely what plating is to metal. The wood by some process is made to resemble marble, and has all the beauty of that article with much of its solidity. It is even asserted by persons who have made trial of the new mode that water may be spilled upon it without staining it.[211]

In 1829 it was still seen as a comparatively modern process which was beneficial to the furniture:

> The method of varnishing furniture by means of rubbing it on the surface of the wood, is of comparatively modern date. To put on a hard face, which shall not be so liable to scratch as varnish, and yet appear equally fine, the French polish was introduced.[212]

However, although it was a highly popular finish with the public, design critics hastened to condemn the process. Eastlake compared it to hand (wax) polishing:

> The present system of French-polishing, or literally varnishing furniture is destructive of all artistic effect in its appearance, because the surface of wood thus lacquered can never change colour, or acquire that rich hue which is one of the chief charms of old cabinet work.[213]

Whereas French polish supposedly enhanced the attractiveness of a fine quality timber, there were other methods that improved the look of furniture made from cheaper materials. Bitmead noted three processes that he considered under the title of 'cheap work'. These included three methods of glaze coating, a process of stencilling using lamp-black on oak, and charcoal polishing which gave a black finish like ebony.[214]

Disguising and imitating timber

The benefits to both maker and consumer in having a 'high-style look' without the associated expense are obvious. Many of the most inventive activities centred on attempts to achieve the appearance of a high-quality timber without incurring high costs. Since ancient

Egypt, stains and colouring agents had been used to imitate costly timbers, and there are many recipes for staining and graining inferior woods from the seventeenth century onward. At the beginning of the nineteenth century the processes were all prepared by hand. As the century progressed the possibility of mechanical application arose. In 1842 a correspondent of the *Mechanics Magazine* described a process he had devised to achieve the appearance and texture of bird's-eye maple. The process simply involved placing veneers of common woods such as plane, birch, etc., between warmed wave-grooved rollers which distorted the fibres of the wood sheets. When they had set and been cleaned off they had the appearance of bird's-eye maple.[215]

In 1850 Samuel Jacobs took out a patent for wood-graining by machine,[216] and in 1854 Clayton patented a machine for embossing and ornamenting woods. In this instance, 'inferior woods' were passed between heated rollers engraved with the design either in relief or intaglio. Pressure then transferred the design to the wood surface.[217] In 1856 there were two more patented processes. F. Whitehead patented a method of decoration using heaters and tracers,[218] and T. Williams devised a process to imitate costly woods.[219] Yet another method, reported in 1868, relied on printing on to wood surfaces using Indiarubber blocks. Attempts to transfer the facsimile of fine grains to otherwise plain wood were devised by William Dean in 1869. His process enabled copies of fine-grained wood to be transferred to any flat or irregular surface.[220] The process was brought to a fine art by the Grand Rapids Panel Company in the United States, who manufactured 'Elastic Graining Plates' designed to produce fine imitation French burl (walnut) veneer and imitation mahogany crotch veneer. It is worth noting that hand-operated graining instruments had been used by house decorators for a long time and were also used to impress a grain pattern on to a painted surface. The hand roller was carved in relief with the required design and rolled into the wet paint.[221]

The craze for pseudo-scientific names for wood treatments and finishes abounded. The prefix xylo- (from Greek, *xulon*, wood) was adopted by a number of inventors for their particular processes. One of the most widely reported of these grain transfer processes was an operation called 'xylography'; it was based on the idea that designs could be transferred to furniture by printing or impressing.

The first reference to xylography appears to be in the *Society of Arts Journal* published in January 1869.[222] The technique was based on taking a decorative wood board and applying a coat of oil paint to it. A paper sheet was then rolled over this, and the print was transferred to the paper. It was then a matter of rolling the print on to the inferior surface. The ability to produce many copies from the same plate contributed to its success. Further developments occurred in October 1873 with the granting of a patent to Thomas Whitburn of Guildford for his process of printing decorative designs on wood.[223]

Whitburn presented his findings to the Society of Arts in December 1873.[224] The process used engravings or electrotypes which were printed on to a wood surface, using a printing press. Whitburn was at pains to distinguish between his decoration and the imitation of surfaces, and declared that his process was definitely decorative, its role being subordinate to the construction. This was welcomed by Dr Christopher Dresser, who expressed the opinion that if too great an elaboration were given to furniture, the general effect of the design would suffer.[225]

In 1876, another report in the *Furniture Gazette* further explained the Whitburn process, and lamented the fact that it had not been generally adopted by the trade.[226] However, in the following year there appeared a series of advertisements for the process made by Messrs Whitburn and Young. These, and the fact that the process was shown at the Paris Exhibition of 1878, could indicate some commercial success. Paterson noted that:

> Among the specimens [of xylography] are some panels of pine with representations of flowers and leaves, in which the natural brilliancy of the wood is not deadened by any process of dyeing. This greatly heightens the effect produced, and if the process is a cheap one, as one would suppose it should be, it might become a very valuable addition to the means at the disposal of the decorator or cabinet-maker.[227]

Another process called xylotechnography, devised by the cabinet-making firm of Trollope and Sons, was shown at the 1871 Exhibition. It consisted of staining the wood surface with certain transparent colours to produce a result similar to inlaying.[228] The *Art Journal Catalogue of the 1871 Exhibition* (1871, p. 50) noted that 'the process gives it all the elegance of combined ebony and ivory'.

New techniques and processes appeared regularly in exhibitions and in the pages of the trade press. It is evident that many of them fall into the category of those patented ideas that were rapidly superseded by others in the continuing cycle of invention. A successful decorative process was developed by H. C. Webb of Worcester. It was called diachromatising, and was a method of staining colours in a pattern into a wooden surface which enabled the colours to penetrate right through the solid wood. This method had the benefit of not being prone to wear and abrasive removal. The technique was exhibited at the South Kensington International Health Exhibition in 1884.[229]

The Pixis process involved another type of copying process: the transferral of photographs to wood. It appears to have been an extremely complicated process, and yet another example of a precursor of a twentieth century method.[230]

Various other strange attempts ensued. Thermography was a process devised by Felix Abate of Naples in 1854. Here the veneers were exposed to the action of hydrochloric acid or sulphuric acid, either in vapours or in dilution. A press, with the appropriate pattern, was applied to the treated veneer and immediately the wood was heated a 'most perfect and beautiful representation of the printing instantly appears.'[231] A process of imitating sepia drawings by charring the surface of the wood with heated engraved cylinders was invented by Mr Brigg in 1859. A cylinder was heated by gas to allow some control over the temperature of the charring process; once the shadow effect had been obtained, the surface was rubbed down and polished.[232] Perhaps one of the most bizarre finishing processes was that invented by H. Buyten. This was a method of artificially ageing wood by a sand blasting process. Patented in 1897, it was clearly designed to help satisfy the demand for 'antique' furniture.[233]

Apart from machine methods, there were some processes developed for hand application. Bitmead (1876) referred to a process of applying paper imitations of fancy woods onto polished pine work.[234] Other more common methods included pyrography, stencilling, and painting.

Critics were constantly aware of the possibility that new techniques were open to abuse as they often seemed to undermine concepts of honesty and skilful workmanship. For example, Wyatt denounced the process invented by a Dr Boucherie for injecting dyes into woods that were to become part of marquetry panels, saying that these processes 'have presented a dangerous facility to the designers and workmen'.[235] This really is difficult to reconcile with the normal trade practice of dyeing wood for marquetry in bowls of stain. However, not all the new processes were condemned by critics. In fact some were espoused as being positively beneficial.

One such major improvement, patented in 1861 by John Dyer, was a process that produced an imitation of marquetry on the surface of deal or pine furniture.[236] John Dyer established a furniture manufacturing company that won medals at many international exhibitions. His method consisted of coating a cheap wood surface with gum, size, or wax and then applying blocks, stencils or transfers to the surface. The dry surface was then French-polished. The process was acknowledged as being an exciting development by Booth (1864), and he praised the partnership of Dyer and Watts for their 'honest intentions':

> These gentlemen have directed their attention, first to treating a common material with first rate workmanship and superior design; and secondly they have involved and introduced a decorative system, which is simple, effective and expressly suited to their common material.[237]

The *Art Journal* (1863, p. 80) had been even more glowing in its account of the firm's products:

> Messrs Dyer and Watts claim from us a most decided expression of our approval and admiration – not only because of its intrinsic elegance, but also because, being so excellent, it is in every respect adapted to both the requirements and the means of the community at large.

Finally, G. W. Yapp, commenting on the painted furniture of Dyer and Watts, pointed out that painted ornament should not necessarily be made to imitate inlaid work: 'on the contrary, it is capable of effects quite beyond the reach of marquetry.'[238] This was perhaps the vindication of a machine process that was a success in its own right.

Decorative finishes

Apart from copying timber grains and creating artificial effects, cabinet-makers sought methods of decoration which were applicable as surface ornament. The *Furniture Gazette* ran a short series of articles entitled 'Cheap artistic decoration for deal and pine furniture', which detailed three processes of simple decoration for surfaces.

The first process was leaf work. The article acknowledged that although nature was the basis of the design, this particular technique was a revival of one that had been overlooked for many years. It entailed selecting suitable natural leaves, pressing them and then gluing them to a previously stained carcase. A final coat of copal varnish sealed the surface.[239] Apparently, the attraction of this process was that it used natural materials that were not only artistically acceptable, but were also cheap and novel.

The second process noted was straw mosaic. After pointing out that much straw work was imported from Germany (where convict labour, combined with extensive steam-powered machinery, was used to make it), the article details the full process of making a straw-work finish by hand to be applied to small articles of furniture. Straw mosaic work closely resembled very superior Tunbridge ware and it was in this comparative context that it was seen as novel but inexpensive.[240]

The third method was the application of watercolour painted designs on to plain wooden surfaces. When dry, it was polished to make it permanent.[241] One of the problems associated with buying this type of painted furniture was spelt out in the section devoted to wardrobes in *Hints on Houses and House Furnishings* (1851):

> In order to meet the great desire for cheapness cabinet-makers give a coat of size to such articles as they wish to paint and upon this a coat of water-colour of any required shade.

The purpose of this process was to allow the colour to dry on the surface which was then varnished and appeared as good as japan. Only when the varnish wore off and the paint soon followed, did the cheapness of the process reveal itself. According to the writer this problem was particularly associated with common wash-stands. Painted furniture had not always been accepted so readily. In 1826 Whittock wrote:

> In painting chairs it is sometimes the practice to marble them; nothing can be in worse taste, as no imitation should ever be introduced where the reality could not be applied if persons chose to go to the expense – and who would choose a marble chair?[242]

Surface finish and the quantity of work were two of the major attributes required by customers. It is little wonder that attempts to interest the general public in the merits of plain oiled oak met with little response when it was possible to buy furniture with a bright, shiny, new surface.[243]

Notes

1 Ingold, 'Tools, minds and machines', p. 158.
2 C. Mitcham, 'Types of technology', *Research in Philosophy and Technology*, I, 1978, pp. 229–94.
3 Ingold, 'Tools, minds and machines'.
4 Staudenmaier, *Technology's Storytellers*, p. 140.
5 Staudenmaier, *Technology's Storytellers*.
6 *England's Workshops*, 1864, p. 311.
7 These divisions include cabinet-makers, fancy cabinet makers, frame-makers, chair-makers.
8 Dodd, *Days at the Factories*.
9 Booth, *Life and Labour of the People of London*.
10 Productivity can be increased when a manufacturer is producing a limited range of objects using the same raw material and processes. In these cases, the large concern has a benefit over the small by, for example, increased purchasing power.
11 Richards, Treatise, p. 47.
12 *Ibid.*
13 Pollen, 'Furniture and woodwork'. p. 212.
14 *Furniture Gazette*, 21 April 1877.
15 Mateaux, *Wonderland of Work*, pp. 147–8.
16 Reid, *Furniture Makers*, p. 31.
17 *Scientific American*, October 1880.
18 C. Hooper, in [Paris 1867b] *Reports of Artisans* p. 6.
19 Mateaux, *Wonderland of Work*, pp. 147–9.
20 H. Mayhew, *The Morning Chronicle*, Letter LIX, 4 July 1850.
21 For the history of mass production of gunstocks see J. W. Roe, 'Interchangeable Manufacture', *Newcomen Society Transactions*, XVII, 1936. Also Rosenberg, *American System of Manufactures*.
22 See Advertisement in the *Furniture Gazette*, 1 January 1889 (C.M.). The insurance records of a small business in Essex from 1900 indicate the use of machines. The insurance cover was for four benches, carding machine, mortising machine, combination saw all of which were hand powered only.
23 See G. L. Molesworth, 'Conversion of wood by machinery', *Minutes of Proceedings of Institute of Civil Engineers*, XVII, 17 November 1857, pp. 17–51; Richards, *Treatise*; Sims, *200 Years of History and Evolution of Woodworking Machinery*, 1985; M. P. Bale, *Woodworking Machinery*.
24 Patent No. 1152, 11 April 1777.
25 Sims, *200 Years of History and Evolution of Woodworking Machinery*, p. 3.
26 Patent No. 2844, 7 May 1805.
27 For details of the Portsmouth block-making machinery and factory organisation see Cooper, 'Production line at Portsmouth block-mill', and Gilbert, *Portsmouth Block-making Machinery*.

28 Bitmead, *London Cabinet-Makers Guide*, p. 67.
29 Patent No. 1125, 21 May 1776.
30 Patent No. 5502, 1 June 1827.
31 See Tice, 'The Knapp dovetailing machine', pp. 1070–2.
32 Clark, *Exhibited Machinery of 1862*.
33 Bitmead, *London Cabinet-Makers Guide*, p. 74.
34 Holland's records in the Archive of Art and Design show a purchase of a boiler, engine and gearing for lathes, vertical and circular saws, and mortising machines. AAD folio 364, 13/39.
35 Wyatt, *On Furniture and Decoration*, p. 308.
36 *Post Office Directory*, London, 1866.
37 Arkell and Duckworth, 'Cabinet-makers', p. 183.
38 *Second Report of the Royal Commission on Technical Instruction*, IV, Cmd 3981–III, 1884, p. 7.
39 *Cabinet Maker*, 1 October 1883, p. 66.
40 Wyatt, *On Furniture and Decoration*, p. 311.
41 *Furniture Gazette*, 7 November 1874, p. 1228.
42 *Furniture Gazette*, 28 July 1877, p. 53.
43 Paterson, 'Cabinet work', p. 96.
44 *Cabinet Maker*, 1 March 1884, pp. 174–5. These machines included log saw, circular saw, universal jointer, band-saw, fretsaw, lathes, boring, mortising, and tenoning machine, carving and incising machines and a papering-up machine.
45 *Cabinet Maker*, 1 August 1883, p. 39.
46 Paterson, 'Cabinet work'.
47 *Ibid.*
48 Examples include High Wycombe factories as well as outworkers.
49 For a thorough history of the early use of plywood, see Knight and Wulpi, *Veneers and Plywood*.
50 Perry, *Modern Plywood*, p. 28.
51 For more details on the Renaisssance and veneers, see Knight and Wulpi, *Veneers and Plywood*.
52 Quoted in MacQuoid and Edwards, *Dictionary*, p. 363.
53 This extract is taken from *The Decorator*, May 1864.
54 These included Sir Harry Hamilton Johnston, *The Veneerings*, 1922, and Grace Furniss, *The Veneered Savage*, 1891.
55 W. Maclerie, 'Veneer', *Tinsley's Magazine*, XIX, 1876, pp. 591–5.
56 Sheraton, *Cabinet Dictionary*.
57 *Furniture Gazette*, 20 August 1873, p. 378.
58 Eastlake, *Hints on Household Taste*, p. 57.
59 *Ibid.*
60 *Cabinet Maker*, October 1883, p. 66.
61 Patent No. 87, 31 October 1635.
62 Patent No. 120, 20 October 1638.
63 Patent No. 2968, 23 September 1806.
64 The Sun Insurance Company records identify Marc Isambard Brunel, John Collingdon and Thomas Mudge all of Battersea, Surrey, as having: 'Insurance on their manufactory stables, carthouse, £700. Steam engine therein – £600. Fixed machinery and utensils – £600. Moveable utensils and stocks and goods in trust – £100. Total £2000 On another policy the same plus Sophia Drummage,

the proprietors of Battersea Bridge for the time being, on the dwelling house of Thomas Mudge – £700, house adjoining in tenure to John Collingdon – £700, a manufactory for machinery – £1000 Total £2400.' I am indebted to Frances Collard for this reference.

65 Holtzapffel, *Turning and Mechanical Manipulation*, p. 806.
66 *Ibid.*
67 *British Register*, Local History Collection, Battersea District Library.
68 *House Decorator and School of Design*, 15 April 1881, p. 285.
69 *Ibid.*
70 *Ibid.*
71 H. Mayhew, *The Morning Chronicle*, Letter LXII, 25 July 1850.
72 Himmelheber, *Biedermeier Furniture*, p. 93.
73 *Ibid.*
74 C. F. Hummel, *With Hammer in Hand*, footnote no. 253.
75 Greeley, *Great Industries of the United States*.
76 US Patent No. 1758, 3 September 1840.
77 Perry, *Modern Plywood*, pp. 32–3.
78 Holtzapffel *Turning and Mechanical Manipulation*.
79 *Mechanics Magazine*, 3 March 1849, p. 1904.
80 Patent No. 11716, 25 May 1847.
81 *Mechanics Magazine*, 10 March 1849, p. 218.
82 *Ibid.*
83 *Mechanics Magazine*, 12 February 1848, p. 155.
84 G. Dodd, *Novelties, Inventions, Curiosities in Art and Manufacture*, London, 1860.
85 *House Decorator and School of Design*, 15 April 1881, p. 285.
86 *Practical Magazine*, V, 1875, pp. 207–8.
87 *Ibid.*
88 Advertisement in *Post Office Directory of Cabinet, Furniture and Upholstery Trades*, 1877.
89 *Furniture Gazette*, 19 October 1878, p. 265.
90 *Cabinet-Maker's Assistant*, pp. 49–57.
91 Bitmead, *London Cabinet-Makers Guide*.
92 *Engineer and Mechanics Encyclopedia*, 1836.
93 Patent No. 2362, 21 September 1861.
94 Patent No. 533, 25 February 1863.
95 *Practical Mechanics Journal*, III, March 1859, p. 314; also *Furniture Gazette*, 18 August 1877, p. 120.
96 Mateaux, *Wonderland of Work*, p. 153.
97 Patent No. 12791, 27 September 1849.
98 *Cabinet-Maker's Assistant*, p. 54.
99 *Ibid.*
100 Patent No. 308
101 Patent No. 3632.
102 T. Kelly, *The Practical Carpenter, Joiner and Cabinet-Maker*, 1826, p. 21.
103 Martin, *New Circle of the Mechanical Arts*, p. 116.
104 Bitmead, *London Cabinet-Makers Guide*, 1873, p. 78.
105 Wyatt, *On Furniture and Decoration*, p. 302.
106 *Ibid.*
107 *Ibid.*, p. 305.

108 [Paris 1878] *Society of Arts. Artisans Reports*, p. 420.
109 *Ibid.*
110 Eastlake, *Hints on Household Taste*, p. 127.
111 *Ibid.*
112 Talbert, *Gothic Forms Applied to Furniture and Decoration*, p. 1.
113 *Ibid.*, p. 2.
114 [Paris 1878] *Society of Arts. Artisans Reports*, p. 434.
115 Bitmead, *London Cabinet-Makers Guide*, p. 46.
116 *Ibid.*, p. 67.
117 *Ibid.*, p. 74.
118 *Furniture Gazette*, 19 October 1878, p. 265.
119 The *Builder*, 21 December 1878, p. 1326.
120 *Cabinet Maker*, 2 August 1880, p. 20.
121 H. F. Keevil, *The Cabinet Making Trade in Bath, 1750–1964*, 1965.
122 *Furniture Gazette*, 27 December 1873, p. 528.
123 *Furniture Gazette*, 8 November 1873, p. 491.
124 William Billingsley, Patent No. 121, 10 December 1638.
125 Joseph Jacob, Patent No. 1065, 14 February 1774.
126 Thomas Rogers, Patent No. 1568, 7 November 1786.
127 John Skidmore, Patent No. 1552, 5 August 1786.
128 Patent No. 423, 14 March 1818.
129 *Furniture Gazette*, 27 December 1873, p. 628.
130 *Mechanics Magazine*, 1 May 1830, p. 130.
131 M. Levy, 'Bullocks Stock-in-Trade Sale', *Furniture History*, 1989, p. 202. The auction record shows that this was sold for £5, a not inconsiderable sum in 1819.
132 Ure, *Dictionary of Arts Manufactures and Mines*.
133 Wyatt, *On Furniture and Decoration*, p. 296.
134 *Ibid.*, p. 294.
135 Siddons, *Cabinet-Makers Guide*, p. 120.
136 Wyatt, *On Furniture and Decoration*, p. 294.
137 H. Williams, *Workers Industrial Index to London*, 1881.
138 *Furniture and Decoration*, 1 October 1890, p. 280.
139 [Paris 1878] *Society of Arts. Artisans Reports*, p. 419.
140 G. Maddox, *An Illustrated Catalogue of Bedroom Furniture etc*, London, *c.* 1865.
141 Wyatt, *On Furniture and Decoration*, p. 311.
142 G. Colomb, Patent No. 905, 1863.
143 Patented in the UK, May 1867, Patent No. 1598.
144 *Cabinet Maker*, 1 December 1890, p. 162.
145 Smith, *Mechanick*.
146 *Practical Magazine*, VI, 1876, p. 108.
147 *Ibid.*
148 See *Royal Society of Arts Transactions*, LIV, 1843.
149 *Civil Engineer and Architect's Journal*, July 1841.
150 *Furniture Gazette*, 26 October 1878, p. 280.
151 Bitmead, *London Cabinet-Makers Guide*, p. 66.
152 *Practical Magazine*, VI, 1876, p. 108.
153 *Ibid.*
154 Patent No. 2232, 5 October 1855.
155 Bitmead, *London Cabinet-Makers Guide*, pp. 64–5.

156 Pinto, *Tunbridge Ware*, p. 123.
157 *Furniture Gazette*, 24 October 1883, p. 253.
158 *Furniture Gazette*, 14 January 1882, p. 24.
159 O. A. Nathusisus of New York, 1877, trade catalogue, Henry Francis du Pont Winterthur Library Collection.
160 *Cabinet Maker*, 1 May 1882.
161 For example, fretted trusses are illustrated in the *Journal of Design*, XII, 1851, p. 193, supplied by Samuel Sandy, 8 Upper Smith Street, Northampton Square, London.
162 Paterson, 'Cabinet Work', p. 96.
163 Pollen, 'Furniture and woodwork', p. 210.
164 *England's Workshops*, 1864, pp. 306–7.
165 Dodd, *Days at the Factories*, p. 405.
166 Patent No. 15518, 1885.
167 Audsley, *Art of Polychromatic and Decorative Turning*. 1911.
168 P. G. Hamerton, 'Furniture: An after dinner conversation', *Macmillan Magazine*, June 1863.
169 Ettema, 'Technological innovation and design economics'.
170 Joy, 'Woodworking and carving machinery', XII; Hughes, 'Mechanical carving machines'.
171 T. Jordan, 'On carving by machinery', a paper read to the Society of Arts, 17–24 February 1847, see Transactions of the Society of Arts, supplementary vol. 1852, pp. 124–36.
172 'On the applications of Science to the fine and useful arts', *Art Union*, 1848, p. 193.
173 J. Buckle, Patent No. 4652, March 1822.
174 See Hounshell, *From the American System to Mass Production*, which includes a full discussion of the semi-automatic turning of interchangeable parts. See also C. C. Cooper, 'The role of Thomas Blanchard's woodworking inventions in nineteenth century American manufacturing technology', unpublished PhD thesis, Yale University, 1985.
175 Patent No. 5871.
176 Exhibited at the Polytechnic Institution Regent Street, 1839. Carving of Alexander in marble and carving of Milton in ivory.
177 Patent No. 10756.
178 P. Stanton, *Pugin*, London, 1971, p. 39. I am grateful to Dr P. Kirkham for this reference.
179 W. Irving, Patent No. 9962, November 1843. In addition to the carving machine, Irving patented two other cutting and shaping machines after 1843, involved himself in patent brick and tile manufacture, and in the patenting of a corn drill.
180 See *Dictionary of English Furniture Makers*, Furniture History Society, 1986, for fuller details of the Pratt family, but note that Samuel Pratt had patented six inventions of his own relating to furniture or camp-équipage.
181 *Art Union*, v, 1844, p. 111.
182 The *Builder*, 4 May 1844, p. 223.
183 *Ibid* p. 232.
184 The *Builder*, 20 June 1846, p. 295.
185 *Patent Journal and Inventors Magazine*, CIV, 20 May 1848, p. 637.
186 Dodd, *Curiosities of Industry*.

187 *Art Journal*, II, 1856, p. 241.
188 *Builder*, XIII, 1855, p. 47.
189 Commissioners of Patents Museum at South Kensington. Catalogue of items exhibited 1863.
190 *Illustrated Builders Journal*, 28 November 1865.
191 *Engineering and Building Times*, 15 March 1871.
192 Richards, *Treatise*, p. 44.
193 *Scientific American*, 6 October 1880.
194 M. Powis Bale, *Woodworking Machinery, Its Rise Progress and Construction*, 1880.
195 W. J. Loftie, *A Plea for Art in the Home*, London, 1877, p. 23.
196 Eastlake, *Hints on Household Taste*, p. 58.
197 *Ibid.*
198 [Paris 1889] *Reports of Artisans*, pp. 206–7.
199 *Ibid.*, p. 207.
200 *Cabinet Maker*, 1 December 1890, p. 162. *Cabinet Maker*, 1 June 1891, p. 331. *Furniture and Decoration*, 1 January 1892, p. 11.
201 *Cabinet Maker*, 1 December 1890, p. 162.
202 *Cabinet Maker*, 28 September 1907, p. 510.
203 *Cabinet Maker*, 1 July 1889, p. 25.
204 In 1876, *the Practical Magazine* reported 'an improved carving and panelling machine that was capable of producing carvings, recessed or relief panels or fretwork.' It was noted that there was a demand for the facility to produce designed mouldings in the solid to avoid having to attach them separately: *Practical Magazine*, VI, 1876, p. 29.
205 *Furniture and Decoration*, January 1894, p. 14.
206 D. Goss, *History of Grand Rapids and its Industries*, Chicago, 1906, pp. 1037–8, quoted in Ettema, 'Technological innovation and design economics'.
207 See, for example, *The Painters, Gilders, and Varnishers Manual, c.* 1835; Siddons, Cabinet-Makers Guide; G. Smith, The Laboratory or School of Arts, 1810.
208 *Complete Cabinet Maker and Upholsterers Guide*, pp. VII–VIII.
209 Herve, *French-Polishers and their Industry*, p. 39.
210 Gill, 'On French varnish for cabinet work', pp. 119 and 371–2.
211 *Mechanics Magazine*, 22 November 1823.
212 *Complete Cabinet Maker and Upholsterers Guide*, pp. 100–1. An identical paragraph is found in A. Phelps, *The Cabinet Makers Guide*, Greenfield, Massachusetts, 1825. See R. Mussey, 'Transparent furniture finishes in New England 1700–1820', in *Proceedings of the Furniture and Wooden Objects Symposium*, Ottawa, July 1980.
213 Eastlake, *Hints on Household Taste*, p. 83.
214 Bitmead, *London Cabinet–Makers Guide*.
215 *Mechanics Magazine*, 9 July 1842, p. 21.
216 Patent No. 13,300, 24 October 1850.
217 Patent No. 2070, Clayton, 26 September 1854.
218 Patent No. 2352, Whitehead, 8 October 1856.
219 Patent No. 2112 Williams 1856.
220 Patent No. 3184 Dean 1869.
221 *Practical Mechanics Journal*, VIII, 1855, p. 78.
222 *Society of Arts Journal*, 29 January, 1869, pp. 155–9.

223 *Furniture Gazette*, October 1873.
224 *Society of Arts Journal*, 12 December 1873, pp. 59–65.
225 *Ibid.*, p. 65.
226 *Furniture Gazette*, 21 October 1876, p. 241.
227 [Paris 1878] *Society of Arts. Artisans Reports*, Report on Furniture by Thomas Paterson, p. 390.
228 *Furniture Gazette*, 13 December 1873, p. 592.
229 *Official Catalogue of International Health Exhibition*, 1884, Class xxx, p. 895.
230 R. Haldane, *Workshop Receipts*, 1883, pp. 193–4.
231 *Furniture Gazette*, 13 December 1873, p. 590, and *Practical Mechanics Journal*, viii, 1866, p. 78.
232 *Furniture Gazette*, 13 December 1873, p. 590.
233 H. Buyten, Patent No. 24381 1897.
234 Bitmead, *Practical French Polisher and Enameller*, p. 42.
235 Wyatt, *On Furniture and Decoration*, p. 294.
236 Patent No. 1661, 29 June 1861.
237 L. Booth, *Original Design Book for Decorative Furniture*, London, 1864, p. 16.
238 Yapp, *Art, Furniture, Upholstery, and House Decoration*, plate cxix.
239 *Furniture Gazette*, 23 August 1873, p. 312.
240 *Ibid.*, 13 Sept 1873, p. 360.
241 *Ibid.*, 4 October 1873, p. 480.
242 N. Whittock, *The Decorative Painters and Glaziers Guide*, London, 1826, p. 77.
243 See, for example, Eastlake, *Hints on Household Taste*, p. 129: 'The foolish practice of varnishing new oak before it has acquired the rich and varied tint which time and use alone can give it.'

3 Materials

Introduction

During the nineteenth century there was a tremendous growth in the choice of materials available to producers of furniture. It is important to use this general term here rather than cabinet-maker or upholsterer, because many of the new materials and techniques were used by those who had previously been unassociated with traditional furniture-making. At the same time, in addition to the growing range of materials available, there was also a gradual change in the nature of substances used in furniture-making. These changes included the imitation of one material by another; the use of completely artificial material; the adoption of seemingly incompatible materials which had been alien to the cabinet-maker's craft; and the revival of craft materials that had been neglected. Research into these matters is useful for the historian, not only because it is a neglected area of furniture history, but also because such study gives some insight into how the use of materials influenced the look of objects, reflecting society's taste as well as economic concerns.

In this work, the investigations into the use of new materials in furniture-making during the nineteenth century have been conducted within a framework that comprises a variety of perspectives: technical developments, the question of choice and usage, the relationship of material to production, and the question of materials and style. In each case study, the nature of the substances has been examined to establish the process of obtaining raw material and then converting it into an end-use product.

Technical developments

To analyse the development of materials and the distinctions between them, it can be useful to look at the degree of technical interference that altered their make-up. The selection of materials by furniture-makers was usually based on the shape to be imposed upon it. If the design demanded a curved wooden member then the appropriate substances had to be cut out of solid, built up from smaller pieces or bent to shape. The actual chosen technique for fabricating the material is generally determined by its nature. For example, with unamended natural resources such as solid wood, a shape is often achieved by tracing or following the grain or similar natural phenomenon. With synthetic matter a form may be given which relates to its plasticity. An example of this might be the moulding of gutta percha into shapes that could be applied in place of carving.

Although all materials have an original natural basis, what varies is the degree of interference by man and this can be divided into three convenient divisions. The first includes those commodities that are left in their natural state, i.e. timber from the tree. These are manipulated in many ways but usually retain evidence of their origin. In the second group, the materials are transformed in some way to disguise their origin, i.e. papier mâché or imitation wood grains. The third group consists of synthetic materials that have no apparent relation to their origin, i.e gutta percha decoration or bois-durci.[1] Furthermore, these three divisions relate respectively to concepts of recognition, partial recognition (surface), and complete loss of recognition of the original material, each one serving a different purpose in the hierarchy of furniture design. There comes a stage where the 'appearance' is the only reality that can be related to. This important question of the blurring of distinctions between the illusory and the real is discussed in Chapter 6 Design, below.

Choice and usage

The second perspective relates to the reasons why certain materials were used in preference to others. This entails reference to the economics of the trade with its expanding markets but lower profit margins, and its ingenious use of once useless products, but it can also refer to the socially and culturally perceived images of materials, their symbolism, and their status. As is well known, these images are endowed with meanings broader than their natural qualities. For example, stone signifies strength and durability, wood signifies warmth and tradition, and even within the genus certain timbers have a significance unrelated to their natural properties. In their natural state they tend to symbolise tradition; in a transformed state they signify an illusion which may only bear a passing resemblance to the real thing, e.g. veneer or scagliola. This is often enough to create the desired effect, but in the use of synthetics there can be an ambivalent significance which may be seen to be progressive or regressive, depending on its use and the point of view.

Connected with these issues of significance is the ever-present search for novelty, prompted by the expansion of the market and its subsequent need for diversification, and by manufacturers looking to either create or meet these demands. Bitmead (1873) thought that the search for new products 'not only calls into action a great deal of mechanical ingenuity and employs considerable capital but [the result] gives even the humblest a sort of self respect.'

The desire to improve one's position in society was the continuation of a process that had been well established in the eighteenth century, and one of the easiest ways of showing this improvement was in the consumption of an ever-growing choice of furniture and furnishings, in an ever-widening range of materials. This process was understood by contemporary commentators, who noted the chain reaction spurred by the demands of various social groups, which in turn encouraged the use of certain materials as signifiers of differentiation. Knight (1830) pointed this out:

> But the general adoption of articles of luxury, such as well-made furniture, by the bulk of the people, has a natural tendency to make the wealthy desirous of procuring articles not so accessible to the many; and in this way there is a constant demand not only for new patterns of furniture, but for new materials of which such furniture should be made.[2]

This clearly links the growth in trade to the demand for new designs and the use of new materials.

Materials and production

The analysis of materials and their relationship to the maker and his production techniques is of equal importance. Prior to the technical advances of the later nineteenth and twentieth centuries, the choice of raw material was limited to that which could be reasonably worked and controlled. The skilled craftsman had to manipulate materials that were naturally resistant to forced handling into an artifact.[3] The materials involved had become part of a traditional system, and as such were predictable and acceptable. This resulted in an accepted relationship between materials, design, and process (or technique) that had essentially remained the same in respect of furniture since the mid-seventeenth century.

Craft techniques had established a relationship with tools of varying sorts from very early days, so that the use of mechanised tools, i.e. machines, in the conversion process was tempered by an understanding of their nature: what could and could not be done, how materials reacted in certain circumstances, and how far a craftsman could 'push' the potential of the material in his design. This understanding gave rise to objects that exploited the natural advantages of raw materials and disguised their disadvantages. In some cases of course, understanding of the material's potential was partial and there was room to improve existing techniques, so as to develop a new product type. Bentwood was perhaps the classic example of a technique that was well known but little understood in terms of controlled manipulation. As the demands on resources became more precise, there grew a need for homogeneous and isotropic materials which would be stable in all directions and be free of natural imperfections. This demand led to a search for components that were, for example, inherently more stable than wood, easier to apply than wood veneer, and less heavy than cast-iron. In conjunction with this was the drive towards a 'workmanship of certainty' which would be achieved through the use of prefabrication of elements, and the use of precision machines: the aim was to produce furniture from stable materials, using semi-skilled labour to meet the demands of a mass market.

Materials and style

Finally, what role did materials play in the search for a recognisable nineteenth century style? Two influences are evident. The first is the apparent continuation of a functionalist tradition, represented by the use of established materials and methods; for example, in the making of a Windsor chair. This recognition of the vernacular was supported by the demand from design critics for furniture to be made using serviceable materials, often in a utilitarian design, as opposed to the creation of 'art' objects.[4]

Second, most nineteenth century attempts at reproducing (other) material types or designs with different ingredients were based on the idea that resemblance would equal recognition and this was the crux of the 'illusion and reality' question. Throughout the century there are numerous examples of substitution and impersonation of expensive components by more mundane ones. In fact materials did little to create a true nineteenth century style. Discounting revivals, and special cases such as papier mâché and iron, the majority of furniture produced was uninfluenced by major changes in materials. However, like many changes over time, the innovations that were gradually introduced grew to transform the trade in the twentieth century. In the twentieth century, furniture design began to move away from 'image-related' performance to concentrate on 'actual' performance. The following case studies demonstrate these changes in various ways, and while each one stands on its own, collectively they illustrate the wide range of new and altered materials introduced in the nineteenth century.

Wood

It might seem unnecessary to devote much space in a work investigating materials and techniques in the nineteenth century to the oldest furniture-making material. However, changes in the use of wood were part of a crucial development process that altered the nature of furniture-making and design. Of course the very character of wood, i.e. its fragility and unpredictability, meant that it imposed certain restraints on the industry that should not be underestimated. There is no doubt that a search for a more stable and reliable wood-based product was a nineteenth century imperative to which I shall return.

One major feature of nineteenth century furniture-making was the increasingly large range of timber options available to the cabinet-maker. Although exotic woods had been available to cabinet-makers in previous centuries, during the nineteenth there was an expansion of sources of fine timber. The development of the Colonial and the South American forests during the century encouraged the use of a wide range of exotic as well as standard timbers.[5] These new sources of supply gave cabinet-makers the ability to introduce new colours and grains to their work, although they did not necessarily affect the design of objects. It could be argued that the

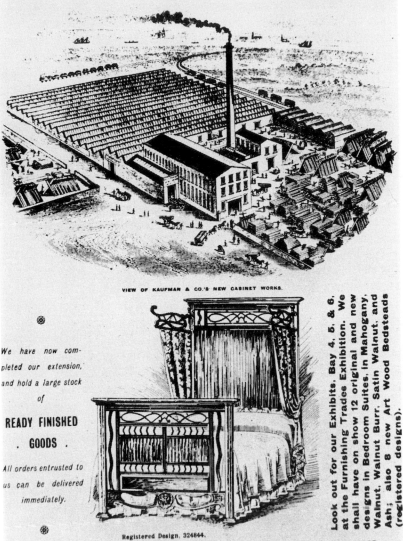

KAUFMAN & CO., WEASTE, near MANCHESTER.

Solid Hardwood Bedroom Suite & Bedstead Manufacturers.

VIEW OF KAUFMAN & CO.'S NEW CABINET WORKS.

We have now completed our extension, and hold a large stock of

READY FINISHED

. GOODS .

All orders entrusted to us can be delivered immediately.

Look out for our Exhibits. Bay 4, 5, & 6, at the Furnishing Trades Exhibition. We shall have on show 12 original and new designs in Bedroom Suites, in Mahogany, Walnut, Walnut Burr, Satin Walnut, and Ash.; also 8 new Art Wood Bedsteads (registered designs).

Registered Design, 324844.

KAUFMAN & CO., CABINET WORKS, WEASTE, near MANCHESTER.

14 An advertisement for the Kaufman Co. of Manchester. Although artistic licence is evident in the factory illustration, by the end of the century there were a number of large factory establishments making furniture in bulk

combination of improved veneer-cutting and reliable timber sources led to an increase in designs that incorporated large (flat or curved), plain surfaces. The development of the American 'pillar and scroll' style and the European Biedermeier style have been cited as examples of this.[6]

What was most important were developments in the techniques of manipulating wood or wood-based products by laminating, bending and veneering. The beginning of a scientific approach to satisfy the requirements of wood-users in general, very gradually led to the ability of producers to take control of wood and dictate the shapes and forms it might take, rather than fighting its natural resistance to manipulation. To achieve this the search for timber substitutes or ways of using the cheaper species of woods became a priority for timber merchants and dealers. The most successful development was the making of strong boards or sections with layers of wood which have become known as plywood.

Plywood

Plywood is a term devised to describe the building-up of layers or slices of wood to make a board that is stronger and more flexible than the original parts. Some authorities consider that the use of veneers on solid timber cores constitutes plywood. Others suggest that a number of veneers glued together with a criss-cross grain to make a board is the more correct definition.[7] If one takes the first definition, then the history of plywood, or more correctly, veneers, can be traced to Ancient Egypt; if the second is more realistic, then the history appears to start later. Wherever the origins of plywood were, the concept was well established by the mid-eighteenth century. Cabinet-makers were commonly using three-ply veneers to create pierced chair splats, and fretwork galleries on tables and candlestands.[8] The reason was that this laminated or ply process was stronger than solid wood of equivalent dimensions, especially when the designs that were to be fretted into it were very finely drawn. This pragmatic use of materials had little deliberate invention in it: it was simply the best solution to the problem, and was only used to help create a fashionable style uninfluenced by the technicalities of the material itself.

Thomas Sheraton's *Cabinet-Maker and Upholsterer's Drawing Book*, designed for use by practising cabinet-makers, described the practical benefits of built-up plywood work. In a design for a Universal Table, Sheraton describes its making:

> the framing is three inches broad, and mitred at the corners; and the panels are sometimes glued up in three thicknesses, the middle piece being laid with the grain across and the other two length ways of the panel, to prevent it warping.[9]

Sheraton also suggested that bookcase pediments should be made up in a similar way: 'The facia or ground board, glued up in three thicknesses, having the middle piece with the grain right up and down.'[10] In this case the plies were used to restrain the movement of the timber, in addition to giving strength and rigidity. Again, in the nineteenth century the process of building-up plies was generally to achieve a stable surface rather than be used as a technique to create new shapes in furniture, although there are examples of the latter which I discuss below.

Plies, while giving strength to cut-out surfaces, were also useful in creating a flat surface that did not warp which was particularly important for marquetry and boulle workers. Martin (1819) gave instructions on how to achieve a satisfactory base for marquetry work:

> The ground whereon the pieces are to be ranged and glued is ordinarily of oak or fir, well dried, and to prevent warping, is composed of several thicknesses glued together, with the grain of one layer intersecting the direction of the other.[11]

In the 1860s it was noted that the finest Parisian ébénistes prepared their 'placage' or base for marquetry or boulle work, by using plies of poplar and oak-wood glued together with crossed grains. The plies were then veneered with the appropriate ground wood for the final surface finish.[12] Both these examples of established relationships illustrate the 'normal' and unselfconscious use of a practical solution to a technical problem.

The development of design and manufacturing processes that deliberately exploited plies of wood, either in plywood or laminate form, may have started in Germany in the early part of the nineteenth century. Indeed, the two most famous makers of ply-laminated furniture originated from Germany around the same time – John Henry Belter and Michael Thonet.

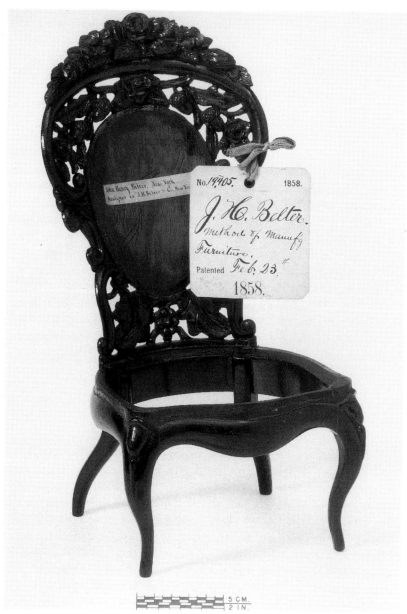

15 Patent model of chair by John Henry Belter, 1858, showing the constructional use of laminations. His technique was often hidden by exuberant carving

Originally from Württemberg in Germany, Belter emigrated to the United States in about 1840, and began experiments with laminations to create shaped forms for the frames of sofas, chairs, and beds. The benefits of using plies or laminates in furniture-making were expressly stated in Belter's remarks about his patent bedsteads; benefits included the ability to be dismantled in case of fire; space-saving by the elimination of posts and frames; a rigidity and solidity not achieved with other bedsteads; and a veneer cover which bugs could not penetrate[13] (which must have been of considerable importance to a population obsessed with bugs). While the bedsteads showed the simple smooth surfaces resulting from the process, Belter's work on chair frames used the lamination process to produce furniture in the Rococo Revival style. According to Vincent, Belter's furniture 'provides a striking example of the way in which the demands of design literally commanded developments in production technology.'[14] This suggests that the demand created by the Rococo Revival style encouraged technical developments in wood manipulation to allow furniture-makers to achieve hitherto unknown forms. The design was reliant on technology for the amazing effects that would have been extremely difficult to execute in traditional ways. There is no doubt that the popularity of the style, and the process that promoted it, led other manufacturers into the field, and some adapted Belter's process for their own use.[15]

Alongside these specifically patented developments was a more general method of ply construction called press work. Press work describes the process of building-up furniture constructions by layering a number of veneers in a criss-cross fashion in a mould or on a caul. The process allowed shaped frames to be produced from thin sections of 'plywood'. In 1866 it was new enough to receive comment in Tomlinson's *Encyclopaedia of Useful Arts*: 'Among the recent applications of this art [i.e. veneering] may be noticed press-work'.[16] He further describes 'a machine recently constituted for moulding the thin veneers into curves of single or double curvature so as to enable them to be employed for making dished and spheroidal articles'.[17] As late as 1877, press work was still regarded as new enough to be reported in the British trade press. It appeared that it was often made from 'some strong plain wood such as black walnut and rosewood or other fancy wood for the exterior'.[18]

The application of these new methods was not limited to furniture, for there is evidence of their use in other woodworking industries. In a description of workshop practice in a piano factory, published in 1864, it was noted that the 'solid carcases are formed of five or six thicknesses of timber, the grain of each laying transversely to the other, and the whole pressed together in a similar manner to veneering.'[19] This method, also called 'built-up veneer work', was used to manufacture sewing-machine cases.[20] The standardisation of material made it ideally suited to the production of large numbers of similar objects, and it was for this reason that it was most successful in the sewing-machine industry. The process, developed by the French Manufacturing Co. of Cincinnati, started in 1865. In 1867, Mr E. F. French obtained a patent, and in the following five years, another four patents were granted, all relating to the plywood construction of sewing-machine cases:

> The process consists in the making of the cases and the tables each from one board; in the former instances the corners being rounded without joints, the two ends of the boards being securely glued together on one side, each board being composed of seven layers of veneers, each one-eighth of an inch thick, five of whitewood and two of walnut, also glued and pressed together, the grains of the veneers running alternately transversely, by which a firm board is made that cannot, as with solid wood, warp or crack.[21]

Other inventors employed plywood's own special qualities in furniture design. The patent taken out by John Mayo of New York in 1865 appeared to be prophetic:

> By adopting the well-known process of wet and dry heating in course of manufacture, the several scales of wood may be brought to such a state of pliability as to assume any desired form by compression in a matrix or upon formers and by using different degrees of thickness, in connection with cements of different kinds, the character of the article made can be either rigid or flexible.[22]

This description could be applied to the experiments, and productions of twentieth century furniture designers such as Marcel Breuer, Gerald Summers, and Alvar Aalto, and illustrates the idea that the nineteenth century was the seed-bed for many twentieth century innovations.

Further experiments on the lines patented by John Mayo continued. The patent of Isaac Cole, taken out in March 1874 in the United

States, has been seen as a landmark in the history of design.[23] Cole designed a 'new and improved veneer chair' which used plies of veneer to create a continuous seating surface, a back, and a support. Although there is no evidence to suggest that this chair was ever put into production, it is another very early example of the possibilities of plywood that were to be re-discovered by some twentieth century designers. Its apparent lack of success suggests that even if technology is sufficiently advanced, customer demand must exist or the product will fail. In the case of furniture, where traditional conventions of style tend to determine the consumer's choice, it is not likely that the introduction of experimental furniture will be commercially successful until the design has been absorbed into the repertoire. If new technology is used, it often has to be cloaked in a conventional disguise to be accepted. (An example of this could be early railway carriages which conformed to road carriage design for some time: the style for the new object therefore directly related to the familiar.)

The history of plywood and its use in furniture took a significant step forward in 1872, when George Gardner was granted a patent for a three-ply veneer or plywood seat.[24] The aim of this patent was to protect the production of a replacement for the traditional cane seat. The principle was very simple: a piece of shaped three-ply was prepared to whatever form was required to create the seat and then it was simply nailed on to the chair frame. It was soon obvious that the labour-intensive process of caning was to decline as a general practice, as a direct result of this new seat. The Gardner chair range of domestic and contract items was hugely successful, exemplifying how certain materials and techniques appealed to the public.

The concept of the ply-seat was developed in a slightly different way by the Thonet company. Their experiments led them to apply the technology of plywood, together with machine-impressed designs (raised, plaited, or with pierced holes), to produce a 'thermoplastic' seat. The use of perforations in both Thonet and Gardner seats was not only for ventilating purposes, but also to increase the decorative appeal of an otherwise plain seat.[25] In addition to these, the choice was widened further by the use of seats produced in 'imitation intarsia', which was a process of branding a seat with a design in two colours.

Not only was this process applicable to new furniture, but there

HUTCHINS & MABBETT,

123 South Second Street, Philada.

CANE SEATS BREAK DOWN.   OURS NEVER WILL.

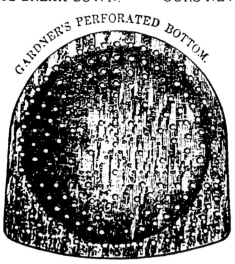

Patented May 21, 1872.

16 An advertisement for chairs made with Gardner's patent plywood seats. The favourable comparison with cane seats is clearly demonstrated

was a growing market for replacement seats for caned chairs. The survey in London (published in 1903) noted that 'there is also less demand for cane seats for chairs of the common sorts; they have been ousted by perforated wooden seats which can at any time be renewed at the neighbouring general store for a small sum.'[26]

The value of plywood as a substitute for solid wood in the construction of furniture, was fully recognised once the rotary cutting of logs into continuous veneers became a commercial proposition. Although there were many patents and inventions during the century pertaining to rotary cutting, it only became cost-effective in the 1880s. The corollary to this invention was the realisation that a suitable glue would be essential. Experiments in Russia produced a blood albumen and casein cement that was water-resistant and strong enough to completely bond the veneers together, so that the resulting plywood was stronger than the timber itself.[27] These experiments and developments were part of the European reaction to the success of the Gardner company in the United States. Christian Luther set up a firm in Reval, Estonia, to exploit the demand for plywood. Based on the vast timber reserves of the country, the European plywood industry was born. Around 1884, Luther's experiments with three-ply led him to develop chair seats, and then, by 1892, fully-assembled bentwood and ply furniture. It has been suggested that the first production of steam-pressed plywood sheets occurred around 1895, when pieces suitable for tea-chests were imported into London by E. H. Archer, the founder of the Venesta Company.[28]

It is not surprising that most of the inventiveness in the development of easily manipulated raw materials should have come from the United States, where demands were greater, and skills relatively less than in Europe. Indeed, in England, plywood was reputed to be cheap and inferior, an opinion that continued into the twentieth century. It is paradoxical that the designers of the Utility scheme, responsible for administering furniture production during World War II, should have embraced plywood as the best material available, while the general public still considered it to be 'tea chest furniture'.

Bentwood

Apart from plywood, two other important processes involving wood technology were developed in the nineteenth century. Indeed any discussion about technology and furniture in the period would be incomplete without the mention of laminated wood and bentwood. The bentwood chair, the archetypal 'well-designed' product, seen by some as the saving grace of the Victorian era, and an inspiration to twentieth century furniture designers, has been the focus of many studies in the past few years.[29]

Although the origins of bentwood furniture can probably be traced to Ancient Egypt, it was the primitive techniques used by Windsor chair-makers in the eighteenth century that formed the basis for later improvements. The difficulty with bending solid wood was due to the uneven tensions in the wood fibres. On the outside of a curve the wood split; on the inside the fibres compressed and buckled. Therefore the impact of the technology necessary to solve these problems was to be enormous. According to Hughes, attempts were made to overcome the problem. The Windsor chair back-bows had the bark removed from the inside of the bend only, which had the effect of stabilising the timber to some degree. The bent bows were then steamed and left to cool in a primitive clamp.[30] More precise technology was applied to trades such as ship-building and wheelwrighting, both of which used curved wood sections in their products.[31] In fact, the earliest patent for bending wood, planks, and ships' timbers was taken out by John Cumberland in 1720.[32] Another patent for a wood-bending process, taken out by John Vidler in 1794,[33] referred to: 'Bending timber for circular work without injury to the grain'. This applied particularly to cabinet-makers (as well as shipwrights), as it used a series of 'concaves and convexs' (or formers) with weights and balances to bend the wood to shape. These processes used a type of former that was to be perfected by Thonet in the 1850s.

The most spectacular bending of solid wood in the early years of the nineteenth century was made in the United States by Samuel Gragg.[34] The details of his patented method of bending side rails, seat, and back stiles, and even complete sides, have been lost. Nevertheless, the essential point is that the innovation was used to create a chair design that was fashionable and not just a virtuoso technical achievement. According to Ostergard, Gragg 'subordinated his technological genius to his own subdued expression of the classical mode of design'.[35] This supports the idea that furniture-makers will use whatever technology is available to produce a profitable

17 Wood-bending machine used for preparing parts for bentwood chairs

line, and in these cases the process is often subordinate to the design. The forms are the prime consideration, and it would be the look of the object that the customer was purchasing, rather than the ideas behind the production.

Contrary to Gragg's approach, where process was subordinate to design, the work of Michael Thonet had process as the pivot. Thonet's ability to combine technical developments with elements of style, resulted in one of the most successful furniture businesses in the nineteenth century. Thonet's furniture has been admired and acknowledged as the true conjunction of concept, material, technology, and style. Thonet became a byword for good design for several reasons: the chair was made in the KD method from a few sections;[36] the material was available cheaply and in quantity, and had ideal

18 A Thonet circular table used as a demonstration model at the 1851
International Exhibition

bending capabilities; he used the technology of patent methods of
forming bends with steel straps; and the simple style was applicable
in domestic or commercial situations and was infinitely adaptable.
Although Thonet is associated with bending solid wood, his early
experiments were with making furniture from laminations (see
Laminations, below). His success came from the gradual change from
the use of laminations of wood to bending solid wood. If Thonet's
aim was to introduce an industrial system into Austrian furniture-
making, then the desideratum of an easily disassembled object made
from a limited number of simply-produced parts was only to be
achieved in the 1850s. Thonet had learnt the lessons of batch production, the economics of the furniture trade, and the maxim that
high-style is a luxury that has little to do with cheapness and comfort.
The matter-of-fact report on the firm's exhibit at the 1878 Paris Exposition perhaps says it all: 'There is of course very little attempt at
art, the matter is one rather of cheapness combined with comfort'.[37]

Laminations

Another important technique used by cabinet-makers to shape wood was to cut timber into veneers or slivers that could then be glued together with the grain running in the same direction, and then shape them while still hot and wet. Again this process was not new: eighteenth century cabinet-makers had used the technique to make rims for tables and other items. As in the case of bentwood and plywood, attempts were made to develop the laminating process, but these had little immediate influence on furniture design.

The patent lists record that in 1793, the inveterate inventor, Samuel Bentham, devised a method of 'giving curvature to wood by dividing it into thicknesses'.[38] A few years later, *c.* 1802, the ébéniste Jean-Joseph Chapius built chairs using quarter-inch thick wood slats which, when glued together, bent, and then shaped, made semi-circular legs for chairs.[39] Again, like Gragg, the technology was subservient to the neo-classical design and can really only be seen as a means to an end.

In the 1840s, Michael Thonet began to construct chairs out of laminates of thin wood so as to achieve hitherto unknown degrees of bending. Again the technique reflected the contemporary taste, in this case, first Biedermeier, and then Rococo Revival styles. Thonet soon discovered that the laminating process was time-consuming, expensive, and could not survive the extremes of temperature that furniture might be subject to. For these reasons he moved towards the bending of solid wood. Nevertheless, the laminating process remained important for traditional cabinet-making. In a treatise on cabinet-making published *c.* 1865, the instructions for making curved or 'sweep-work' are revealing. For the best results it suggests 'to glue up our stuff in thin thicknesses in a caul or mould.' This was alleged to give both accuracy and strength, and certainly shows the practical matter-of-fact approach of ordinary craftsmen to finding the solution to a particular problem. The Thonet company returned to experimenting with laminates for chair-making in the 1880s. This time they tried to produce a chair which was cut out from sheets of laminations rather than building up thin sections, but again it was not successful. However, a laminated chair frame suitable for upholstering was commercially produced. Nevertheless, the successful development of laminated furniture had to wait until the 1930s for

19 Laminated-leg chair by Chapius, *c*. 1802, shows the revival of laminating in the early part of the century. From these experiments grew the important bentwood industry

Alvar Aalto to perfect the sculptural possibilities offered by the process of bending laminated wood.

The new technology that manipulated wood into bent, laminated, and ply forms coexisted with traditional methods, so the developments in timber use must be seen in the context of an industry that was unlikely to embrace any new methods until they were well proven.

Upholstery springs

Upholstery springs provide a wonderful example of the nineteenth century's propensity to enjoy the comforts of modern inventions but at the same time to have them clothed in a disguise of some description. The desire for a comfortable seating support and a good night's sleep seems to have been the driving force for improvements in upholstery and bedding manufacture. Springs, originating in the requirements for carriage suspension, found their first upholstery use in chamber, or exercising, horses.[40] The English chamber horse was not the only example of the use of springing in the eighteenth century. In fact, the idea of introducing springs into seat upholstery may have come from Germany. Some accounts propose that a German blacksmith was responsible for the invention of the coil spring, and suggest that it was first used in the making of sprung bed bases.[41]

Mattresses were indeed made with interior springs, but it is difficult to show whether they preceded upholstered chairs or vice versa. Himmelheber has suggested that true sprung upholstery was a Biedermeier invention, and points out that Georg Junigl, a Viennese upholsterer, was granted a patent in 1822 for upholstery springs. This patent was

> for his improvement on contemporary methods of furniture upholstery, which, by means of a special preparation of hemp, and with the assistance of iron springs, he renders so elastic that it is not inferior to horsehair upholstery.[42]

However, this was probably a codification of previous practice and not a major advance. The phrase 'improvement on contemporary methods' would suggest that this is so. Little more seems to be known about this development and its later success or otherwise, but the comparison with the comfort qualities of curled horsehair was not exclusive to Austria.

From 1841, the Heal Company were offering 'Austrian sprung chairs', the description emphasising that the stuffing was all hair.[43] It was another example of the tried and trusted methods of hair upholstery being combined with the new developments in comfort, the emphasis being on the established materials again. Interestingly, the Austrian upholstery connection continued into the late nineteenth century. In evidence to a Select Committee investigating the sweating system, Arnold White commented on the origins of spring upholstery: 'Going back as far as the Great Exhibition of 1851, Germans from Vienna came in and introduced spring stuffing, and this revolutionised the upholstery trade.'[44] He continued his evidence by describing how they attempted to keep the secrets of their trade (unsuccessfully as it turned out): 'These Germans formed a society of their own and they were accustomed to work in rooms by themselves. They earned large wages so long as their secret was undiscovered: once discovered they were soon no longer around.'[45]

In England the acceptance of upholstery springs seems to have grown rapidly.[46] In 1826 Samuel Pratt took out a patent for 'improvements in the application of springs to beds, couches and seats to be used on ship-board for the prevention of sea sickness.' This consisted of wire springs, twisted into circular or angular coils in the shape of an hourglass, which were attached to webbing inside the upholstered seat.[47] In the same year, John Gillespie patented a 'spring or combination of springs for forming an elastic resisting medium'.[48] In 1828, Pratt developed the spring further, and his new patent was for 'elastic beds, cushions seats, and other articles of that kind'.[49] This latter development was applied to sprung cushions and simple spring units for upholstery rather than sea-sickness prevention. Pratt's patent defined the spring unit in such a way as to indicate that it had the advantages that would be its selling points for many years: the sprung edge, the advantages of reversibility, and the fact that they could either be built into furniture or be fitted to a removable cushion.

Although the use of springs in upholstery has been traced to at least the mid-eighteenth century,[50] it can be assumed that spring upholstery for general domestic use was not widely introduced into the furniture trade until the 1830s. The reasons for this were twofold: firstly, although a knowledge of springs existed from the early eighteenth century, there was an inadequate ability on the part of the upholsterers to use them properly, and secondly, the poor quality of the material used in spring manufacture led to customer dissatisfaction. By the 1830s, however, the commercial application of springs to upholstery was beginning to make strong headway.[51] Loudon (1833) confirmed that the use of

> spiral springs as stuffing has long been known to men of science; but so little to upholsterers, that a patent for using them was taken out, some years ago, as a new invention. Beds and seats of this description are now, however, made by upholsterers generally . . . [52]

He continued: 'springs may be had from Birmingham by the hundred weight'. His statement indicates the very few years' delay before the trade wholeheartedly embraced the idea of springs.[53]

In 1834, John Crofton codified the various methods used by upholsterers to make chairs, but more importantly he wrote a section devoted to 'The art of spring stuffing, with all its late improvements'.[54] He suggested that there were few workmen who had a sound knowledge of spring upholstery:

> They [the upholsterers] will be found pretending to know, rather than [being] really and truly acquainted with the art; the necessary result of which has been that the public have been dissatisfied with the spring-stuffed sofas, and they have, consequently, grown into disuse.[55]

This implies that spring seats were available generally before 1834, but upholsterers had little idea as to their correct application. Crofton hoped his book would enable young upholsterers to learn so that 'the art of spring-stuffing may then be reinstated in its original perfection'.[56]

Cooke and Passeri pointed out that it was not only the quality of the wire and spring making, but also the technique of fitting that caused difficulties for early upholsterers. The earliest attempts at fitting were to secure springs to the solid boards used in chamber horses, with the result that they did not have the same degree of resilience that came with the later use of webbing. Cooke and Passeri have shown that some early nineteenth century American sofas exist with iron coil-springs stapled directly to board or slatted bottoms in the manner of the chamber horses of the eighteenth century.[57] Grier has shown that this method of fixing was in fact patented in 1831 by Josiah French of Ware, Massachusetts.[58] Although his patent referred to bed bases, the cost advantages were obvious, and Grier pointed out that solid or slatted wooden bases with springs attached, were an 'important design compromise' in the making of inexpensive furniture.[59] The resultant upholstery was inevitably heavier and less resilient than the conventional methods of using webbing, but it enabled spring upholstery to become available to another level of the market.

Whatever patents or processes were devised to simplify the methods of spring stuffing, the problem for chair manufacturers still remained: the full upholstering of an easy chair or sofa was a skilled trade that successfully resisted mechanisation for a long time. The most difficult parts consisted of the tying of the spring bed and the processes of even stuffing and tufting. However, various techniques were invented to assist in the making of upholstered chairs. The first was simplifying the setting of springs in the interior seat. In 1853 Finnemore patented a method of fixing springs in upholstery and mattresses, using springs with loops formed at the top and bottom.[60] The springs were held in place by straps that passed through the loops on the spring. A simple solution to the problem of seat springing was to make a spring unit which just had to be inserted into the frame. An important process was patented by Louis Durrieu in 1864: a set of springs was connected at top and bottom using spiralled wire to produce a linked but flexible unit.[61] The obvious advantages of this process over individual knot tying by hand resulted in not only a consistent product but also the possibility that the unit could be developed so as to fit on to chair backs and sides as well as in loose cushions.

Apart from spiral springs, other endeavours were made to provide an 'elastic base' for upholstered chairs. In 1841 John Wilkie, an upholsterer, and Charles Schiewso, a musical-instrument maker, patented an early form of tension spring,[62] which used the principle of expansion and contraction of small springs mounted on straps. It was an important development as it avoided the need to have a deep seat to accommodate the original hourglass-shaped springing. This concept was developed further when in 1856 George and William Hooper patented 'improvements in springs for carriages, and for the cushions of carriages, chairs, mattresses, beds and similar articles'.[63] The patent relied on compensating springs made from rings or strips

20 A view of a London upholstery workshop *c.* 1899

of vulcanised Indiarubber. Yet another example, and a precursor of the modern 'No-sag' spring,[64] was invented by William Searby in 1857; it consisted of a piece of elastic metal, wood, or bone compressed into a curved form. Each end was attached to a buckle and strap fixed to the frame of the furniture, and used lateral tension to create a spring.[65] Yet again these patented methods are forerunners of mid-twentieth century concepts.

The manufacture of springs remained a manual operation for most of the century. In 1871, the *House Furnisher* could say that this was not for want of machines but rather for the 'want of uniformity in the wire'.[66] The problem was that soft spots in the spring wire needed to be removed before it could be made-up into springs. This could be done manually because the maker could see the flaws, but machine processes could not develop until reliable supplies of wire were available. These problems were reflected in consumer complaints. In 1877, Rhoda and Agnes Garrett wrote that iron springs

113

were 'always out of order and cannot have their anatomy readjusted without the intervention of the manufacturer, by whom alone the complexity of their internal structure is understood'.[67] Even later, complaints were still being voiced about the poor quality of English springs, especially in comparison to French ones. A report on upholstery from the Mansion House Committee visiting the Paris Universal Exhibition in 1889 (Paris 1889, p. 658), complained that all this was even more annoying as the cost of springs was a nominal part of the cost of an upholstered job. It has been suggested that it was as late as 1901 that machines were introduced for the machine winding of springs, instead of the previous process of hand winding them on to shaped wooden blocks.[68]

Whatever the technical difficulties in making them, the impact of the internal spring revolutionised upholstery practice and design in the nineteenth century – a clear case of a technical improvement that affected the look of an object. Seats upholstered with a base of webbing and a simple mixture of fibres as padding, did not need to be of very great depth. Spring-seated upholstery designs usually needed to take account of both the depth required for the construction of the padding/spring system and the increased tension on the frames. As soon as springs were introduced, a completely different profile had to be used to accommodate the rise and fall of the spring, the main result of which was the fully upholstered chair. This style of chair, built-up on a sprung base with layers of filling, an intermediate cover, and a top covering material, has become a hallmark of Victorian furnishings. The main design feature to occur as a result of the new method of stuffing was the buttoned seat and back which gave a particularly plump look to easy chairs of the time. The buttoning was a technical imperative to hold the stuffing in place, but it soon became a distinct feature of upholstered furniture, not least, perhaps, because it again indicated the amount of 'work' that the customer had purchased.

It is indeed difficult to see how these processes might be mechanised. The sewing of covers was aided by the use of the industrial sewing-machine, but otherwise it seemed that the mechanical assistance that became available in other parts of furniture-making was not possible with upholstery. However, as buttoned or tufted upholstery was a major feature of the period, it is not surprising that attempts were made to try and simplify the process by mechanised means. But it was not until the end of the century that a satisfactory method was marketed. The tufting machine produced a 'blanket' of backing, stuffing, and material top-cover together, which could then be applied to a sprung frame with much more speed and ease than the traditional built-up process. This encouraged the division of labour, and consequently caused a reduction in the skill required for upholstering chairs and sofas. There was also an attempt to mechanise other parts of the upholstery process. In 1878 it was reported that Paul Roth of New York was exhibiting machinery that could produce a stitched edge, pack the hair into a seat and tie the springs.[69]

Whatever the merits of these machines, they were not exploited commercially, and it is fair to say that the upholstery trade remained generally unaffected by changes in technology until the introduction of man-made fillings in the twentieth century. The production of a fully upholstered chair was based on the craftsman constructing the shape on to a pre-formed wood, or sometimes iron, frame. This called for considerable skill in technique, as each chair had to be built up in carefully balanced layers. The main change in the process was the gradual division of labour into the three stages of stuffing, cutting out the covers, and covering.[70] However, as chairs were usually made to order in a wide variety of fabrics, the integration of the upholstery business into the factory situation was a slow process that remained based on workshop practice well into the twentieth century.

Metal furniture

The use of metals in furniture-making can be traced to Ancient Egypt; surviving examples of furniture from this period indicate the high quality of the founder's art. Other examples over the centuries include Dagobert's throne and curule-shaped Gothic chairs from the fifteenth century, fabricated from wrought iron.[71] There has always been a relationship between metal and wood, for example metal was often used to fix and decorate wooden furniture. In this context, however, I want to discuss furniture that had metal of some sort as its primary constructional or decorative material, a development that occurred to a great extent in the nineteenth century.

Metal furniture is a prime case of another industry encroaching on the traditional preserve of the furniture trade, in order to create and exploit a new market demand.

There were two types of metal used in volume furniture-making: cast-iron, and metal tubing. The benefits of cast-iron had been acknowledged in the eighteenth century, particularly for architectural applications requiring multiple castings of the same object, e.g. railings, balconies, and panels. To accommodate the demand for finer-quality work, changes had to occur in the manufacturing technology. By the 1780s, two-thirds of furnaces making iron had switched from charcoal to coke-burning which thus increased temperatures and produced a more fluid iron.[72] This resulted in the makers being able to produce finer castings. In conjunction with this improvement in quality, was the use of steam engines for air blasting, and the introduction of the puddling process which helped to reduce costs. Such changes made the cast-iron material suitable for bulk production of household items, including various ranges of furniture.

One of the first commentators to be enthusiastic about the possibilities of cast-iron was John Claudius Loudon. The designs in the *Encyclopaedia* include traditional examples but also illustrate a novel approach to chair design shown in the early application of iron tubing to chair-making (none of which are known to have been made). Although he published these very simple chair designs, he was also aware of the demand for inexpensive ornament. Loudon pointed out that 'where carved work or much ornament is to be executed in furniture, cast-iron will always be found cheaper than wood, even though small numbers only of the article were wanting.'[73] His only objection to cast-iron would appear to be the cost of the patterns. Nevertheless, he forced the point home about improving design and lowering costs, by using cast-iron: '... that power of invention which seems to be now almost exclusively occupied in contriving bad fireplaces' [ought to be put] to the improving of the designs and lowering the price of cabinet furniture by the judicious introduction of cast-iron.'[74] Loudon suggested that by employing iron in the furniture of farmhouses for simple sideboards, tables, bedsteads, and hall chairs, great economies could be made. He further suggested that the combination of slabs of marble or slate for tops, combined with enriched cast-iron brackets, would make very desirable sideboards, and tables could easily be produced with mahogany tops and bronzed cast-iron bases.[75]

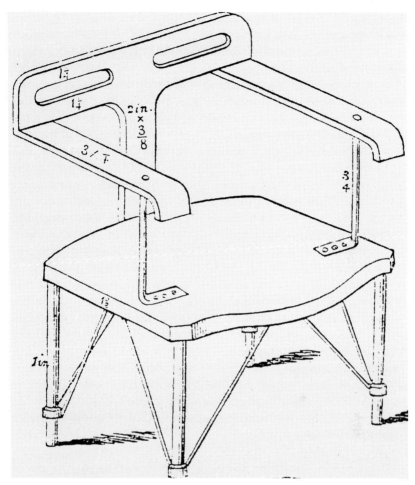

21 The possibilities of using metal tubing for chairs were considered by Loudon. There is no evidence that this design was ever produced

The most important commercial name to be associated with cast-iron objects is the Coalbrookdale Iron Company. The company, which was founded early in the eighteenth century, began to make ornamental castings in the 1830s. During the 1840s the firm exhibited their range of cast-iron products: firstly, in 1846 at the Exposition of British Industrial Art at Manchester, and again in 1849 at the Society of Arts' Exhibition of British Manufacturers, where they won the Gold Isis medal. These exhibits raised a number of questions about the role of iron in furniture. Some commentators were not sure of their own reaction to iron furniture. Reviewing some iron-topped tables produced by Coalbrookdale Co., the *Art Union*, in July 1845, suggested that 'their connexion with Art raises too many questions to be summarily discussed in a cursory notice'. (It never actually addressed any of the questions raised!) However, it continued by commenting on the contrast between 'the fragility of patterns of light open work, and the real indestructibility of the material', saying that 'iron has been conquered by artistic skill, and compelled to do homage to decorative power: the most stubborn portion of the mineral kingdom has been annexed to the realm of taste.'

This great emphasis on the ornamental rather than functional attributes of iron products, led to difficulties with questions of finish. Cast-iron products were often decorated so that the ironwork would imitate other materials in attempts to make them acceptable to domestic consumers. For example, Loudon had suggested that iron chairs should be painted in imitation of oak, and that table pedestals might be bronzed.[76] In addition to wood grains and metallic finishes, the great variety of surface treatments might include imitation bamboo, silvering, or painting red, brown, or black. One firm even produced iron-framed bedsteads that were in imitation of papier mâché.[77] All this led some contemporaries to regard the whole process of disguised finishes as ludicrous. Discussing a Coalbrookdale cast-iron hall chair that was painted to imitate bamboo, the *Journal of Design* commented:

> no bamboo chair could ever exhibit the ridiculous bits of ornament which disfigure this, nor could it have been made without ties and points of connexion, all of which are here omitted. We really had imagined that society was getting tired of the conventional upholsterer's bamboo with its three black strokes and splashes to indicate foliations; but here it is breaking out in the most inveterate form, upon a material least of all calculated to support the attack.[78]

These supposedly unsuitable treatments were not confined to England. In the United States, Gervase Wheeler admonished the practice of graining iron furniture to look like wood. He favoured the bronzing and gilding of iron furniture because he thought such processes did not suggest another material, but rather a higher or different quality metal.[79]

Apart from questions of finish and the whole argument about imitation and reality, the cast-iron furniture makers had another design problem. The plebeian connotations of cast-iron, and its associations with military, agricultural, and industrial tools and objects, had to be overcome if the material was to be accepted in the middle-class home: perhaps this could be achieved by making the product more 'artistic', rather than purely functional.

By employing well-known designers or by choosing subjects for copying that were considered to be inherently 'artistic', this objective was achieved. Apart from the well-known collaboration with the painter and sculptor, Alfred Stevens, Coalbrookdale employed John Bell, RA, to design a deer-hound table which was exhibited in the Paris Exposition of 1855. From the mid-1860s, the same company engaged Dr Christopher Dresser as designer, an association that lasted some twenty years. In 1867 hall furniture designs were registered and were followed by other designs in the 1870s. Dresser's enthusiasm for the material is suggested in *Principles of Decorative Design*: 'Cast-iron should be formed in the easiest manner it can be worked and as perfectly to suit its means'.[80] Although manufacturers tried hard, not everyone saw the artistic merit in cast-iron furniture and by 1876 H. J. Cooper could declare: 'cast-iron stands and hall tables with plate glass mirrors and marble tops we abhor; you can never make an artistic room with iron furniture.'[81]

While cast-iron was being developed for house furnishings, the possibilities of using iron tubing for furniture construction were also being investigated. Around 1828, Gandillot and Cie in Paris began to develop chairs with iron tube frames. They were soon able to produce chairs from reinforced hollow iron tubes, which were, however, painted in imitation of wood, ebonised, or painted with flowers or other designs.[82] Even these finishes were insufficient to maintain a commercial interest, and the idea failed. In Austria, the firm of Kitschelt used metal tubing to create the internal frames of sofas and chairs but the design of the whole suite remained in a traditional form.[83]

The use of metal tube was soon to be applied to a chair type that has since become a design icon for modernists in particular, as it does not appear to follow any prior models: it was the metal-framed rocker chair. The earliest reference to the rocker appears in an entry for an exhibition held at the London Polytechnic Institute in 1839.

22 A. Kitschelt's Austrian iron-tube framed furniture, exhibited at the 1851 International Exhibition

In the following year, the first pictorial evidence can be found in John Porter's iron-founder's brochure. The model illustrated in the company's broadsheet is very similar to those that were to be available for the next thirty years or more.[84]

The earliest of these chairs were undoubtedly made from cast-iron, often in tube form. The use of iron was referred to in an article on invalid furniture in Webster's *Encyclopaedia* published in the United States in 1845. A very simple representation of the metal rocker had the concise caption: 'a rocking chair for exercise . . . It is made wholly of iron, with a stuffed covering but not very heavy' – an early reference to the supposed therapeutic qualities of the chair.[85] Although there have been some other names mentioned above in connection with the metal rocker, the most well-known firm associated with these chairs remains R. W. Winfield of Birmingham. Winfield exhibited a brass tube and morocco leather chair at the

23 The display stand of Winfield and Co. at the 1851 Great Exhibition. The metal rocker in the foreground was not considered to be especially important

Great Exhibition; interestingly, his stand was classified as general hardware rather than furniture. Winfield and Co. were major manufacturers of brass tubing, and beds in particular, and their venture into furniture-making was a natural extension of skills towards a new market, in a similar way to the papier mâché manufacturers. The corollary is that there is little doubt these chair-types were mainly produced and retailed outside the recognised channels of furniture manufacture and distribution. For example, in a catalogue of *c.* 1850–60, Deane and Co. of London Bridge, who were general iron-mongers and wholesalers, advertised an 'Improved reclining chair with chintz furniture' for three guineas, on the same page as patent bed frames.[86]

These rocker chairs were nothing if not international. An American connection existed with a chair made for Peter Cooper, and at least two European countries had these available. In France, Charles Leonard offered 'fauteuils américains' from his iron-furniture factory in the 1860s.[87] The chairs were very similar to those of Winfield, in that they offered both a tube and a strap-framed version. Apart from France, there is evidence that these chairs were popular in Denmark. The National Museum in Copenhagen has an iron-framed 'American rocking chair', upholstered in red plush with an embroidered panel; and in the Hans Andersen Museum in Odense is a chair of similar description which once belonged to the writer.[88]

Apart from rocking chairs and hall or lobby chairs, there was another use for iron in seat furniture: to improve comfort by its use for upholstered chair frames. The origins of this method of framing are difficult to trace, although it seems that the earliest mention of iron-framed upholstered chairs occurred in France. In the 1830s, the construction of a 'bergère en gondole' used an iron frame to give a shaped contour to the back. It was then completely upholstered, and the only evidence of the iron support was the slight give in the back when the chair was used. In 1834, Le Bouteiller illustrated an example of a 'Fauteuil en fer garni' in his furniture pattern book.[89] Iron frames continued to be used throughout the century and were still being illustrated in text books into the twentieth century.

Exposed iron frames were yet another matter in the design and manufacture of upholstery. The Birmingham firm of Peyton and Peyton, leaders in the manufacture of brass and iron beds, exploited the 1860 patent of Angelo Sedley. This patent used a metal rack and pin mechanism to allow the user of their chairs to adjust the rake of the chair-back from an upright to a fully reclining position. The more sophisticated Equilibrium couch with an iron frame, japanned bronzed or made in brass, was partially demountable as well as having a reclining backrest.[90] These folding metal chairs were popular for many years: their light weight, their portability when folded, and their relative cheapness led to a long life.

The acceptability of metal as a material for chairs in domestic interior use may at first appear surprising, but the delight in new uses of materials, the lightness of tubular frames, and the decorative effects that could be obtained at relatively low expense were reason enough for the popularity. The possibilities of iron for chests of drawers, bookcases, and bureaux were considered as early as 1809 by Benjamin Cook. According to him, they could be japanned to imitate costly woods, or the panels could be painted; the mouldings might be Gothic or any other form, and the drawers 'might be made

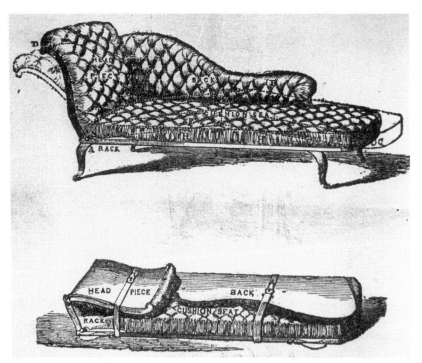

24 Sedley's equilibrium couch: an example of patented furniture which uses 'new' materials combined with a space-saving intention, two of the major concerns of the nineteenth-century furniture trade

with light iron framing: filled up with wire work, which would make them very light.'[91]

With Cook's idea the contradictions persist. The need to imitate other materials, and the question of weight and brittleness inherent in the material, affected its acceptance into the wider repertoire of furnishings. It is really no surprise that, with the exception of lightweight portable chairs, interior furniture made of cast-iron should be mainly limited to tables and hall-stands that remained in one position all the time. The Coalbrookdale catalogues have many entries for hall-stands, hat and umbrella stands and a few for hall tables, but other articles are very limited.

The use of metal seems to have had two results. The first, an ephemeral style, and the second, the beginnings of a completely

25 Hat and umbrella stand in cast iron by Yates and Drabble of
Rotherham, shown at the 1862 International Exhibition

new way of using metals in furniture-making which was only to be
exploited fully in the twentieth century.

Papier mâché

Papier mâché was an ideal material for the neo-rococo and natural-
istic styles that were popular for much of the middle years of the

nineteenth century. It was ideal in that its smooth surface finish was a perfect ground for painted and applied decoration, and its plastic qualities allowed it to be manipulated into a wide variety of shapes.

The use of paper, in a mashed or layered sheet form, indicates a degree of technical interference whereby the origin of the base material is completely hidden and the object produced is only recognisable from its shape and familiar surface decoration. The attractiveness of the material to manufacturers was its plasticity and malleability, and the fact that once set, it could be sawn and polished in a manner similar to other solid materials. The development of the moulding process gave the manufacturers a potential control over form that was unheard of in furniture-making prior to this development, and the way in which it could be easily manipulated made it a potentially useful material for new design initiatives. However, the process was not generally exploited for its plastic potential. Papier mâché manufacturers often took traditional shapes for their designs, and in many cases reproduced shapes that had been executed in wood. The decorative possibilities offered by a blank surface were often used solely as a basis for demonstrations of the skills of the japanning artist. Therefore the production of machine-moulded blanks, combined with the hand decoration and finishing of the pieces, could be seen as a method of diversifying the trade of the japanning firms and was not a deliberate and fundamental design change.

The origins of papier mâché can be traced to India and other parts of the Orient. But the earliest mention of the material in England is in Robert Boyle's essay *Of Man's Great Ignorance of the Uses of Natural Things*, published in 1672. Boyle referred to the use of papier mâché as being suitable for 'frames of pictures and divers pieces of embossed work and other curious movables'.[92] However, there is no evidence that the material was much used before the mid-eighteenth century. In 1749, William Duffour of Soho claimed to be the original maker of papier mâché, and Kirkham suggests that his French surname may give some credence to the suggestion of others that the craft of papier mâché manufacture was first established in France.[93] Other evidence also supports this assertion.

Eighteenth century commentators, like Robert Dossie in *Handmaid to the Arts*, refer to French snuff-boxes made from papier mâché, and in 1763 Peter Babel, a papier mâché worker, refers to his raw

26 An example of the extravagant work achieved in papier mâché. This bed frame by Bettridge's was considered a pièce de résistance by the *Art Journal*

material as 'an invention of modern date, imported by us from France and now brought to great perfection'.[94] However, it was not only England that profited by the French initiative. It is supposed that a Frenchman, Lefèvre, passed on the secret of manufacturing varnished paper ware to Martin, a German varnisher, who developed the famous 'vernis Martin' process. The trade in these wares was so extensive that in 1765 Frederick II established a manufactory in Berlin to avoid importing papier mâché goods from France.[95]

Henry Clay is credited with producing papier mâché goods, including furniture, on a commercial scale in England. Clay was an apprentice of John Baskerville, a famous paper-maker and japanner from Birmingham. In 1772 Clay took out a patent for making 'high varnished [paper] panels for rooms, doors, cabins of ships, cabinets, bookcases, screens, chimney-pieces, tables etc.'.[96] The fashionable acceptance of Clay's work can be seen in the *Description of Strawberry Hill*, published in 1784. It mentions a highly varnished table made by Clay, with a Gothic design by Paul Sandby, and also a 'Tea-chest of Clay-ware painted with loose feathers'.[97] A fascinating description giving a clear impression of the manufacturing process employed by Clay, was written in 1791 by the traveller Edward Clarke:

> A number of sheets of paper are pasted together and dried; they are then carried into a room, resembling a little timber yard, contiguous to which is a very large workshop: cabinet makers form every article as it is required, sawing it out of paper and planing it with the greatest exactness. It is then japanned and polished, and this is always done by hand.[98]

The cyclical nature of this fashionable business is illustrated by the suggestion that at one time Clay was alleged to have employed 300 hands, but by 1802 the number had diminished to less than 100.[99] The resurgence of demand during the second quarter of the nineteenth century was too late for Clay, but encouraged developments in processes of manufacturing and ornamentation that allowed the trade to boost its production.

Papier mâché is a broad classification of five different, though related, processes. The first is the original process that Clay patented. It consisted of pasted sheets of paper laid over variously shaped cores, and was found to be the best form for furniture as the moulds could be made from iron or brass, ensuring a consistent form. The second variety was formed into thick sheets or boards by pressing paper pulp between dies. The resultant panels were generally flat and could be used for interior decoration: bedstead ends, door panels or other flat cabinetry. In addition, the panels were employed by the carriage-making trade. The process was further developed by pressing pulp into matrices to form a variety of shapes which were especially suitable for architectural work. The third process consisted of making a fibrous slab from coarse fibres, earthy matter, chemical agents, and cementing size. This mass was passed through rollers to produce a uniform board which could then be finished and decorated like papier mâché. Carton Pierre was the fourth process; it was made from pulp paper mixed with whiting and glue, pressed into moulds, backed with paper, and then hardened and dried. It was usually destined for use as architectural ornament. The fifth process was known as ceramic papier mâché. This was made from paper pulp, resin, glue, drying oil, and sugar of lead. The resulting plastic material could be moulded into any form and was especially used for architectural decoration.

Papier mâché furniture was generally made from either Clay's patent process or from the panel method. It is important to stress that papier mâché was seen as a raw material which had to be embellished. The decorative processes of japanning and 'inlaying' were the furniture's main selling points, therefore a variety of methods of decoration were important. One of the very earliest patents was taken out by John Skidmore in 1786, for 'Ornamenting japan wares with foil stones, Bristol stones, paste, and all sorts of pinched glass, sapped glass, and every other stone, glass, and composition used in or applicable to the jewellery trade.'[100] This is a very early indication of the impending mid-nineteenth century penchant for inlay and glass decoration in papier mâché. Two more patents, one in 1809 by Charles Valentine for producing landscapes on japanned surfaces, and another in 1812 by Thomas Hubball, for replacing pigments with coloured metallic ores, further developed the ornamenters' repertoire.

However, the names of Jennens and Bettridge, the successors to Clay's business, remain as the most successful of the papier mâché manufacturers and ornamenters. The reason for their fame perhaps rests on their use of unusual materials to decorate the blank shapes. Their patent of 1825[101] signalled the most well-known phase of papier mâché furniture decoration – the so-called pearl-shell 'inlay'. Aaron Jennens and John Bettridge took out their patent for 'preparing and working pearl-shell into various forms, applying it to ornamental uses in the manufacture of japan ware'. In fact, the process was not inlaid, but rather applied to the surface at a particular stage of the decoration.[102] At the height of their success Jennens and Bettridge were employing sixty-four men solely as full-time decorators.

To protect the processes invented to satisfy the demand, there was a major burst of patent activity in the 1840s, with fourteen patents being taken out in that decade. Of course, not all of them were directly related to furniture, but the volume of interest is an indication of the popularity of the product. How ironic then that the early success of papier mâché furniture decoration eventually contributed to its subsequent failure.

As early as 1835, Samuel Wiley, an employee of Jennens and Bettridge, gave evidence to the *Select Committee on Arts and Manufactures*, where he said: 'I could frequently sell bad articles, bad in execution and design, for the same money as I could sell the best.' The popularity of the product was to continue for a number of decades before the final demise, so why were makers able to sell bad articles as well as the best? The Great Exhibition of 1851 may hold a clue. The Jury for Class xxvi (the class that included papier mâché goods), commented on the nature of the problem even if they did not really grasp the nettle. Discussing Jennens and Bettridge's exhibit, they said: 'The style of work of some of the large objects, such as a reclining chair, a cot, tables etc. however well designed and ingeniously executed, did not appear suitable to the material.'[103] In other words, using designs originally created for wooden products was not going to achieve the full potential of the material.[104] These arguments were picked up by Redgrave. In his report on the Great Exhibition, he commented on this question of the nature of the material, and suggested that although it was admirably suited to furniture-making, makers must take into account the nature of the material itself and not refer to other furniture material types for inspiration:

> There is no apparent reason why this material should not be used for chairs, couches, tables or cradles; but the art of designing for it is not yet attained: as the material possesses peculiar properties of strength and lightness, without needing any framing it should be considered purely for itself, and the designer must forget all other constructive forms.[105]

These remarks are all the more telling when it is considered that that which Redgrave advocated was being developed by Thonet with his bentwood process, i.e. the material with its own special qualities

27 The *Day Dreamer*, a papier mâché chair by Jennens and Bettridge, shown at the 1851 Great Exhibition

should be considered for itself, and should not be fitted to pre-conceived ideas, styles or designs. In addition to his remarks on construction, Redgrave also had a comment to make on the decoration of papier mâché furniture:

> As to its ornamentation the sooner it has a thorough revision the better, since at present it is a mass of barbarous splendour that offends the eye

and quarrels with every other kind of manufacture with which it comes into contact. The simple lacquered work of India may afford an example for the ornamentation of papier mâché.[106]

His requirement for simplicity yet again ignored the desire of many consumers for objects that exhibited a large amount of 'work'.

An alleged decline in the quality of design, in both the United States and Europe, was also noted by George Wallis in his report on industry in the United States, published in 1854. He considered that

> in papier mâché the productions are all below mediocrity, being chiefly imitation of the worst style of pearl inlaying and japan work executed in this country. Everything approaching to purity of design, or in the inlaid work, to geometric arrangement of the parts is as carefully avoided as it generally is in Europe.[107]

Some years later the same criticism was again raised. Lindsey (1876), referring to the history of papier mâché products, noted the tendency to produce papier mâché goods embellished with 'work':

> Shortly after the introduction of this material there arose a morbid taste in the Birmingham japan trade for placing great blotches of pearl upon articles made of pulp, and finishing them in the gaudiest of colours . . . While this tendency to over-elaboration of ornament, fostered principally by the production of goods for the United States and other foreign markets was undermining the trade, there were other mischievous influences at work in the same direction. The public had been taught to believe that the quantity of material was the test of value and they naturally asked for more pearl and gold.[108]

Not only did the quality of work suffer, but there was also difficulty in finding appropriate new designs. The extent of the problem was defined by Lindsey:

> The old showy gaudy unnatural style of flower decoration will now only sell at most unremunerative prices, among the lower classes of society in Europe, and amongst the uncivilised masses in other countries.[109]

The final indignity for papier mâché was perhaps when a particular example (a tray) was exhibited in the Department of Practical Art's Museum at Marlborough House. The catalogue entry described it as 'an example of popular but vulgar taste, of a low character, presenting numerous features which the student should carefully avoid.'[110]

Perhaps some thought that popular taste was to blame, but others thought improvements in design should be initiated by manufacturers. In other words, the problem lay in the education of workers who were responsible for the art manufactures. In 1856, George Wallis, the director of the Birmingham School of Design, bemoaned the lack of training for japanners and considered that 'the higher qualities of design will remain dormant for want of educated power in the worker.'[111]

Apart from the education of the designer, there was another problem in the way of good design. The ever-widening choice of materials and techniques available to the manufacturer led to a surfeit of means from which the producer could choose, and this led to the orgy of applied decoration described above. George Wallis touched on this question of too wide a variety of materials for the maker to choose from:

> there is a tendency certainly to a somewhat severer style of decoration, but we fear that the very facilities for producing startling effects is a constant temptation to the manufacturers to cater to the desire of the public.[112]

The connection between the developments in chemistry (technology) and their influence on taste were not lost on Wallis either:

> The various coloured metallic powders, the facilities for painting rainbow tints with ordinary pigments 'ad libitum' are all so many stumbling blocks in the way of cultivating a purer taste as applicable to the decoration of papier mâché.[113]

Eleven years later, in 1866, W. Aitken, in his survey of papier mâché manufacture, pointed out the real commercial reasons for the continuation of gaudy decoration:

> so long as the popular tendency is in favour of ornamentation in which show and glitter preponderate, and articles decorated in accordance with true principles are only selected by buyers of educated taste; it is too much to expect that producers should deliberately shut themselves out of the more extended and profitable market.[114]

It was not only design commentators and writers who saw the problem facing papier mâché designers. David Sarjeant, one of the artisans reporting on papier mâché at the 1867 Paris Exhibition, discussed the work of Jennens and Bettridge of Birmingham, and Loveridge of Wolverhampton, and commented on the 'sudden decline of the papier mâché trade in Birmingham'.[115] He claimed that 'the real cause of disaster is to be found in a period of unhealthy prosperity, which culminated some thirteen years back' (i.e. 1854). He thought that the prosperity caused by the fashionable nature of the product had led to an increase in the number of workmen who were unskilled in the trade, thus echoing the concerns of the witness to the 1835 Select Committee. Sarjeant wrote:

> It soon began to appear that buyers did not mind this [use of unskilled labour] being unable to discern between the qualities of good and bad work; as for the Americans they had a decided liking for the latter kind.[116]

Sarjeant described the phenomenon of that desire by customers for applied 'work' to furnishings which was to be seen in other product categories. It seemed that the more the public had, the more they wanted:

> Worse yet, the public conceived the notion that the quantity of material was the test of value and began to ask for more pearl and gold. This extra cost had to be met by a reduction of the workman's price, and further disregard for the quality of the work, so that children came at last to be employed.[117]

After the financial crash in the United States, the papier mâché manufacturers had to return to the English market to try and regain their position. As Lindsey noted above, the over-ornamented designs were now unsuitable for the home market. The delight in highly decorated surfaces had declined and it seemed that this was coincidental with

> the very time when Schools of Art were beginning to influence the public mind, and it became a favourite practice with art critics and lecturers to point to the papier mâché trade as a shocking example of the untaught condition of English workmen.[118]

As if in confirmation of this change of attitude, G. W. Yapp (1879), an Assistant Commissioner of the Great Exhibition, suggested that the exuberant decoration of papier mâché 'has at last been nearly annihilated by its own extravagance'.[119] In a way Yapp was just confirming the natural end to a cycle of taste. Papier mâché, introduced as a novel material, became a best seller. As its popularity moved down the social scale, new desires took over and papier mâché went into a decline. The public's rejection of papier mâché as a furniture material seemed complete when a new phrase entered the language: a false politician or a dishonest tradesman was called a 'man of papier mâché'.

Other materials

The significant materials I have already discussed were supplemented by an amazing variety of other products that were of varied importance. Patent and non-patented substances alike are examples of the fertile mind and imagination of the nineteenth century's obsessive search for 'something new', as well as for a more profitable use of existing resources. Although these processes and materials varied very considerably, it is convenient to analyse them briefly under group headings. I have arbitrarily divided them between those used for construction and those used for decoration.

Perhaps the search for wood substitutes was the most important. I have noted elsewhere the desire of inventors to produce a stable substitute for wood (see Wood, above), so it is not surprising that a large number of patents were taken out for this category.[120] Most of the wood substitutes attempted to use wood waste in combination with chemicals, to produce a paste that could be moulded and then set. The processes varied from chipped wood, boiled in caustic soda and then pressed and rolled,[121] to wood pieces, ground down on a grindstone, then mixed with water and moulded under pressure.[122]

Others were more exotic. In 1852, Mr Pidding patented an amalgam of coal, peat, shrubs, shells, bark, etc. which was mixed with glue and carbonised.[123] In the same year, Moses Poole patented an improvement based on vulcanised Indiarubber. The resulting product was then either made into veneer form for wooden frames or wrapped round iron-framed furniture.[124] The success of these processes is unknown. Between 1855 and 1865 there were another nine patents taken out for veneer substitutes. One of the most promising developed vulcanised rubber or vulcanite to produce veneer. The process involved using a rubber solution rolled into thin sheets which could be plain or embossed; they were then dipped into boiling water until they were very flexible and could be applied to carcases as veneer. The obvious advantage was that they would mould to curves and angles.[125] A final example of this interest in substitutes for veneers was published in a notice in the *Furniture Gazette* (16 November 1878). It details the formation of a company to exploit the patent of James Budd who devised a method of using a 'varnish' of glass as a veneer in place of wood, the object being to reduce the cost and at the same time produce a high finish that could imitate any other surface type, while remaining impervious to atmospheres, etc. It apparently attracted considerable interest, and the Duke of Norfolk was included amongst its patrons.

It is difficult to assess the true impact of these substitute materials as there is very little evidence of their use, apart from the initial patent details. However, the trade journals do not appear to have any advertisements relating to any of these products, and the trade directories do not mention any enterprises that produced such materials in commercial quantities, so it can be assumed that these attempts were doomed precursors of other efforts made in the twentieth century. Other materials used in construction included coal, which is yet another example of a specialised use of material to produce an exotic product. It was never really meant for the retail trade market; rather, it was used for demonstration or presentation pieces. It is, nevertheless, another indication of the Victorians' fascination with unusual uses for common materials.[126]

It would appear that the materials used to decorate furniture and furniture-making materials were much more successful. In many cases these processes were related to the search for substitutes for expensive and luxurious original materials. One of the most popular finishes was marble, and it is therefore not surprising to find a number of attempts to reproduce it. The most obvious method was to enlist the painter-grainer to imitate the look of marble. The Kershaw panels demonstrate the high point of the painter-stainers' art and are a perfect example of the skill that could be achieved in the production of deceptive treatments.[127] However, Kershaw did use some mechanical means to achieve his effects. In 1860 he took out a patent for 'imitating fancy woods, marbles etc.', which clearly showed the tools of the grainer's trade and demonstrated how they were achieved.

Apart from the use of painting techniques to imitate marbles and stones, the use of slate as a base material was successful. Originally invented and patented by George Magnus in 1840,[128] the process involved floating mineral colours in prepared water on to a slate bed, and then firing the decorated slate so as to create a glazed surface. The fired finish not only looked like marble, but bore a tactile resemblance to it as well. Wyatt (1856), in his report on the 1855 Paris Exhibition, commends Magnus for taking an ordinary material and 'giving to it form and ornamentation' and for 'raising a school of artists and for applying to it hundreds of new purposes which it could be better and more cheaply adapted than those which it displaces.'[129] Magnus was not the only person experimenting with imitations of marble. In 1848, Elizabeth Wallace patented a process that used coloured glass to replicate marble.[130] It was used to decorate wall linings, picture frames, tombs, and furniture, and was shown at the 1851 Exhibition.

The possibilities of gutta percha as a furniture material created much excitement.[131] Discovered in 1844, gutta percha, a plastic substance derived from a latex, showed great promise for some years until the expense of supplying it in large enough quantities rendered it uneconomical. It was thought that gutta percha would be an ideal substitute for wood where carving and ornament were required. Its malleable and elastic qualities made it a strong contender. However, it never really became part of the furniture-makers' repertoire as it was vulnerable to direct heat and was easily marked by fingernails and other abrasions.[132] Nevertheless, the Great Exhibition showed a large sideboard decorated with gutta percha ornament which was described as 'combining the three-fold advantage of lowness of price, elegance of form, and absence of fragility.'[133]

The middle years of the nineteenth century were fertile ones for the imagination of inventors. There seemed to be no limit to the possible sources of materials for furniture-making or decoration. For example, in 1853 a patent was issued for a process using liquefied quartz and other compositions to imitate wood for table tops; and in 1861 Brooman introduced a mixture of lava material fused with other compounds, which was designed to be used for table tops and the like. The use of natural materials from exotic locations is also evident in Alexander Prince's patent for decorating furniture with the lace-like remains of Opuntia, a cactus which, when its leaves are boiled, produces a vein-like skeleton similar to lace. How successful this was may be gauged by the patent specification which says that 'In some instances it may be necessary to strengthen the lace-work with iron or brass wire or with pieces of plain or carved wood.'[134]

28 Sideboard demonstrating gutta percha as a decorative medium, shown at the 1851 Great Exhibition

Less exotic, but with a similar aim, was Eliza Cunnington's process of decorating table tops with ferns pressed under glass, sometimes with the addition of feathers, to create an image of pictorial inlay.[135] Other natural materials used to imitate more costly materials were patented by Thomas Ghislin. In 1862 he patented a complicated process of converting seaweed, mixed with glue, gutta percha and Indiarubber, to form a 'plastic' material that was alleged to be a good substitute for ebony.[136] He also proposed boiling the mixture in a solution of sulphuric acid to harden the material and this he called laminite or 'laminarian stag-horn'. It would then be used as a substitute for horn, ivory, and bone.

Comfort was also considered by patentees and inventors, with the search for a substitute for expensive horsehair upholstery being a priority. In 1862 again, Thomas Ghislin patented 'Improvements in the treatment of certain foreign plants and the application of fibres derived therefrom'. These plants were broken down and their fibres used as stuffing, or they might be woven into cloth as a substitute for horsehair.[137] For upholstery fillings, anything from pigs' hair to seaweed was considered as a possible contender, although one of the most unlikely fillings was sea sponge. In c. 1868, a company in the United States offered for sale 'patent sponge' as a substitute for curled horsehair. By a process of mixing natural sea sponge with water and glycerin, and allowing it to evaporate to leave a stable product, they produced an upholstery stuffing that was apparently cheap, easy to use, and germ-free. Their catalogue is full of testimonials relating how wonderful the material was but unfortunately there are no illustrations or samples![138]

Unlike some of the experimental materials, there was one that had been in use for hundreds of years but was enjoying a revival in the period. Wicker is a generic term that embraces a number of natural materials that have at various times been made into furniture by weaving processes. The materials include cane, reed, willow, osiers, and rattan. Rattan is the most important: it is derived from a climbing palm found in the East Indies and had been known to furniture-makers for a long time as the source of cane used for chair seats and backs. Cane is the outer bark of the rattan palm and has been used in furniture since the 1650s. The reed, the inner part of the plant, was discarded until the nineteenth century. The story of Cyrus Wakefield and the development of reed furniture is well known, and from the 1840s there began a massive revival of interest in wicker.[139]

Wicker furniture met a very wide range of criteria thus making it acceptable to various consumer groups. For designer reformers, for example, its simple material, which was generally left natural or at worst stained, together with its obvious revealed construction, were important markers of the honesty of both the material and the style. Rather than being applied to the surface, any ornamental design could be woven into the material and become an integral part of the furniture. From a stylistic point of view, the material lent itself to a wide range of designs, and it could be decorated as extravagantly as required. More importantly, the public's growing awareness of sanitation and health issues saw wicker as a natural, clean material, synonymous with country living and good health: it was, for example, associated with baby carriages and invalid chairs. Lastly, the growth of a market for furniture designed to be used in a summer setting, either in the garden or in a conservatory, encouraged lightweight, easy-to-handle suites for which rattan was an ideal material. Wicker furniture was very popular in the United States, and enjoyed a vogue all over Europe as well; indeed, traditional woodworking machine suppliers developed special machinery for this particular trade.[140] Essentially though, wicker was not associated with technological breakthroughs or the use of new materials until the development of Marshall Lloyd's loom for weaving a wicker-type material in large and regular quantities. In fact, Lloyd Loom, as it was known, was a man-made material constructed from kraft paper-wrapped steel wire woven into sheets and then fitted on to bentwood frames.

Many of these exotic materials were never serious contenders for a share of the furniture-makers' repertoire. With the exception of wicker, which was often made by a specialist company, most of these materials remained experimental or of limited application. Nevertheless, they do illustrate the continuing interest and, indeed, the demand for novelty in the period, and in some cases formed the basis for further developments in the twentieth century.

Notes

1 Bois-durci was a wood-based plastic material introduced into England from France in the 1860s. It was chiefly used to imitate ebony carving (see Chapter 2, under Imitation carving).

2 Knight, *Description of Vegetable Substances*, pp. 174–5.
3 This relates to David Pye's ideas on the workmanship of risk.
4 Soden-Smith, in [Paris 1867c] *Reports*, p. 221.
5 For example, the Australian timber, Heron Pine, which had many small knots in its surface showing as dark spots, was considered an example of the 'absolute novelty' of Colonial timbers. See also Bitmead, *London Cabinet-Makers Guide*, p. 83.
6 These two examples relate to the combination of stylistic trends and a desire for functional objects. The fact that veneers were available in larger sheets was useful but not essential to the design.
7 For a discussion of the etymology of the word plywood, see P. Morton Shand, 'Timber as a reconstructed material', *Architectural Review*, LXXIV, February 1936, p. 75.
8 Examples may be found in many collections of eighteenth century furniture. Percy Macquoid noted that Chippendale made chairs for Osterley Park with back splats 'composed of layers of mahogany in three plies': P. Macquoid, *A History of English Furniture*, IV, 1908, p. 105.
9 Sheraton, *Cabinet-Maker and Upholsterer's Drawing Book*.
10 *Ibid.*, p. 352.
11 Martin, *New Circle of Mechanical Arts*, p. 112.
12 Hamilton Jackson, *Intarsia and Marquetry*, p. 113.
13 Vincent, 'John Henry Belter', pp. 220–1.
14 *Ibid.*, p. 209.
15 Ernest Hagen discusses the infringement of Belter's patent by Charles Baudouine of New York, in the 1850s. See Ingerman, 'Personal experiences of an old New York cabinet maker', p. 578.
16 Tomlinson, *Encyclopaedia of Useful Arts*, III, 1866, p. 712.
17 *Ibid.*
18 *Furniture Gazette*, 18 August 1877, p. 120.
19 *England's Workshops*, 1864, pp. 306–7.
20 See Hounshell, *From the American System to Mass Production*, pp. 125–46.
21 *Furniture Gazette*, 31 January 1874, p. 109.
22 Quoted in Perry, *Modern Plywood*, p. 35.
23 See Hanks, *Innovative Furniture in America* p. 56.
24 US Patent No. 127045, 21 May 1872.
25 See Ames, 'Gardner and Company of New York', pp. 252–5.
26 Arkell and Duckworth, 'Cabinet Makers', p. 215.
27 Morton Shand, 'Timber as a reconstructed material'.
28 Wood and Linn, *Plywoods, Their Development, Manufacture and Application*, 1942, p. 188.
29 See, for example, Wilk, *Thonet*; Ostergard, *Bentwood and Metal Furniture*.
30 G. B. Hughes, 'Windsor chairs', *Country Life*, 25 May 1962, pp. 242–4.
31 Early patents for wheel sections include Joseph Jacob, 13 July 1769, Patent No. 932; and for architectural items, John Bevans, 4 April 1791, Patent No. 1799.
32 John Cumberland, 14 April 1720, Patent No. 42.
33 John Vidler, 5 November 1794, Patent No. 2020.
34 I am indebted to Patricia Kane's article, 'Samuel Gragg'.
35 Ostergard, *Bentwood and Metal Furniture*, p. 201.

Materials

36 KD refers to the 'knock-down' process where the components are joined by various metal fittings and shipped in an unassembled state.
37 H. R. Paul, in [Paris 1878] *Society of Arts. Artisans Reports*, p. 408.
38 Samuel Bentham, Patent No. 1951, 23 April 1793.
39 See Kane, 'Samuel Gragg', p. 31.
40 For an introduction to the early use of springs, see Holley, 'Upholstery springs'. For chamber horses, see E. Pinto, 'The Georgian chamber horse', *Country Life*, 20 October 1955.
41 J. Deville, *Dictionnaire du Tapissier de L'Ameublement Français*, Paris, 1878–80, p. 179. See also P. Thornton, 'Upholstered seat furniture in Europe in the 17th and 18th centuries', in E. S. Cooke (ed.), *Upholstery in America and Europe from the 17th century to World War I*, New York, 1987, p. 38, no. 11.
42 Himmelheber, *Biedermeier Furniture*.
43 Holley, 'Upholstery springs', pp. 66–7.
44 *Select Committee on the Sweating System*, 1888, xx, Q.2143.
45 *Ibid.*
46 See the *London Chair-makers' Book of Prices*, 1823, p. 68, where details of spring-making are listed.
47 Samuel Pratt, Patent No. 5418, 18 October 1826.
48 John Gillespie, Patent No. 5349, 25 April 1826.
49 Samuel Pratt, Patent No. 5668, 25 June 1828.
50 H. Havard, *Dictionnaire de L'Ameublement et de la Décoration*, Paris, 1887, p. 326. Havard mentions a mid-eighteenth century example of a 'bergère a ressorts' (sprung chair), mentioned in the *Memoirs of Madame Campan*.
51 This was not only in Europe. In 1834 the McIntyre business of Ontario offered sofas 'spring stuffed in the best manner'. See McIntyre, 'From workshop to factory', p. 30. See also Grier, *Culture and Comfort*, who states that in Philadelphia in 1840 'a spring seat was then a luxury – almost a novelty'.
52 Loudon, *Encyclopaedia*, 1833, p. 336.
53 *Ibid.*
54 Crofton, *London Upholsterers' Companion.*
55 *Ibid.*, p. 47.
56 *Ibid.*, p. 60.
57 E. Cooke and A. Passeri, in *Upholstery in America*, p. 239 (see note 41).
58 Grier, *Culture and Comfort*, p. 227.
59 *Ibid.*
60 Patent No. 1652, 12 July 1853.
61 Patent No. 1054, April 1864.
62 Patent No. 8861, 2 March 1841.
63 Patent No. 282, 1 February 1856.
64 A No-sag spring is made in a serpentine shape which is then held under tension between the rails of the chair frame.
65 Patent No. 2939, 24 November 1857.
66 *House Furnisher*, 1 May 1871, p. 42.
67 R. and A. Garrett, *Suggestions for House Decoration in Painting, Woodwork and Furniture*, Philadelphia, 1877, quoted in Grier, *Culture and Comfort*, p. 117.
68 Edmund Flowers of the Pullman Spring Company. Lectures to the Furniture Development Council Conference, 28 June 1967.

141

69 *Furniture Gazette*, 23 February 1878, p. 106.
70 Kirkham, 'London furniture trade', p. 36.
71 Ostergard, *Bentwood and Metal Furniture*, pp. 7–10.
72 Snyder, 'Victory over nature, Victorian cast-iron seating furniture', p. 233.
73 Loudon, *Encyclopaedia*, 1839, p. 318.
74 *Ibid.*, p. 349.
75 *Ibid.*, p. 654.
76 *Ibid.*, p. 564.
77 *House Furnisher*, 1 June 1891, p. 65, Peyton and Peyton advertisement.
78 *Journal of Design*, ii, 1850, p. 202.
79 Wheeler, *Rural Homes*, p. 208.
80 C. Dresser, *Principles of Decorative Design*, London, 1873, quoted in W. Halen, *Christopher Dresser*, Oxford, 1990, p. 75.
81 H. J. Cooper, *The Art of Furnishing*, 1876.
82 G. Halphen, *Rapport sur L'Exposition Publique des Produits de L'Industrie Français de 1844*, Paris, 1845, pp. 55–6.
83 See Ottillinger, 'August Kitschelt's metal furniture factory', pp. 235–9.
84 I am indebted to Francis Collard of the Furniture Collection, Victoria and Albert Museum, for this reference.
85 Webster, *Encyclopaedia of Domestic Economy*, p. 306.
86 Deane and Co., London Bridge, Trade Catalogue, *c.* 1850–60, Henry Francis du Pont Winterthur Museum Library.
87 C. Leonard, *Fabrique de lits et meubles en fer*, Paris, *c.* 1860, Henry Francis du Pont Winterthur Museum Library.
88 I am indebted to Adrian Heath for this information.
89 Le Bouteiller, *L'exposition Journal de L'industrie*.
90 Angelo Sedley, Patent No. 2742, 1860.
91 'A chapter in the early history of iron bedsteads', *Furniture Gazette*, 10 June 1882, p. 361.
92 Quoted in Macquoid and Edwards, *Dictionary*, p. 24.
93 Kirkham, 'London furniture trade', p. 117.
94 Macquoid and Edwards, *Dictionary*, p. 14.
95 Lindsey, 'Papier mâché', p. 165.
96 Henry Clay, Patent No. 1027, 1772.
97 Macquoid and Edwards, *Dictionary*, p. 14.
98 E. Clarke, *A Tour Round the South of England, Wales and Part of Ireland Made During the Summer of 1791*, London, 1793.
99 Aitken, 'Papier mâché manufacture', p. 567.
100 John Skidmore, Patent No. 1552, August 1786.
101 Jennens and Bettridge, Patent No. 5137, 29 March 1825.
102 For a full description of the manufacturing processes, see *Georgian and Victorian Japanned Ware of the West Midlands*, exhibition catalogue, Wolverhampton Art Gallery, October–November 1982.
103 *1851 Exhibition Jury Reports*, Class xxvi, p. 548.
104 One of the more bizarre examples of using technique to imitate one material in another was the use of papier mâché to resemble ivory. Between 1864 and 1866, Bettridge and Co. produced such a chair decorated with gold leaf in an Indian style.
105 Redgrave, *Supplementary Report on Design*.

106 *Ibid.*
107 Whitworth and Wallis, *Industry of the United States*, p. 148.
108 Lindsey, 'Papier mâché', p. 176.
109 *Ibid.*, p. 177.
110 Department of Practical Art, catalogue of articles of ornamental art in the Museum, quoted in Huth, *Lacquer of the West.*
111 G. Wallis, 'Recent progress in design as applied to manufacturers', *Society of Arts Journal*, IV, 14 March 1856, p. 297.
112 G. Wallis, 'The artistic, industrial and commercial results of the Universal Exposition', *The Exhibition of Art and Industry, Paris*, London, 1855.
113 *Ibid.*
114 Aitken, *Papier Mâché*, p. 573.
115 D. Sarjeant, 'On papier mâché', in [Paris 1867b] *Reports of Artisans.*
116 *Ibid.*
117 *Ibid.*
118 Lindsey, 'Papier Mâché', p. 105.
119 Yapp, *Art, Furniture, Upholstery and House Decoration*, p. 26.
120 Between 1855 and 1876 there were sixty-eight patents relating to wood substitutes.
121 C. Stevens, Patent No. 112, 1861.
122 J. Clark, Patent No. 217, 1861.
123 C. Pidding, Patent No. 13911, 1852.
124 Moses Poole, Patent No. 14299, 18 September 1852. Poole was a prodigious patentee, having no less than 106 patents granted between 1825 and 1852.
125 *Furniture Gazette*, 18 August 1877.
126 See D. Jones, 'Coal furniture in Scotland', *Furniture History*, XXIII, 1987, pp. 35–8.
127 Kershaw panels are on display in the Victoria and Albert Museum.
128 G. Magnus, Patent No. 8383, 1840.
129 Wyatt, *On Furniture and Decoration*, p. 318.
130 E. Wallace, Patent No. 12075, 1848.
131 'The application of gutta percha to the arts', *Universal Decorator*, 1858, p. 35.
132 *Ibid.*
133 *1851 Exhibition Jury Reports*, Class XXVIII, p. 598.
134 A. Prince, Patent No. 157, 1853.
135 E. Cunnington, Patent No. 882, 1853.
136 T. Ghislin, Patent No. 2035, 1862.
137 T. Ghislin, Patent No. 1953, 1862.
138 American Patent Sponge Co., 1868.
139 For recent publications, see Thompson, *Complete Wicker Book*, 1979; R. Saunders, *Collecting and Restoring Wicker Furniture*, New York, 1976; A. di Noto, 'The presence of wicker', *Connoisseur*, June 1984, pp. 78–84.
140 The machinery manufacturer, Ransome of Chelsea, made a cane-splitting machine, which produced a round rod from the rattan centre and split the outer cane surface into strips: *Spon's Encyclopaedia of the Industrial Arts, Manufactures and Commercial Products*, division II, London, 1880.

4   Patents

Many aspects of furniture history are encapsulated in patents and their relation to furniture. These include the nature of the demand for furniture; the design of the objects; the manufacturing processes (often themselves subject to patent); the particular materials used; and the distribution and consumption of the objects produced. The subject of patents can also lead the cultural historian into wider areas of investigation. Patents are important because they reveal something more than a technological detail of a process or design. The sort of areas appropriate to furniture studies (apart from the obvious attribution of objects), could include innovation and invention within and outside the trade; the use of illusion in place of reality; attitudes to tradition and reform in furniture design; and the paradox of traditional designs using innovative processes and methods.

   Before investigating the effect of patents on the furniture industry, it is necessary to bear in mind three points that relate to working with this material. The first is that not all patents granted were applied to actual products for sale, and that those that were may not have been successful in the marketplace.[1] Of course, the granting of a patent and the subsequent production of the item is no guarantee of commercial gain or successful production. To explain why some patent furniture was extremely successful, while other ideas literally never got 'off the drawing board', is very complex. But at least part of the answer may be in attitudes to innovation. The purchasing public was 'constrained by traditional conceptions of propriety and by definitions of what constitutes newness'.[2] These boundaries of public acceptance are arbitrary but very real, so if an invention extends or falls short of the accepted boundaries of newness or propriety, it will fail. Equally, if it falls within these boundaries it might be very successful. In addition, Ettema has suggested that innovative furniture was also a manifestation of the adoption of mechanisation as a 'pervasive cultural value'.[3]

The second point is that the patentee would often sell or licence another party to exploit the patent for commercial use, therefore the maker might be different from the patentee. In a number of cases the patentee is completely unconnected with the trade, although the evidence suggests that the most successful patents were taken out by craftsmen.

The third point is that there were many innovations in method and design that never had a patent to protect them because of the cost and time involved in the patenting process. This was often due to the fragmentary nature of the furniture business and the great number of individual makers, so changes in the way objects were produced were often made in a piecemeal way and there were only a limited number of widely recognised specific advances. Furniture trade practice was not governed by the continuing advance of patents and inventions in the same way as iron and steel or textile production might have been.

By analysing the number of patents granted during the period 1620–1885, it is possible to draw some conclusions about the patent system and its operation in relation to the furniture trade. A quantitative analysis reveals that the greatest number of patents granted relates to furniture castors,[4] and this is followed by bedsteads and upholstery stuffing materials.[5] These facts are not surprising and can be explained by the three main motivations behind patent furniture design: mobility, hygiene, and comfort. Of the true furniture patents, those that relate to chairs, both easy and folding, are the most numerous,[6] closely followed by folding bedsteads and invalid bedsteads,[7] and expanding dining tables.[8]

A diachronic analysis confirms the belief that certain periods were more active in producing patents than others. The quantity of patents related to furniture issued in the period of 265 years (1620–1885) amounted to 3880. The breakdown of this total reveals that in the first 120 years there were only four patents granted. By 1820, a total of seventy-four were granted. Between 1820 and 1852 there were an additional 153, bringing the total to 227, and after 1853, due in some respect to the Patent Law Amendment Act, the number of patents grew very rapidly. To put these figures into perspective, the work of

Dutton on patents and industrial activity is useful.[9] He has prepared a ranking of patent activity by process, for the period 1750–1851. In his table, the furniture category ranked twenty-eighth out of one hundred. Apart from textiles, furniture is the highest domestic category on his list. The reasons for this growth in patent protections were partly due to the potential economic advantages of applications accruing to the inventors, hence the noticeable amount of non-furniture trade patentees who patented furnishing-related inventions; and partly due to a growing domestic market that was demanding a wider choice and variety of furniture, combined with other domestic requirements related to mobility, hygiene, and comfort.

The patent system

The earliest patent was granted to John of Utynam by Henry VI in 1449, for coloured glass to be supplied to Eton College. The British patent system (based on rewarding inventors by granting them limited monopolies for their efforts) was properly constituted by the Statute of Monopolies in 1624. For over two hundred years this was the basis for anyone wishing to file a patent application. It became increasingly apparent that with the growth in inventing activity in the eighteenth and nineteenth centuries, the system would need to be overhauled.[10] The object of patent law was that the exclusive rights for a patent should encourage manufacture and stimulate investment. However, a major stumbling block for patent designers was the time and cost involved in acquiring a patent; the process could take up to thirty-five separate stages and cost around £300 for fourteen years' protection.[11] In addition, the process involved seven different offices of the Crown and required two personal signatures of the Sovereign. It is therefore perhaps surprising that there were so many patentees who could afford both the time and the money to go through the process. With the rapidly increasing patent activity, due to a perceived need to benefit industry, the problem eventually became intolerable, and after a great deal of public pressure, by Henry Cole and Charles Dickens amongst others, changes were made. The 1851 Exhibition was a further stimulus to this reform, and in 1852 the Patent Law Reform Act came on to the statute book.[12]

Innovation and invention

The distinction between innovation and invention helps one to understand the role of patents in the nineteenth century. Whereas invention is a well-defined concept which involves individual effort to devise a new or improved method of producing an item or process, innovation has three different meanings. The first is the introduction of novelties: a new object can be an innovation. The second is to make changes: these changes can be very small, and indeed the role of innovation in the way styles of ordinary objects change is based on an accretion of minor changes. The third is the use of old materials in new forms. All these definitions are useful in discovering the relationship of innovation to furniture history. Indeed innovation in the development of new product types and the use of new materials and processes is not a well-known aspect of furniture history.

There have been some attempts to chart the progress and development of certain aspects of furniture materials or methods, and one or two of these have used patent records as a source, but furniture studies have usually tended to be design and provenance based.[13] Even though the patent lists are a valuable source of record for ideas and inventions of an innovatory nature, they do not mean much by themselves. As I indicated above, the context is as important as the invention itself if any historical value is to be drawn out of the patent.

Perhaps the first point to note is that comparatively few patents relate to completely new ways of making or designing an item. In most cases, a principle had already been established and it was the development and application of this principle that was the subject of patent rights.[14] Naturally, the continual development of, and improvement to, existing patents, tended to cause short-term advances, which were themselves superseded at a later date. In the middle of the century Gottfried Semper wrote:

> Nowadays inventions precede real need and are withdrawn before their technical let alone artistic possibilities can be recognised and fully used, being replaced by new and only occasionally superior inventions.[15]

Ames (1983) noted the same phenomenon: 'Most patented furniture turned out to be less an enduring amelioration of the human condition than a short-lived solution replaced by newer innovations more responsive to changed conditions.'[16] Ames went on to suggest that few patented furnishings outlived their patent life, thereby implying that innovation was a continual process, which produced a constant stream of products and methods that sought to improve upon previous productions. This may have been the case with many objects, either where a state of perfection was difficult to achieve, or where there was a wide variety of types (such as castors), but many successful patented designs or processes did continue to be produced in their original form for many years. Examples of these continuing products would be Jupe's extending dining tables[17] and Daws's reclining chairs.[18]

The reasons for innovation in the furniture trade can be considered in various ways, and should be divided between production and design factors. The first production factor relates to the question of innovations to save costs. The introduction of cheaper materials, methods, and machinery is basic business economy planning. The potential use of new and improved machines, materials, and processes that might reduce unit costs will therefore be a prime consideration in developing new designs and models. However, for much of the nineteenth century demand exceeded supply which meant it was only internal trade competition that had to be matched, and that had a stifling effect on serious innovation. While the basic economic unit in the furniture industry remained the small workshop, savings from cost and expense control were not significant. In the second half of the century the development of factories and their inherent cost centres made financial savings more important. The economies of scale had to be matched by tighter financial controls.

In technological terms, the discovery of improved materials, new uses for older ones, and the development of economically produced substitutes is the second consideration. The use of substitute materials to supply a particular look at a less expensive price led to the development of new methods and materials which were used in many furniture productions. The most well-known processes might be papier mâché and bentwood, but throughout the nineteenth century there were a vast number of different attempts to introduce new materials. Many of these were successful, many more were not. It was a question of which ones fell within the boundary of public acceptance.

29 Daws's reclining chair, patented in 1827, is an example of a successfully patented mechanism that remained in production for many years

Public demand also influenced upholsterers. The search for comfort has been a continuing feature of furniture design since the later eighteenth century. However, it was in the early nineteenth century that upholsterers really took advantage of the improvements that were becoming available, including spring seating, and metal chair and bed frames. These improvements allowed them to satisfy the demand for a more relaxed and easy private life-style, as well as to meet the demand for the formal public front.

There are two other forces in this analysis of innovation and they are not complementary. The first is the interest in the mechanics and variability of furniture which had been a feature of a number of eighteenth century cabinet-makers' works:[19] an interest that filtered down into the nineteenth century. Again the novelty of innovative products has always been a selling point, particularly when the 'patent' label has been appended to them. Often the furniture was required to have a dual purpose for reasons of space and economy, and this encouraged inventive processes. In most cases the dual nature of the innovation was not prized simply for itself, but was seen as a necessity that had to be cloaked in a shroud of 'tasteful' clothing to make it acceptable. This was the metamorphic principle of objects looking normal but actually concealing a novel mode of operation to convert their use. Therefore, innovative aspects of furniture design that were hidden behind conventional exteriors, suggest an ambivalence towards change that explains why many patented inventions relating to furniture were attempting to replace older methods or materials without looking too new. This illustrates the question of illusion and reality which was part of much of the nineteenth century psyche. Extreme examples of the duality include beds hidden in pianos, chairs that convert to bath-tubs, and tables with hidden mangles and wringers. Other more realistic examples from everyday use would be sofa beds, extending dining tables and reclining chairs.

The second force relates to items of furniture that were to remain utilitarian in design and finish simply because they were part of an established continuum. Bentwood furniture is perhaps the best example of this. Ostergard (1987), in his opening essay, made the point that early innovations were not necessarily used to proclaim a new or improved form, rather they were hidden behind an 'aesthetic determined by people ignorant of method'.[20] In other words, the innovation, whether patented or not, was hidden by the ruling taste of the period. He used the examples of Chapius's chair, which although made from bent laminated wood, was designed using a Roman precedent, and Samuel Gragg's bentwood chair, which exploited the bentwood process to make a continuous leg seat and back stile, but was essentially a traditional seat form, decorated with painted motifs. Both these chairs have similar technology to the Thonet bentwood but their design is retrospective, whereas Thonet's designs are directly related to the nature of the material. The extraordinary success of the Thonet innovations illustrate how a simple concept, patented technology, and selected materials produced a 'timeless' design that is still recognised as a design classic.

Demand for and consumption of patent furniture

An increase in demand for all types of furniture and furnishings was activated by a rapid population increase from the late eighteenth century onward. This growing market was to be satisfied in a number of particular ways by patent furniture. There were various demands made upon furniture for which 'patent' type objects were ideal. The demands included space-saving, portability, hygiene, and comfort.

The practical aspect of constructing furniture for different tasks that could be combined into one item, shows how furniture-makers responded to the problem of lack of space. Joy (1977) has suggested that the space-saving requirement arose from a rise in population and a demand for furniture convenient for use in crowded town dwellings. Is this a reasonable assumption? The large quantity of patents that refer to space-saving would appear to support the idea; however, it has been argued that many patent furniture items would be found in well-to-do interiors where the need to save space was not a requirement. It is suggested that in these and other cases, it was the elements of novelty or ingenuity that were enjoyed.[21]

There are a number of patents that relate to various modes of combining functions within one piece of furniture. There are equally a number of items of furniture, incorporating space-saving facilities, that were not patented. The first patent with a specific space-saving intention was Eckhardt's portable table and portable chair of 1771, which was 'so contrived as to answer all the purposes of the common tables and chairs, and at the same time to lay in the compass of a small box';[22] it was evidently designed for ease of transport as much as movement within the home. The most ubiquitous space-saving items, and the subject of a number of patent applications, were extending dining tables. The first was Sweetman and Higgs' 'improvements in the construction of tables'.[23] The principle of this patent was that a double-flap top would be able to flip over, swivel round and extend the table to twice its original size. The table also had a hollow-framed top which was apparently designed to hold shaving, dressing, or writing requisites.

Dining tables whose size could be adjusted continued to gain the attention of patentees, and in 1800 Richard Gillow designed an extending dining table, using wood or metal sliders to pull apart the two tops ready for insertion of extra flaps.[24] Between 1802 and 1807 four more patents were taken out. Brown's patent extension table was based on the concertina or 'lazy-tongs' principle with a cross rail and legs between each pair of tongs; it was successfully marketed by Wilkinson & Co. of Ludgate Hill. Another improvement on the extension of dining tables was invented by George Remington in 1807: it consisted of a lazy-tongs motion which expanded tables in a concertina motion similar to Brown's patent two years before; however, Remington's patent relied on a pair of legs being attached to each set of tongs.[25]

One of the less well-known table extending devices was patented by William Doncaster in 1814. Doncaster was not a cabinet-maker and this may be the reason for the eccentric nature of his patent. It was based on the principle of hydrostatic bellows that operated the rising and lowering of a rotary centre in a table. It seems highly improbable that it was ever made. Other examples of attempts to extend tables include the use of pulleys, endless chains and developments of the lazy-tong and screw motions.

Further space-saving developments had to wait until the patent of Robert Jupe in 1835. Jupe's patent table was based on enlarging a dining table by the addition of segmental pieces. His patent specification included designs for circular, oval, square, and rectangular table shapes. He also showed two differing methods of enlarging the table frame: one was a straightforward pull-out mechanism based on sliding sections; the other was a more sophisticated arrangement which included a mechanical contrivance to swivel the sections out from the centre.[26] This was one of the most successful patented tables, and was still available some thirty years later.

Not all inventions related to space-saving involved dining tables. The requirement was further advanced by the patent of John Elwick[27] in 1800, which was for a new and improved method of framing 'together chairs and sofas of every kind and sort whatsoever and which invention is intended to be applied to every description of household furniture'. This patent, designed to help the needs of exporters, was made by the son of Edward Elwick of the firm of Wright and Elwick. His invention was based on the 'knock-down' principle by having screw-tapped holes and stretchers with screws inserted into them to enable the item to be assembled at its destination. This method of assembly seems to pre-suppose a carefully and accurately cut series of joints that would be certain to fit together upon arrival. The essential part of knock-down construction is the accurate preparation of all the parts. Considerations for military space-saving requirements are reflected in a patent taken out by James Hakewell in 1809; the patent described a system of collapsible tables and chairs designed especially for 'domestic, military and naval service'.[28]

Portability was another practical aspect; it partly related to the need for space-saving, especially with folding tables and chairs that could be brought out into a room when needed. It was also important in designs for travelling or campaign furniture. The need for portability in furniture design, like other innovations, seems to have stemmed from someone perceiving a demand and then planning to meet it. The needs of an army and navy that were more often abroad than at home, obviously demanded furniture that could be taken on tours of duty. Some families liked to take furniture with them as they moved around, or when they emigrated and would require furniture for the journey and for the new home. In 1809 James Hakewell patented a novel arrangement specifically for constructing chairs and tables for military use.[29] The patent was based on a folding joint that could be incorporated into a number of differing styles of chair or stool or table. The concept of flat-packing chairs and table together was no doubt appreciated on board ships where space was at a premium.

These patents illustrate the interest in folding furniture that was to continue as a part of the furnishers' repertoire through the century and beyond. The majority of patents for portable furniture related to methods of fastening and fixing so as to secure it as rapidly as possible when assembled. Apart from the consumer demand for knock-down furniture, a number of manufacturers realised the benefits in the process, especially when exporting. The ultimate example of the economy in design, linked with the KD concept, is the Thonet No. 14 chair, which comprises only six wooden elements held together by four bolts and two screws.

In addition to the extending and knock-down furniture, there was a demand for dual-purpose objects which was often related to the size of the family. A large family with a small number of bedrooms would need special arrangements for extra beds. Press beds or beds in cupboards had been in use for a long time. However, sensibility and social pressure suggested that 'a bed in a dining room is not nice'. This problem was tackled by Thomas Gale in 1772 when he invented a bedstead that when shut resembled a bookcase or wardrobe. In the early nineteenth century, J. C. Loudon discussed and illustrated a bed which was built into a cupboard.[30] His comments reveal that although they were considered objectionable because they harboured vermin, these beds had the advantage that persons sleeping in them generally had to get up in the morning! He further suggested that such beds were held in little repute because they indicated a deficiency of bedrooms. Despite their reputation, this type of press bedstead was being offered for sale at least until the 1860s. More obvious as an example of bedroom deficiency were the half-tester beds which allowed the bed to be lifted up under its tester and have a curtain pulled around it during the day so as to give the occupant of the room more space.[31] Other space-savers were the bed-chair or convertible sofa, both of which were known prior to the nineteenth century but their production for general sale and use was a new phenomenon in the period. Figgins's palanquin couch is a good example. Patented in 1812, the palanquin was a couch by day and a bed by night[32] (a clear example of metamorphosis). When the bed was housed in a sideboard or, more extremely, a piano, it moved into the realms of parody.

Whatever the camouflage, the notion of decorum, in which the alternative use of a piece of furniture is hidden, was part of a wider feeling that the specialised use of space, rational systems of storage, and the careful planning of limited resources was both practically and morally superior.

The practical demands created by two medical issues also furthered the cause of patent furniture. The toll of wartime and the subsequent need for invalid care, together with a strong desire to have hygienic beds, acted as stimuli for inventions. One of the first concerns of patentees was to produce furniture that would relieve the suffering of patients who were bedridden or incapable of self-propulsion. Indeed the very first furniture patent listed in July 1620, relates to a back frame designed to relieve sick persons who were always lying down. In the nineteenth century the developments in

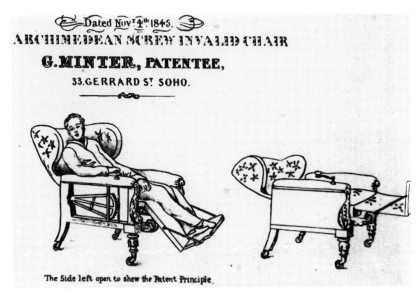

Dated Nov 4th 1845.

ARCHIMEDEAN SCREW INVALID CHAIR

G.MINTER, PATENTEE,

33.GERRARD S! SOHO.

The Side left open to shew the Patent Principle.

30 G. Minter's patent 'Archimedean screw invalid chair', one of a wide range of specialist chairs made by Minter between 1830 and 1860

invalid furniture were to influence designs for other forms of seating. In 1810, Parker and Cluley patented an adjustable bedstead, based on a frame with a fourfold motion.[33] In 1813, Samuel James enrolled his patent for a 'machine for the ease of invalids or others': the design was based on a Classical sofa shape but with a mechanism built in for adjusting the reclining or support of the occupant.[34] Both these examples show how the possibilities found in the invalid furniture began to filter into the mainstream of upholstery design and the search for comfort, especially in situations that supported a posture between sitting and lying.

Although the most important invention associated with comfort is arguably the development of the upholstery spring, there were other items designed for the enjoyment of the public. The reclining chair was a ripe area for patent furniture producers. Between 1828 and 1863 there were no less than sixteen patents relating to improvements in reclining chairs.

In addition to the requirements of space-saving, portability, hygiene, and comfort, patents could provide objects that were considered modern, new, and exciting. Roth pointed out that:

to the public the patented object perhaps suggested the latest, if not the best in its field, it had something none of its competitors had, and was so 'valuable' that it had to be protected by patent.[35]

It also explains the use of the patent label for furniture designs that had never had the benefit of legal protection. Patents were a very potent sales promotion tool which, combined with the idea of fashion changes, must have encouraged a lively market. A guide, published in 1829, gave advice to new entrants to the furniture trade:

> In a business where change and caprice rule with unbounded sway – in which the fashion of today may become obsolete tomorrow – an inventive genius and discriminating judgement are certainly essential qualifications.[36]

This notion of the need to be an 'inventive genius' confirms the idea that patent furniture and its consequent innovations in material, process, and technique were a distinct part of the furniture trade from the early nineteenth century.

Notes

1 The main body of material relating to this type of furniture is the Patents of Invention listings that give full details of all patents granted from 1620 to date.
2 Barnett, *Innovation: the Basis of Cultural Change*.
3 M. J. Ettema, 'History, nostalgia and American furniture', *Winterthur Portfolio*, XVII, 1982, p. 140.
4 Seventy-seven patents for castors were issued between 1620 and 1866.
5 Fifty-two patents for bedsteads and thirty-eight for upholstery stuffing were issued between 1620 and 1866.
6 Twenty-eight easy chair and twenty-eight folding chair patents were issued in the period 1620–1866.
7 Twenty-five folding and twenty-three invalid bedstead patents were issued in the period 1620–1866.
8 Twenty-three expanding table patents were issued between 1620 and 1866.
9 Dutton, *Patent System and Inventive Activity*, pp. 206–8.
10 For the history of the patent system, see Gomme, *Patents of Invention*.
11 Hughes, 'Day Gunby and patent furniture'.
12 The re-organised Patent Office identified a number of the problems. One of the most pressing was the need for a listing of the specifications of existing patents so that effort would not be wasted in re-inventing some item or process that was already subject to patent rights. This was achieved by the efforts of Bennett Woodcroft, first Superintendent of the new Patent Office established in 1853.
13 See Kirkham, 'London furniture trade'.
14 A good example of this is recorded by R. Roth, 'Nineteenth century American patent furniture', *Innovative Furniture in America from 1800 to the Present*, New

York, 1981, p. 31. She shows how the United States Patent Office rejected Belter's patent for press work or laminated wood as it was a 'prior art'. He eventually received his patent for the process and method of using laminates that were peculiar to his products.

15 G. Semper, preface, 'Theory of formal beauty', quoted in W. Herrman, *Gottfried Semper, In Search of Architecture*, MIT Press, 1984.

16 K. L. Ames, introduction, *Wooton Desks*, exhibition catalogue, Indiana State Museum, Indianapolis, 1983.

17 R. Jupe, Patent No. 6788, 11 March 1835. This table was still being exhibited as late as 1886 (Paris).

18 R. Daws, Patent No. 5490, 28 April 1827.

19 See Merlin (1985).

20 Ostergard, *Bentwood and Metal Furniture.*

21 Kirkham, 'London furniture trade', p. 131.

22 A. G. Eckhardt, Patent No. 995, 29 July 1771.

23 R. Sweetman and J. Higgs, Patent No. 2007, 13 August 1794.

24 R. Gillow, Patent No. 2396, 1800.

25 G. Remington, Patent No. 3090, 16 December 1807. His patent also describes a globe table with two moving quarters which can act separately.

26 R. Jupe, Patent No. 6788, 11 March 1835.

27 J. Elwick, Patent No. 2420, 1 July 1800.

28 J. Hakewell, Patent No. 3217, 20 March 1809.

29 *Ibid.*

30 Loudon, *Encyclopaedia*, 1833. For a more detailed examination of press beds, see C. Edwards, 'Press beds', *Furniture History*, xxvi, 1990.

31 Loudon, *Encyclopaedia*, 1833, pp. 329–33.

32 T. Figgins, Patent No. 3539, 19 February 1812. Palanquin appears to be a Hindu term for a portable throne carried by bearers.

33 Parker and Cluley, Patent No. 3387, 8 October 1810.

34 Samuel James, Patent No. 3744, 1 November 1813.

35 Roth, 'Nineteenth century American patent furniture', p. 23.

36 Stokes, *Complete Cabinet Maker*, p. 4.

5   The United States

It is worth making a brief investigation into the similarities and differences between the United States and the British furniture trades. Both were characterised by a number of specific economic features: a growing population; the development of a wage-based economy; the development of a national transport and communication system; the growth of a large middle class; and the increasing sophistication of marketing techniques. However, in contrast to Britain's generally slow acceptance of technology, it was the United States, with its vast natural resources, limited skilled labour, and growing markets, that encouraged the embracement of new technology, especially machines and machine processes. In the United States, the division of labour and the standardisation of prefabricated parts gradually combined to reduce costs and improve efficiency from early in the nineteenth century. The change in the young republic's base, from a craft and agrarian system to a modern industrial-based economy, could not help but alter the nature of the furniture trade. Factories were established in the upper midwest, particularly in Indiana, Ohio and Illinois.[1] These factories were characterised by large-scale investment in premises and machinery; division of labour; use of duplicated parts; and the distribution of finished furniture through wholesalers and warehousemen. The combined access to raw materials and expanding markets as well as the growing use of machinery, enabled these businesses to reproduce the fashionable styles of Europe and the East Coast at popular prices. The eastern furniture centres, such as Boston, Philadelphia and New York continued to develop both the large-scale export companies and the small-scale or custom-making businesses.

Design

On the East Coast, the fluctuations of international fashions in furniture were most skilfully interpreted by small-scale workshops, often run by French and German immigrant master craftsmen. Cabinetmakers like Ernest Hagen,[2] continued in small workshops, while others such as George Henkels of Philadelphia,[3] Pottier and Stymus,[4] and Alexander Roux,[5] in New York, developed medium-scale enterprises which maintained the small-shop ethos. Technical skills of a very high order were evident in the work of John Henry Belter[6] and Charles Baudouine, both of whom embraced a technique that served them well in producing fashionable Rococo Revival furniture. In some cases the bespoke businesses such as Daniel Pabst,[7] and Herter Bros.[8] developed into artist-craftsmen concerns, who executed projects for architects as well as distinguished private customers. In some cases cabinet-makers were instrumental in introducing European styles: the firm of Leon Marcotte, whose father-in-law was the Parisian decorator Ringuet LePrince, was associated with a Louis XVI revival. It is important to recognise that many of these businesses employed new techniques and steam-powered machinery (lathes, routers, etc.), in conjunction with their traditional craft skills to maintain their position at the top end of the market. The undoubted success of these businesses was nothing compared to the giant enterprises in Chicago, Grand Rapids, and Cincinnati. However, from a design point of view, the mid-western products apparently left much to be desired. Sloan, in *Homestead Architecture* (1861), complained about the cheap, showy furniture coming from the western and southern states, and Andrew Jackson Downing advised the working classes to furnish their homes with simple, inexpensive and 'nicely painted cottage furniture'. This was produced quickly by specialists, who perfected freehand brushwork and stencilled patterns that often created an illusion of more highly priced timber and carved effects. Technology did improve lives and made furniture accessible to the lower classes despite its mediocre quality and decoration. It created an illusion of material well-being and began to fulfil the democratising ideal of decorative arts for all.

Tools and techniques

The period is known for its eclecticism in visual sources and their application, and it was the ability of machine-assisted manufacture to meet these demands that made their role important. The availability of abundant and cheap furniture meant disposability, which promoted a continuing pattern of consumption, which in turn led to increased mechanisation. Nevertheless, mechanisation was a slow, infiltrating process and the relationship between machine, material, and maker remained unstructured and variable. The evidence of the use of steam power in the furniture industry, cited by Earl, concluded that as late as 1870 a large proportion of American furniture output was manufactured in relatively small shops without the aid of steam power.[9] However, this does not mean without the aid of machinery, since hand, wheel, foot, and pole-operated machines were all available to makers of furniture on any scale.

The ideal solution was found in a mix of labour and machines. The labour component comprised semi-skilled men who had to be directed towards a 'workmanship of certainty', using specialised machines to perform particular tasks in the production sequence. The results of this were then assembled, fitted and finished by the balance of the workforce. Nowhere can this process be seen better than in the industry of the United States and Canada where acute labour shortages encouraged rapid development of machine technology in the furniture trade, and where a growing market for furniture needed to be satisfied. The difference between the North American and the British experience was hinted at in an article that asked the question: 'Why was England able to export furniture to the West Indies and South America more cheaply than the United States could?' The reply confirmed that machinery could eventually replace the high labour costs in the United States and this would then help to make their product competitive:

> with her cheap labour she [England] can produce, sell and deliver at a less price than we [the US] can. Allowing that labour is the most important item that enters into the cost of manufacturing furniture, it is not everything, and we can even offset it with machinery, for the use of machinery is much more common with us than with our transatlantic neighbours.[10]

Even so, machines did not completely rule the manufacturing scene in the United States, particularly at the top end of the business. In M. and H. Schrenkheisen's establishment, it was found to be more 'economic to do a large proportion of the carving by hand, rather than to fit up the knives and patterns for all the new and elaborate designs in carving [that] are always being introduced'.[11] This was of course the rub between machine and design: the fewer design changes in a product there are, the longer a production run can be, and the simpler the design, the more economically the machine can run.

A considered analysis of the relationship between technological innovation and design economics in the United States furniture trade was made by Michael Ettema in 1981.[12] He suggested that in the case of the United States, 'the degree to which machinery was capable of reducing labour costs in furniture manufacture was inversely pro-portional to the total cost of the product'.[13] This meant that the machinery that was introduced in an effort to reduce labour costs, achieved that aim in the production of simple, batch-produced fur-niture, but the cost savings on better furniture gradually became less and less, as other expensive processes became part of the cost equa-tion. This perhaps helps to explain why many entrepreneurs and inventors were interested in developing methods of mechanical decoration or reproduction of expensive hand processes, so as to balance the equation by reducing the traditionally expensive costs of handwork. In the United States then, the introduction of machines encouraged the proliferation of furniture, while in the United King-dom cheap labour achieved the same end.

In 1850, William Chambers wrote of the advantages of speed and accuracy promoted by the use of machinery in the Canadian factory of Jacques and Hay:

> here for the first time saw in operation the remarkably ingenious machinery for planing, turning, morticing and effecting other purposes in carpentry, for which the United States have gained much deserved celebrity ... So perfect is the machinery, that from the rough timber a neat bedstead can be made in the short space of two minutes![14]

Machinery

It was the United States that led the way with the construction of these labour-saving devices. It is instructive to note that the cumulative figures for patented inventions associated with wood-working show that between 1790 and 1873 there were, for example, thirty-eight patents granted for machines to cut veneers, and in the seventeen years between 1856 and 1873 there were an amazing eighty-two patents related to wood-bending processes. Amongst the most successful were those relating to joint-cutting. For example, the Burley dovetailing machine, patented in 1855, was alleged to have been able to produce seventy-five to one hundred dovetail joints per hour. Improvements continued to occur in these machines but one is worthy of a special mention. In 1870, Charles B. Knapp patented his dove-tailing machine. Tice has pointed out that this machine was significant because it was the first machine that did not attempt to reproduce the hand-cut dovetail, but rather produced its own peculiar 'modern machined joint'. Ironically, Tice suggests that the interest in traditional furniture towards the end of the century contributed to the decline of this obviously modern joint.[15]

In addition to joint-cutting, carving machines became an American speciality. The origins might be found in the copying-lathes employed in armouries which used the Blanchard method, but there is little evidence of this being transferred to the furniture trade. The major development came when bosting or multiple carving machines were developed in the 1870s; they were based on Jordan's invention but were still essentially a preparatory bosting process. The *Cabinet Maker* (1885) commented on the carving machine produced by the Buss company of Grand Rapids:

> A great advance in the decoration of furniture has been made within a few years, mainly by reason of the introduction of such new and improved devices, and the ability to indulge in tasteful designs is now enjoyed by a large number.[16]

A few years later, in 1889, the same journal was suggesting that another model, the Moore carving machine, could be operated by a boy and therefore 'no manufacturer who employs carvers and has any quantity of duplicate carvings to make, can afford to be without a machine, as it will save its cost in three months.'[17] Even more successful were American uses of the spindle carvers which had a cutter mounted on a spinning shaft. These could only be operated by a skilled person, but they could be used in an assembly-line fashion to produce a relatively complicated design.

31 An advertisement for graining plates which produced an imitation wood grain on plain timber surfaces

Of all the processes of furniture-making that could be mechanised, polishing seemed to be the least likely to profit from the inventiveness of the period. Nevertheless, in the United States alone, thirteen processes were patented between 1790 and 1873 for machines to polish cabinets.[18] The United States industry also took what were essentially hand operations and successfully mechanised them. For example, hand-operated graining instruments, with the roller carved in relief with the required design, had been used to impress a grain pattern on to a wet painted surface.[19] This process of grain imitation was brought to a fine art by the Grand Rapids Panel Company who manufactured a machine with 'Elastic Graining Plates', designed to produce fine imitation French burl [walnut] veneer and imitation mahogany crotch veneer.

Production

One of the more contentious arguments of recent years has centred around the question of mass production in the American furniture industry during the nineteenth century. Evidence of apparent mass production can be found in the changes in the Trade Committee price books. The Philadelphia price book for 1811 indicates that variety in design was achieved through the making of uniquely shaped or specialised forms.[20] By 1828 it was evident that variety was achieved by a plethora of furniture parts that could be added to or substituted for another item in the same basic design, thus creating a range of interchangeable items.[21] In some cases though, the arrangements for preparing parts appear to have been similar to the United Kingdom. Ernest Hagen, talking about his early experiences during the 1840s in New York, said:

> The work was all done by hand, but the scroll sawing, of course was done at the nearest sawmill. The employers (boss cabinet makers) having no machinery at all, all the moldings were bought at the molding mill and the turning done at the turning mill.[22]

However, it was soon evident that, despite Hagen's example, full-scale machinery was required to meet the ever-growing demand for furniture, particularly in the lower to medium price range, which was the largest market. The machines in use in the converting mills such as Hagen discusses were important in assisting this sector of the trade, but even more important was the application of technology in the workshop, which was contrary to British experience. For visitors to the United States the cheap end of the trade was thought to be where the most interesting innovations were occurring. George Wallis, the British Commissioner at the New York Industrial Exhibition of 1854, considered it was very regrettable that

> the ordinary class of useful and cheap furniture, so largely manufactured for the Western states, was not represented in the Exhibition. This is to be regretted as much ingenuity and economy of materials is often shown in the production of this class of goods.[23]

In fact, Wallis was so impressed with the 'machine-made' furniture he saw at the New York International Exhibition, he apparently brought back a sample of the work for inclusion in the Victoria and Albert Museum collection.[24] Wallis's comments about the ingenuity of the American makers were confirmed by another British traveller. William Chambers, writing about his visit to a Cincinnati furniture factory in 1854, said that he was astonished to find 'a factory as large as a Lancashire cotton mill for making chairs, tables, or bedsteads by machinery'.[25] He commented on the employees, noting

32 Machine-made work table, *c.* 1854; an American example of machine preparation and hand assembly. Allegedly brought to England by George Wallis to demonstrate the possibilities of machine work

that 'many of these are occupied merely in guiding and superintending machines moved by shafts and belts from a large steam engine on the ground floor.'[26]

The growth of the use of machinery of all sorts continued rapidly, and a report in the [American] *Cabinet Maker* (28 May 1870), used the example of the Boston firm of Beal and Hooper to give a clear

picture of a typical operation. Having discussed the firm's management system and how it was based on the experience of the Springfield
Armoury, the Waltham watchworks, and the Colt arms factory, they
go on to describe the machinery in use. The list included 7 turning
lathes; 4 jig-saws; 1 belt-saw; 2 boring machines; 1 tenoning machine;
1 David's planer; 4 variety moulders; 1 jointer; 1 buzz-planer; and 2
circular saws. In addition to these was a squaring-up machine, built
by the factory for their own framing needs. This inventory seems to
show how a typical American factory relied both on mass-produc-
tion management systems and on the use of extensive machinery for
nearly all processes.

This demand for machines encouraged an expanding woodworking machine industry that served both the home and export markets.
Some claims for the machines were based on the supposed benefits
that their use would bring. Rather confidently, one machine-maker
declared of his product: 'No machine ever invented or introduced to
the public notice is capable of doing so much to benefit the mil-
lions'.[27] The same manufacturer even took it upon himself to suggest
that 'The best style of cabinet work is carved and moulded in every
conceivable direction, and to do this with dispatch is a great gain.'[28]
Needless to say the corollary was that his machine would best achieve
this.

There were those who were not wholly comfortable with the
supremacy of the machine. A cautionary tale regarding the use of
machines was noted in *Tales of the Trades*. Although in support of
machine production, it warned against the possibility of short cuts
used in furniture-making:

> Formerly and not so many years ago, the cabinet-maker made furniture,
> and the machine supplemented his work; nowadays the machines the
> thing, while man puts on the finishing touches. The price has been cut in
> two and the furniture is better. That is, the furniture is better if in none
> of the various stages there is slighting, and if throughout, the right
> material has been used. There is no stage at which a fine piece of furniture
> may be hurried on its way through the factory. It feels even in its early
> stages, the dignity that is in keeping with its finished appearance of
> quality, and it will permit no infringement upon that dignity.[29]

Regardless of any demands to control the machine, it was an indis-
pensable part of the American industry. The most revealing docu-
ment, which illustrates the comparison between machinery and hand

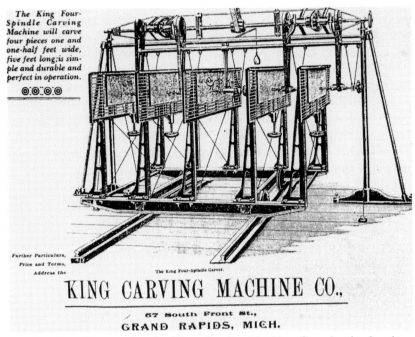

The King Four-Spindle Carving Machine will carve four pieces one and one-half feet wide, five feet long; is simple and durable and perfect in operation.

Further Particulars, Price and Terms, Address the

The King Four-Spindle Carver.

KING CARVING MACHINE CO.,

67 South Front St.,

GRAND RAPIDS, MICH.

33 An advertisement for the King Carving Machine Co., clearly showing the principle of a tracer and four cutters

labour, is the report of the Commissioner of Labor, published in 1898. This massive effort attempted to compare the process of making goods, in a variety of industries, by hand (usually taking details from the mid-century) and the machine-assisted production of the 1890s. In the introduction to the furniture section it was stressed that the difficulties of making comparisons were enormous when the styles of furniture changed so regularly. Nevertheless, the report continued:

> The presentations for this industry have great value in showing the wonderful cheapening of articles that are necessary to the comfort and convenience of every household. In general it may be said that the machine product is superior to the hand-made, but it is claimed in several instances that the latter is of greater durability.[30]

An analysis of the statistics quickly reveals that when using machines, compared to hand processes, there was an increase in the workforce and the number of operations, but a decrease in time and a saving in costs. The most extreme variations were found in simple processes such as sanding, where one man could smooth by hand 240 square feet of timber in sixteen hours, whereas by a machine with two men, it took just one hour and two minutes. Despite these examples of the use of machinery and the obvious attempts to improve efficiency with an increasingly scientific approach to furniture making, the trade was still being criticised for its lack of manufacturing prowess as late as 1921. A mechanical engineer from Grand Rapids wrote:

> lack of engineering ability in the furniture manufacturing organisation shows its effect throughout the entire plant; in fact the writer is convinced that the average manager of a furniture plant is more interested in marketing his product than in manufacturing it.[31]

He suggested that improvements might be made by reducing the variety of parts and limiting the ranges produced. His comments show a lack of understanding of the trade in practice, whereby retailers demanded a wide range of choices, usually changed at six-monthly intervals: this meant that design and marketing had to take priority over actual manufacture. Although it made economic sense to reduce the quantity of parts and limit the ranges, this did not feature within certain sectors of the trade until the later twentieth century.

Notes

1 Mitchell and Rammelsberg of Cincinnati, noted for inexpensive furniture, was one major source of the East Coast's competition.
2 Ingerman, 'Personal experiences of an old New York cabinet-maker'.
3 'A visit to Henkels' warerooms', *Godey's Magazine and Lady's Book*, XL–XLI, August 1850, p. 123.
4 [New York, 1970] *Nineteenth Century American Furniture*.
5 D. Hauserman, 'Alexander Roux and his "Plain and Artistic Furniture"', *Antiques*, XCIII, February 1968, pp. 210–17.
6 Vincent, 'John Henry Belter', pp. 92–9.
7 D. Hanks, 'Daniel Pabst', in *Nineteenth Century Furniture, Innovation, Revival and Reform*, 1982, pp. 36–44.
8 See note 4.
9 In 1850, in Hamilton county, Cincinnati, 27.8 per cent had adapted steam power to operate machinery and by 1870 it was 54.5 per cent. In 1870, Ohio employed more steam power than any other state but its output was eclipsed by many

states. In the New Castle county census in 1870, no makers using steam power were listed. Earl, Craftsmen and machines; Quimby and Earle *Technological Innovation*, p. 315.

10 *Furniture Gazette*, 13 February 1875.

11 *Scientific American*, 6 October 1880. In a discussion on 'general joiners' (multipurpose woodworking machines) the *Furniture Gazette*, 13 May 1875, noted that up to fifty changes per day might be required to adjust the machine, and the time lost was therefore considerable unless the machine-maker simplified the process. It was reckoned that a total of fifty changes in sixty minutes, and one hour for sharpening, would still give an eight hour profitable work time out of a ten hour day.

12 Ettema, 'Technological innovation and design economics'.

13 *Ibid.*, p. 206.

14 Quoted in McIntyre, 'From workshop to factory', p. 31.

15 Tice, 'Knapp dovetailing machine', pp. 1070–2.

16 *Cabinet Maker*, May 1885, p. 234.

17 *Cabinet Maker*, 1 July 1889, p. 25.

18 *Subject Matter Index of Patents for Invention 1790–1873*, Washington, 1874.

19 *Practical Mechanics Journal*, VIII, 1855, p. 78.

20 In 1817, A. Steele's Windsor chair workshop was filled with 151,959 turned spindles, 23,908 stretchers, 4748 bent crest-rails, 305 arm supports and 912 chair bottoms. D. Ducoff-Barone, 'The early industrialisation of the Philadelphia furniture trade 1800–1840', unpublished PhD thesis, University of Pennsylvania, 1985, p. 35.

21 *Ibid.*, p. 54.

22 Ingerman, 'Personal experiences of an old New York cabinet-maker', pp. 576–80.

23 G. Wallis: Rosenberg, *American System of Manufactures*.

24 Work table, Victoria and Albert Museum, Furniture Collection Ref: W2-1944.

25 Chambers, *Things as they are in America*, pp. 151–2.

26 *Ibid.* The factory that Chambers visited was producing 200 dozen chairs per week and 2000 chests of drawers per annum.

27 A. S. Gear and John Gear's pamphlet of machines made by Gear of New Haven, 1868.

28 *Ibid.*

29 *Tales of the Trades*, Philadelphia Merchants and Travellers Association, Philadelphia, 1906, p. 85.

30 United States Commissioner of Labor, *Report on production by hand and machine*, Washington, 1898.

31 B. A. Parks, 'Engineering in furniture factories', *Mechanical Engineering*, XLIII, No. 2, February 1921, p. 85 (abstract from *American Society of Mechanical Engineers Transactions*, XLII, 1920, pp. 881–2).

6   Design

In 1946, a Board of Trade report on the furniture industry laid the blame for its apparent demise firmly in the nineteenth century:

> Our position [as leaders in furniture design] was lost somewhere between the beginning and the end of the nineteenth century, and it seems fairly clear that industrialisation was responsible. On the one hand, production and consumption were separated by channels of distribution, and on the other, the advantage of new machine production was appreciated from the point of view of increased business, instead of from that of improving the furniture as well.[1]

This continuing confusion between the development of the factory and mechanisation, with its supposed impact on design, is also illustrated in a general study of furniture by Grant (1976): 'Technological processes were directly responsible for radically changing the appearance of furniture.'[2]

Is this really possible? Did new techniques and materials really create a style or styles? Is it possible, for example, to show that circular saws were directly responsible for the pillar and scroll of the 1830s, the band-saw for scroll and curve work of the 1850s, and the jig or fretsaw for the bracket and overmantel style, etc.? It may be possible to argue this, but what seems more likely is that designs reflected the cyclical changes that always occurred, ranging from the simple to the complex, whether they were made with the aid of the machine or not. There is little doubt that machines became an enabling factor in the speedier manufacture of furniture, but in the influencing of design they had much less impact. Even in the case of bentwood, in which technique influenced design to some degree, there was always a choice of style that could be applied.[3]

There have been many attempts to define design, and other attempts have been made to analyse the process. For my purposes,

I have divided the design process into four parts: conceptual, stylistic, technological, and material. In any particular case one or more of these criteria may be paramount. The conceptual is the original idea; it might be a new object, such as a 'cosy-corner', or it might be the re-working of an item as traditional as a stool. The stylistic aspect is the input of the decoration, shape, and form that is applied to the material. Technology refers to the knowledge involved in the making process and the associated 'work' that goes with it. The material choice is the decision whether to use, for example, metal or wood. Whatever the process, whether it be traditional cabinet-making, or new ideas such as the use of springs, steam bentwood or machine-printed wood grains, it is evident that technology is only one of a group of stages involved in the design and production of furniture.

However, what is of vital importance is that technology and materials are recognised as the connection between cause and effect in furniture design: they are the link between 'thinking and doing'. They represent the choices or options available to the craftsman or factory-owner, and these very choices determine the relationship between style, material, and technology, which make a design. Indeed it was a feature of the period that the range of choices increased dramatically. In innovative design the forms are not just superimposed: they are the results of a re-thinking of the concept, often to suit new demands or conditions, but the forms also result from an increased understanding of the properties of materials available. Architecture is of course the best example of the inseparability of aesthetics and technology. Therefore the choice of options is circumscribed or aided by any combination of these stages and influences. In other words, technology may be an integral part of changes in design but it cannot be considered solely responsible.

The key to understanding the influences of materials and techniques on nineteenth century furniture is to be aware of the nature of demand, the demand for 'work' in an object, the supply of an appropriate style for the consumer, and the relationship between illusion and reality. Nineteenth century culture is well known for being one of contrasts: for example, the interest in novels of disguise and mistaken identity, the love of games and masquerades, and more importantly, the strict separation of home from workplace, and the distinction between industrial work and amateur work.

The notion of the contrast between illusion and reality will help to explain the impact of materials and technology on furniture design. This approach melds Giedion's constituent and transitory notions of furniture history[4] into one hierarchy of furniture that accepts that consumers' real desires were acknowledged by the trade, who remained uninfluenced by design reforms unless they were commercially viable. These real demands were based on the hierarchy of taste which required tradesmen to offer a range of high-style goods which were suitably differentiated but subtly similar.

The application of 'meaning' to an object by the imitation of particular materials was part of the process of signalling refinement in homes of limited incomes. Sometimes this demanded that furniture objects had more than one treatment and the imagery became very convoluted, e.g. black painted beech-wood in imitation of ebonised imitation bamboo. The imitation of high-style goods was not a new phenomenon in the nineteenth century. Marbling and other paint techniques, scagliola, imitation stone, etc., were all well known to designers and makers in the eighteenth century and before, but it was the ability of the machine to print wallpaper, produce marble linoleum and plated metal, and in the case of furniture, to reproduce parts cheaply, and in increasingly larger quantities, that was significant to the nineteenth century.

It is well understood that nineteenth century cultural commentators were not unaware of this duality. The American novelist Edith Wharton, in *Age of Innocence*, discusses the 'elaborate system of mystification' and noted that 'in reality they all lived in a kind of hieroglyphic world where the real thing was never said or done or even thought, but only represented by a set of arbitrary signs.'[5] In the case of furniture, as long as it looked expensive, fashionable, or whatever other signal was required to be given, it had done its job, its real value and origin was immaterial. Orvell, in his study of American culture in the period 1880–1940,[6] made a comment that has universal application and which explains why materials technology began to have an important role in the period: 'thus the imitation becomes the foundation of middle class culture, exemplifying as Jean Baudrillard would say, the inevitable tendency of technology to substitute the fabricated world for the natural one.'

These ideas of imitation connect with the notions of substitution that Miller discussed in *Material Culture and Mass Consumption*. Miller noted that it was not the actual process of manufacture that was important to the consumer, but the ability of the object to 'stand for' a particular form of production, even though it may be derived from another completely different one.

In addition to this notion of substitution, Orvell noted the Veblenian thesis which was fed by the possibilities of imitation:

at every level of society individuals sought an elevation of status through the purchase and display of goods whose appearance counted for more than their substance. The result was a factitious worth in which the sham thing was proudly promoted by the manufacturer and easily accepted by the consumer as a valid substitute for authenticity.[7]

In 1893, *The Studio* (II, p. 7), in a report on the Arts and Crafts Exhibition, spoke out against the desire to show how much an article cost by its ornament:

Simplicity, in short, is unpopular today when the average advice, if given frankly, would be: 'If you cannot afford a well made piece of furniture discreetly ornamented, choose one badly designed, badly made, with plenty of meretricious ornament, so long as it looks its cost'.

Of course, the actual impact of technology on design or style is dependent upon a number of external factors: historical, cultural, technological, and economic, and any combination of these might restrict the choice of options for a manufacturer or consumer. To understand this, it is necessary to look at the alternatives and see how the evaluation worked.[8] The comparison between the stylistic development of two innovators in bentwood processes, Michael Thonet and John Henry Belter, may give some clues. Belter used his bent veneered panels to create a basis for a carved and decorated piece of Rococo fantasy which, from the front, hid the technique entirely, whereas Thonet successfully introduced a new design vocabulary into furniture-making using bentwood techniques, perhaps originally based on the simple Biedermeier style, which does not hide the technique or the material.

Modernist design critics might have suggested that design standards declined in the example of Belter, while Thonet had not lost faith with the accepted relationships between materials, production, and design. The fact that the Thonet bentwood process had been popular for a very long period of time, signified that it was satisfying demands on the levels of both design and value. However, technical brilliance and design austerity had their price, and this was often as high as in the 'fashionable' furniture that was to be replaced. Cook (1878) thought that:

> One may well despair of getting anything cheap when he finds that even chairs as ostentatiously bare and matter of fact as those made by the Shakers or the Viennese bentwood chairs, cost as much as some to be found in the fashionable shops that make a good deal more show.[9]

The main fear of design reformers was that machines were only capable of copying, therefore progress in design would be slow because the inspiration for machine-made designs would be drawn from the past. The alternative was to return to basic principles. Horatio Greenough, the American sculptor and theorist, distinguished between copyists and the designers who re-thought the fundamental nature of objects: 'Your steam artisans would fill your towns with crude plagiarisms, calques upon the thefts from Pompeii or modern Venice, while the true student is determining the form and proportion of one article.'[10]

Although this passage has sometimes been seen as a precursor of Bauhaus modernism and therefore prophetic, it again misses the point about the nature of the business of making and selling furniture. The customer demanded plagiarisms, copies, and reproductions as symbols, rather than making an objective choice. The way this demand for imitations was satisfied by the industry was not lost on George Wallis. He thought that the alleged bad taste of the public was the result of bad practice, 'fostered to a large extent by a class of persons [manufacturers] whose object it is to crowd as large an amount of work into as small an amount of space as possible and who prefer charging for labour rather than skill and taste.'[11]

More pragmatic reasons identifying the ability of manufacturers to respond to the current taste can be found in other writers. George Dodd, a prolific commentator on the British manufacturing trades, realistically pointed out that 'to command anything like a leading position in decorative art, there must be an untiring attention to new designs, new artistic ideas, new combinations of form and colour and material.'[12] Dodd equated this 'untiring attention' with success for the individual firm, and he also considered it a matter of national pride:

> Among our large establishments, where mechanical skill and fine art meet hand in hand, those which produce the most continuous run of new

designs are those that generally rise to the uppermost place; and it is here that the artistic education of the artisan becomes a matter not merely of individual but of national importance.[13]

Dodd obviously understood the commercial nature of the furniture trade. He also understood the advantages of new technology and choice of materials for both the maker and the consumer.

The role and impact of technology on the design process was noted by the *Cabinet Maker* in 1884:

> ever since the more solid and sensible furniture styles of recent years came into vogue, machinery has played an increasingly important part in the production of cabinet and chair work. The decline of the serpentine forms and the veneering methods of the last decade [1870s] gave an exceptional opportunity to the 'Iron Hand'.[14]

It seems clear that the editor thought that changes in design preceded developments in machine production. The conjunction of the two in the latter part of the century was apparently judicious timing.[15]

However, the continual search for new designs had also created problems for the furniture-makers at the beginning of the century. Martin (1820) discussed the difficulty of producing a design book that would not be out of date even before publication:

> many pieces of furniture are daily falling into disuse, whilst others are introduced, which for a time are considered as indispensably necessary for our comfort ... it must be obvious how impossible it is to lay down precise instructions as to the formation of particular pieces of furniture, where shape and dimensions are continually varying and indeed, were it practicable, it would be necessary, for the reason before stated, that cabinet, [furniture fashions] like female fashions, should be published monthly.[16]

This was only the beginning. By 1853, the author of *Cabinet Maker's Assistant* could claim that 'everyone connected with cabinet-making is aware of the difficulty of obtaining good and novel designs for furniture.'[17] By the end of the century little had changed. In a report on the firm of T. Lawes it was noted that they had a horror of 'running in a rut, by interminably producing articles of the same form and style, and hence the new and artistic designs they are constantly issuing.'[18] Examples of 'novelties' offered by the firm included 'The Handel' combined Music and Writing Cabinets, the

'Louise' Writing and Work Table, and a patent combined Billiards and Dining Table.[19] It was perhaps no coincidence that this firm was also the agent for the machine-made ornamentation produced by an American company.

Reaction towards the introduction of technology and its effect on furniture design and making varied. While some were happy to embrace the machine, others saw it as the beginning of the end. In 1878, the American writer, Harriett Spofford, thought that

> the cabinet-makers and furnishers of today are as capable of producing noble objects as those of the sixteenth century were. They have better woods, better appliances, the best of models, and steam to help them in the rude blocking out. But glue has been their undoing; and they have learned to rely on this fatal steam until it has nearly abolished the individuality of the workman and the life of his work.[20]

Contrary to this were the comments of Lewis Foreman Day. In the *Art Journal* (1885) he wrote that machinery was not bad *per se*, and indeed the link between bad taste and machine-made objects was not a natural one.

> That the great mass of existing manufactured ornament is intolerable need not be denied. But it is not all bad, any more than all handwork is good. Still less is there any inherent reason why a work of Art because it owes something to machinery, should be false in taste or unsatisfactory in effect.

Day went on to point out, however, that machinery has 'opened the flood gates of extravagance', evident in the unrestrained use of ornament. His suggestion that the machine could be an instrument of truth, capable of faithfully representing the designer's plan is revealing: 'A wiser application of the machine to the purposes of the lesser arts might enable us to dispense with the intermediate 'hand' who nullifies in execution whatever in an Art there may have been in the original drawing.' However, his final comments are perhaps the most imaginative and far-sighted: 'The manufacturer's real chance of success lies in showing not only what the machine can do, but what it can do best, better than the craftsman who would compete with it.'

Even so, in 1901, the *Illustrated Carpenter and Builder* was still blaming the machine, rather than the designer of the product, for poor design: 'There are really only two machines in general use which are at war with art, and those are the scroll saw and the shaper, both of which have led to great abuses in design.'[21]

A very perceptive writer in *The People's Journal* (1851) pointed out that it was necessary to raise 'the character of art so as to place it beyond the power of the machine to imitate.' The writer went on to say that if the upper class of society set the trend by fostering art-workmanship, the rest of society would follow: 'for it will be found that each layer of society lives not in itself, but in the one immediately above it.' This in turn encouraged the subsequent moving on of those being emulated and set off a perpetual merry-go-round of styles. Eastlake (1877), however, considered that there had been an improvement in furniture design since the mid-nineteenth century: 'The coarse carving and lumpy machine-made ornament which disgraced our furniture some twenty years ago is being gradually replaced by delicate mouldings and graceful inlay.'[22] It was not only commercial considerations and fear of 'running in a rut' that encouraged changes. Competition and blatant copying led to frequent changes in designs. Whether it was East End scampers memorising designs from the West End shop windows, or neighbouring competitors in Grand Rapids, USA, the problem was the same:

> On account of the rapid growth of our industry in the past few years many persons having invested their money in this business who have no knowledge of, or experience in the trade, they have thought the cheapest way to get designs was to steal them, and they have done so unmercifully, thus compelling the originator to discard them.[23]

As with all design developments, the cyclical see-saw effect that brought previously despised materials or processes back into the limelight, worked in the furniture trade. Solid wood versus veneered surfaces was one of these perpetual see-saws. In a report referring to the Paris workshops of Mamaroz Ribailler et Cie, solid antique furniture was praised over the new productions, using machines as well as veneer as a scapegoat:

> This fashion for antique furniture does rest upon a very reasonable and very logical foundation ... first in its disdain for phantom furniture, which through the perfecting of wood-working machines has arrived at the last degree of veneer, scarcely presenting the slightest degree of solidity.[24]

Contrary to this attitude was the rather matter-of-fact approach recorded during an imaginary dinner conversation, published in the *Macmillan Magazine*. One of the guests said: 'my friend's table is veneered of course, all over, and has two borders of machine carving all round it that are simply glued on.'

The idea that machinery might liberate the designer and enable him to produce inexpensive furniture was an exciting prospect. However there were difficulties. The *Universal Decorator* (1858, p. 106) had this to say about budget furniture:

> a chair, a table, a chest of drawers, or any other article, when sold at a rate to accommodate the purse of the working man, has its intrinsic value even more expressly denoted by its utter tastelessness than by the ticket whose low figure attracts the purchaser. Nothing of the asperity of the thing is even attempted to be softened down by the most trifling graces of ornament.

In an explicit acknowledgement of the requirements of the age, the 1867 Paris Exhibition displayed a class of objects (including furniture) that were supposed to be 'distinguished by the qualities of utility combined with cheapness'.[25] Soden-Smith took little comfort from the displays from a design point of view:

> Utility is the professed aim of everything exhibited; and while it may be admitted that this objective is often ingeniously attained, it is to be regretted in its necessary attainment the workman never deviates into good taste or strays as it were by accident into the slightest appreciation of beauty.[26]

So both commentators demanded that even utility furniture should be softened with some sort of artistic merit. It is little wonder that machine-made ornament was therefore thought ideally suited to meet this demand and at the same time help to keep the cost of the objects as low as possible.

Notes

1 *Board of Trade Working Party Report*, London, 1946, p. 112.
2 Grant, 'The machine age', p. 191.
3 The Thonet catalogue, for example, includes a number of reproduction styles, including imitation bamboo.
4 Giedion, *Mechanisation Takes Command*.
5 Quoted in Orvell, *The Real Thing*, p. 40.

6 Orvell, *The Real Thing*.
7 *Ibid.*, p. 49.
8 It is also useful to inspect records of processes and products that did not reach the market-place. They are indicators of levels of interest even if the objects were never produced. The patent records are of course full of these unrealised ideas.
9 Cook, *The House Beautiful*.
10 Greenough, *Form and Function*, p. 128.
11 G. Wallis: Rosenberg, *American System of Manufactures*.
12 Dodd, *Days at the Factories*, p. 18.
13 *Ibid.*
14 *Cabinet Maker*, 1 March 1884.
15 See the Eastlake style in the USA.
16 Martin, *New Circle of the Mechanical Arts*.
17 *Cabinet-Maker's Assistant*, preface.
18 *Furniture Gazette*, 29 November 1873, p. 543.
19 *Ibid.*
20 Spofford, *Art Decoration Applied to Furniture*, p. 170.
21 *Illustrated Carpenter and Builder*, 21 June 1901.
22 C. L. Eastlake, letter to Spitalfields School of Art, 22 March 1877, reprinted in *Furniture Gazette*, 21 April 1877.
23 [American] *Cabinet-Maker and Upholsterer*, XLI, No. 8, p. 5, quoted in D-A Fillos, 'The American Furniture Trade in the 1890s. The evidence of the furniture trade journals', unpublished MA dissertation, George Washington University, 1982.
24 *Furniture Gazette*, 8 November 1873.
25 Soden-Smith, Report on Class 91, in [Paris 1867] Reports, p. 221.
26 *Ibid.*, p. 222.

7   Conclusion

Imagination demands the real thing and to attain it, must fabricate the absolute fake.[1]

This study of materials, techniques, and technology, and their possible impact on furniture design and style, has identified a number of issues that are relevant to the furniture historian. The re-examination of furniture-making in the nineteenth century has resulted in a re-assessment of processes and materials (see case studies under Chapters 2 and 3); it has also demonstrated that the canonical approach to furniture history, with its celebration of pioneer designers, has tended to ignore (or overlook) the nature of the furniture trade, its processes, and its products.[2] This study has also attempted to relate developments in the nineteenth century furniture industry to wider changes in technology and materials science, by describing what these changes were, and what impact they had on the nature of furniture-making. In this extended conclusion, the three major concerns of this work are summarised, together with some interpretation of their economic and social impact. By analysing these coexisting checks and progressions, it is possible to piece together 'what really happened', thus challenging the misleading statements that have been commonplace in discussions on nineteenth century furniture manufacture.

Machines and associated technology were not responsible for changing the appearance of furniture. They were perhaps, in part, responsible for a proliferation of objects, but they had little influence on the elaboration of decoration or design. They were introduced as an economic measure to assist in meeting a growing demand. An examination of some of the technical aspects of furniture-making in the form of case studies has confirmed this. The construction of cabinets and upholstery, veneering processes, machine carving, and the use of machines have all been examined to show how machines and new processes were only used when there was an economic imperative. The main argument suggests that the enduring nature of the trade allowed it to be bypassed by many potentially useful developments in science and industry. There were, of course, notable exceptions to this process which are discussed in the case studies, but there seems to have been a general 'laissez-faire' tendency which discouraged technical innovation in the trade. Deliberate attempts to be at the 'cutting edge' of design and technology were not considered. This also shows that the notion of technological determinism which argues that there is an inevitable path of progress, does not apply to nineteenth century furniture-making. I have shown that the 'momentum model' of technological change more realistically demonstrates what happened (see Chapter 2, Introduction section). Changes in process were driven by cultural and economic demands and were therefore not the inevitable result of progress.

However, despite the reactionary nature of the trade during the period under review, there is no doubt that it saw a gradual shift from techniques and practices based on individual volition (craft) towards the objective application of knowledge to productions (industry). This had the effect of increasing the options available to the craftsman and the widening of his repertoire. In the case of both material and technique there was a very gradual but inexorable movement towards David Pye's notions of the workmanship of certainty overtaking the workmanship of risk. In other words, there was an underlying trend, albeit slow moving, which gradually influenced the trade towards being a more scientific and structured industry by the early part of the twentieth century. Materials and technology were the enabling factors between the cause and effect of furniture design and making.

In establishing a method or methodology for researching and interpreting the case studies, four main areas for investigation emerged. Firstly, the relationship between new materials and technical developments; secondly, the choice or use of materials; thirdly, the relationship between materials and production methods; and fourthly, the problem of material and style.

Prior to the industrialisation of trades into industries, the choice of materials was limited to a selection of natural timbers, stones, and minor decorative material. Production processes had developed slowly since the sixteenth century and incorporated changes that had been easily assimilated. These could be called 'accepted relationships'. During the nineteenth century, however, the growth in the choice of materials, and in methods of achieving effects, was so rapid that the balance that seemed to exist between material, process, and design was undermined. A greater volume of available material, and more intricate or speedy processes of production meant that 'high-style' designs could be produced more easily. This disturbance of 'accepted relationships' was one of the main impacts of materials science and technology, although it must be remembered that any changes were piecemeal and very uneven.

Records of patents have been one of the key areas of research, since they have helped to indicate the nature of innovation and invention in the furniture business. Case studies of the development of plywood, upholstery springs, metal furniture, papier mâché, and other materials have helped to show that these contributed to a change in the nature of designs; sometimes in a fashionable context which lasted for a limited period, and in other cases as concepts that remained unused until the twentieth century. Whatever the results, the aim of patentees was to use substitutes or improvements to effect cost reductions or advances in product performance. The majority of patents were taken out by non-trade members and were therefore related to the use of non-trade materials, such as metal or papier mâché. The contemporary and subsequent interest in 'patent furniture' is illustrated by the use of the patent label for non-patent objects, and in the preoccupation of historians such as Giedion, with the development of a 'mechanical culture'.

The primary economic factor to have an effect on the use of materials and techniques was the organisation of the trade and its attitude to change. It has often been assumed that most of the later nineteenth century furniture was made in factories.[3] In fact the results of innovation did not bring about this condition. Innovations did indeed do away with some jobs: hand-sawyers, for instance, were in decline due to the introduction of steam-powered saw-mills, but on the whole, innovations appear to have assisted in the creation of a larger workforce.[4]

Secondly, to take advantage of new processes and methods, businesses would have had to invest capital in steam-powered machinery and factory premises. They would also have had to divide their labour by task and process. With certain important exceptions,[5] this was seldom the case in the nineteenth century furniture industry and was only gradually occurring by the beginning of the twentieth century. The trade remained essentially a machine-assisted craft for most of the period under review. The third effect of innovation was the loss of ground by established furniture-makers to other entrepreneurs. The papier mâché, metal furniture, and even the bentwood trade, are all examples of new technology bypassing the traditional businesses. Fourthly, the impact of any development that increased unit value, design or quality was unable to be fully exploited until channels of distribution were better organised, and this had to wait until the early twentieth century when the trade became more centralised.

It has been seen that classic mass production and factory systems were inimical to the organisation of the business and the nature of the demand for furniture. The demand was such that it supported a large number of small-sized businesses who offered a range of differing objects. The lack of integration and amalgamation, combined with a dearth of capital expenditure, worked towards maintaining a status quo. However, a growing turnover meant that some changes had to take place, and it was initially in the primary manufacturing processes that these occurred. This introduction of machines has often been assumed to have made high-class designs available to the general market. It has been shown that this was not the case, and the economic advantages of machines came in cost savings in inexpensive processes, while allowing expensive labour-intensive operations to remain so.[6]

However, this is not to say that some technology was not apparent; it is rather that the results were partial. The nineteenth century produced some very important innovations, for example, upholstery springs and veneer-cutting; others were not effective in the circumstances and remained dormant. All these factors confirm that the trade was a truly traditional one with tralatitious attitudes to innovation and change. With this mental perspective, it is not surprising that any major changes would be slow to become established. The idea of anything like an industrial revolution in the nineteenth century furniture trade is illusory. The evidence has shown that although there were many exciting and innovative possibilities, some of which were developed to a high state of perfection, change was altogether slower than many other trades and industries, and it was not until the second decade of twentieth century that something approaching a modern industry was established.

Notes

1 U. Eco, *Faith in Fakes*, 1986, p. 8.
2 For a further discussion of the new approaches to the study of furniture-making, See E. S. Cooke, 'The study of American furniture from the perspective of the maker', in *Perspectives on American Furniture*, 1988, pp. 113–26.
3 For a clear refutation of this, see Kirkham, 'London Furniture Trade', pp. 166–9.
4 See Table 1 (p. 8) for the growth of employment in the trade.
5 See Table 2 (p. 28) steam power and factories in the cabinet and furniture trades in 1877.
6 Furniture is still not generally seen as a product of high technology: the cachet of 'hand-made', 'solid wood', and 'natural timber' still holds sway over technically more efficient products such as, for example, plywood or veneers.

Bibliography

Ackermann, R., *Repository of Arts*, London, 1809–28.

Adams, J. Q., 'The beauty of machine made things', *House and Garden*, ix, September 1903.

Adburgham, A., 'Give the customer what they want', *Architectural Review*, cli, May 1977.

Agius, P., *British Furniture 1880–1915*, Woodbridge, 1978.

Aitken, W., *The Early History of Brass and Brass Manufacture In Birmingham*, 1866.

Aitken, W., 'Papier mâché manufacture', in S. Timmins (ed.), *Birmingham Resources and Industrial History*, 1866.

Aldcroft, D., 'Technical progress and British enterprise 1875–1914', *Business History*, viii, 2, July 1966.

Amateurs Practical Guide to Fretwork, Woodcarving, Marquetry etc., c. 1875.

Ames, K., 'Gardener and Company of New York', *Antiques*, xcix, August 1971.

Ames, K., 'The battle of the sideboards', *Winterthur Portfolio*, ix, Charlottesville, 1974.

Ames, K., 'Grand Rapids furniture at the time of the Centennial', *Winterthur Portfolio*, x Charlottesville, 1975.

Ames, K., 'Designed in France. Notes on the transmission of French style to America', *Winterthur Portfolio*, xii, 1977

Ames, K., 'Meaning in artifacts. Hall furniture in Victorian America', *Journal of Inter-disciplinary History*, i, summer 1978.

Ames, K., *Victorian Furniture*, Victorian Society of America, 1982.

Ames, K. and Ward, G., *Decorative Arts and Household Furnishings in America 1650–1920. An annotated bibliography*, Henry Francis Du Pont Museum, Winterthur, 1989.

Anstey, B., 'Morgan and Sanders and the patent furniture manufacturers of Catherine Street', *Connoisseur*, clxxxvii, November 1974.

Arbey, F., *Woodworking Machinery Catalogue*, 1873.

Arkell, G. E. and Duckworth, G. H., 'Cabinet-makers', in C. Booth (ed.), *Life and Labour of the People of London*, 2nd series, London, 1903.

Armitage, G., 'Decoration and furnishing', Manchester and Salford Sanitary Association, Lecture, series 8, No. 6, Manchester, 1885.

Bibliography

Art Journal Illustrated Catalogue. The Industry of all Nations 1851, London, 1851.

Aslin, E., *Nineteenth Century English Furniture*, London, 1962.

Aslin, E., 'The iron age of furniture', *Country Life*, CXXXIV, 17 October 1963.

Audsley, G. A., *The Art of Polychromatic and Decorative Turning*, London, 1911.

Ausseur, J., *Tableaux Detailles de la Menusierie*, 1829.

Austen, B., 'Morgan and Sanders. Patent Furniture', *Connoisseur*, November 1974.

Aves, E., 'The furniture trade', in C. Booth (ed.), *Life and Labour of the People of London. The Trades of East London*, London, 1888.

Ayres, W., 'The constructional theory of furniture making; more honored in the breach than in the observance', *Tiller*, I, Bryn Mawr, Pennsylvania, 1982.

Babbage, C., *On The Economy of Machinery in Manufacture*, London, 1832.

Bailey, W., *The Advancement of Arts, Manufactures, and Commerce, or a Description of the Useful Machines and Models Contained in the Repository of the Society for the Encouragement of Arts, Manufactures and Commerce*, London, 2 vols, 1772.

Bale, M. P., *Woodworking Machinery, its Rise Progress and Construction*, London, 1880.

Bale, M. P., *On Saw Mills. Their Arrangement and Management and the Economical Conversion of Timber*, London, 1883.

Bale, M. P., *Handbook Of Sawmills and Wood Converting Machinery*, London, 1899.

Barlow, P., *A Treatise on the Manufacture and Machinery of Great Britain*, 1836.

Barlow, P., *Encyclopedia of Manufactures*, 1861.

Barnett, H. G., *Innovation: The Basis of Cultural Change*, New York, 1953.

Bath, *Furniture Made in Bath*, exhibition catalogue, Holbourne of Menstrie Museum, Bath, September–October 1985.

Batley, H., *A Series of Studies for Domestic Furniture*, The Studio, 1883.

Beckman, J., *History of Inventions and Discoveries*, translated by W. Johnston, 2nd edn, 4 vols, London, 1814.

Beeton, I. M., *Housewifes Treasury of Domestic Information*, London, 1880.

Bemrose, W., *Manual of Woodcarving*, London and Oxford, 1862.

Bemrose, W., *Fret-cutting and Perforated Carving*, London, 1868.

Bemrose, W., *Manual of Buhl and Marquetry*, London 1872.

Bevan, G. P. (ed.), *British Manufacturing Industries*, London, 1876.

Bielefeld, C. F., *On the Use of the Improved Papier Mâché in Furniture, in Interior Decoration of Buildings and in Works of Art*, London, 1843.

Binstead, H., *Furniture*, Pitmans Commodity Series, London, 1918.

Bitmead, R., *The London Cabinet-Makers Guide to the Entire Construction of Cabinet Work*, London, 1873.

Bitmead, R., *The Practical French Polisher and Enameller*, London, 1876.

Bitmead, R., *The Practical Upholsterer*, London, 1876.

Blankenhorn, D., 'Our class of workmen: The cabinet maker revisited', in Harrison, R. and Zeitlin, J. (eds), *Division of Labour, Skilled Worker and Technological Change in the Nineteenth Century*, Brighton, 1985.

Book of Trades or the Circle of Useful Arts, Glasgow, 1837.

The Book of Trades, SPCK, London, 1862.

Booth, C., *Life and Labour of the People of London*, IV, London, 1888 (2nd series, London, 1903).

Booth, L., *The Exhibition Book of Ornamental Designs for Furniture Etc; Arranged for the Hall, Dining Room, Drawing Room, Bedroom Boudoir And Library*, London, 1864.

Boulton, B., *The Manufacture and Use of Plywood and Glue*, Pitman, 1921.

Le Bouteiller, *L'exposition Journal de L'industrie et des Arts Utiles*, Paris, 1834.

Boynton, L., 'High Victorian Furniture. The example of Marsh and Jones of Leeds', *Furniture History*, III, 1967.

Braund, J., *Illustrations of Furniture from the Great Exhibitions of London and Paris*, 1858.

Briggs, A., *Victorian Things*, London, 1988.

Buchwald, H., *Form from Process – The Thonet Chair*, Cambridge, Massachusetts, 1967.

Bullock, W., *Catalogue of Cabinet Fittings*, undated.

Burstall, A., *A History of Mechanical Engineering*, London, 1963.

Buyers Guide to the Manufacturing Towns of Great Britain, 1876.

Byrn, E., *The Progress of Invention in the Nineteenth Century*, New York, 1900.

Bythell, D., *The Sweated Trades. Outwork in Nineteenth Century Britain*, London, 1978.

Bythell, D., 'Cottage industry and the factory system', *History Today*, XXXIII, April 1983.

Cabinet Maker, *A Practical Guide to the Principles of Design and the Economical and Sound Construction of Household Furniture*, London, 1892.

Cabinet Maker, *Furniture and Furnishings 1880–1955*, London, 1955.

Cabinet Maker, *Cabinet Maker Celebrates a Century, 1880–1980*, London, 1980.

Cabinet-Maker's Assistant, Blackie, 1853.

Cassell, *Illustrated Exhibitor and Magazine of Art*, London, 1852.

Cassell, *Cassell's Household Guide to every Department of Practical Life; being a Complete Encyclopedia of Domestic and Social Economy*, London, 1869–71.

Catalano, K., 'Cabinet making in Philadelphia 1820–40. Transition from craft to industry', *Winterthur Portfolio*, XIII, 1969.

Bibliography

Cathcart, R., *The Jacques and Hay Company*, Ontario, 1986.

Chambers, W., *Things as they are in America*, London, 1854.

Chandler, A., *The Visible Hand. The Managerial Revolution in American Business*, Cambridge, Massachusetts, 1977.

Charles, R., *The Cabinet-maker, A Journal of Designs*, London, 1868.

Checkland, S., *The Rise of Industrial Society in England 1815–1885*, London, 1966.

Claney, J. P. and Edwards, R., 'Progressive design in Grand Rapids', *Tiller*, II, Bryn Mawr, Pennsylvania, 1983.

Clark, D. K., *Exhibited Machinery of 1862: a Cyclopaedia of the Machines Represented at the International Exhibition*, London, 1864.

Coe, R., *The Story of High Wycombe Furniture*, High Wycombe Furniture Manufacturers Society, undated (*c.* 1951).

Cohen, L., 'Embellishing a life of labour: an interpretation of the material culture of the American working-class home 1885-1915', *Journal of American Culture*, 1984, pp. 752-75.

Coleman, D. and MacLeod, C., 'Attitudes to new technology. British businesses 1800–1950', *Economic History Review*, 2nd series, XXXIX 1986.

Collins, J., 'Gutta Percha and IndiaRubber', in G. P. Bevan (ed.), *British Manufacturing Industries*, London, 1876.

Complete Cabinet Makers and Upholsterers Guide, London, 1829.

Cook, C., *The House Beautiful*, New York, 1878.

Cooke, E. S., 'The Boston furniture industry in 1880', *Old-Time New England*, LXX, 1980, pp. 82–98.

Cooper, C., 'Production line at Portsmouth block-mill', *Industrial Archaeology Review*, VI, 1, 1981–2.

Cooper, J., 'Victorian furniture. An introduction to sources', *Apollo*, XCVI, 1972.

Cottingham, L., *Smith and Founders Director*, 1823.

Crace, J. G., 'On furniture. Its history and manufacture', paper read of R.I.B.A., 23 March 1857.

Crawshaw, F., *Problems in Furniture Making*, Illinois, 1912.

Crofton, J., *The London Upholsterers' Companion*, London, 1834.

Cyclopaedia of Machine and Hand Tools, 1869.

Dallimore, P., 'Beechwood industry of the Chilterns', *Kew Bulletin*, II, 1911.

Darling, S., *Chicago Furniture. Art and Industry, 1833–1933*, Chicago Historical Society, 1984.

Darrow, F. L., *The Story of an Ancient Art: From the Earliest Adhesives to Vegetable Glue*, Perkins Glue Co., Lansdale Pennsylvania, 1930.

Daunton, M., 'Toil and technology in Britain and America', *History Today*, XXXIII, April 1983.

Davison, H., *The Book of the Home*, I, 1902.

Davison, T. R. (ed.), *Arts Connected to Building*, London, 1909.

Degerdon, W., *The Grammar of Woodwork*, London, 1893.

Dempsey, G. D., *The Machinery of the Nineteenth Century*, part 1–4, London, 1852.

Denning, D., *The Art and Craft of Cabinet-making*, London, 1891.

DeVoe, S., *English Papier Mâché of the Georgian and Victorian Periods*, 1971.

Dickinson, G., *English Papier-Mâché, its Origin, Development and Decline*, c. 1926.

Dickinson, H., *James Watt, Craftsman and Engineer*, Cambridge, 1936.

Dickinson, H., 'Joseph Bramah and his inventions', *Transactions of the Newcomen Society*, XXII, London, 1941–2.

Dickinson, H., 'Origin and manufacture of wood screws', *Proceedings of the Newcomen Society*, 1942.

Dodd, G., *Days at the Factories or the Manufacturing Industries in Great Britain*, London, 1843.

Dodd, G., *British Manufactures*, London, 1844.

Dodd, G., *Curiosities of Industry and the Applied Sciences*, London, 1854.

Dodd, G., *Dictionary of Manufacturing, Mining, Machinery and the Industrial Arts*, London, 1876.

Douglas, B. and Isherwood, M., *The World of Goods*, 1982.

Downing, A., *The Architecture of Country Houses*, New York, 1866.

Duncan, J., *The House Beautiful and Useful*, London, 1907.

Earl, P. A., 'Craftsmen and machines. Nineteenth century furniture industry', *19th Annual Winterthur Conference Report*, 1973.

Eastlake, C., 'The fashion of furniture', *Cornhill Magazine*, July 1864.

Eastlake, C., *Hints on Household Taste in Furniture, Upholstery and Other Details*, London, 1868; revised 1878.

Edis, R., *Decoration and Furnishing of Town Houses*, London, 1881.

Edis, R., *Healthy Furniture and Decoration*, London, 1884.

Ellis, G., *Modern Practical Carpentry*, 2nd edn, London, 1915.

Ercolani, L., *A Furniture Maker, his Life, Work and his Observations*, London, 1975.

Ettema, M. J., 'Technological innovation and design economics in furniture manufacture', *Winterthur Portfolio*, XVI, 1981.

Evans, N., 'A history and background of English windsor furniture', *Furniture History*, XV, 1979.

Exner, W., *Holzarbeitungs Maschinen*, Vienna, 1874.

Exner, W., *Das Beigen des Holzes, ein fur Mobel, Wagen und Schiffbaume Wichtiges Verfarben, mit Besonderer Rucksichtnahme auf die Thonet'-sche Industrie*, Vienna, 1876.

Exner, W., *Osterreiches Holz Industrie*, Vienna, 1907.

Fairbanks, J. C. and Bates, E. B., *American Furniture 1620 to the Present*, London, 1981.

Fairburn, W., 'On machinery in general', in [Paris 1855] *Reports on the Paris Universal Exhibition of 1855*, 1856.

Bibliography

Feinstein, C., *National Income, Expenditure and Output in the U.K. 1855–1955*, Cambridge, 1972.

Fleischman, C., *Trade Manufacture and Commerce in the United States of America*, Stuttgart, 1852.

Flim, M. W., 'Timber and the advance of technology; a reconsideration', *Annals of Science*, XV, 1959.

Flint, R., 'George Hunzinger. Patent furniture maker', *Art and Antiques*, No. 1, January–February 1980.

Floud, P., 'Victorian Furniture', in L. Ramsey (ed.), *The Concise Encyclopedia of Antiques*, I, 1957.

Fores, M., 'Myth of British industrial revolution', *History*, LXVI, 1981.

Forty, A., *Objects of Desire*, London, 1986.

Fraser, H., *The Coming of the Mass Market, 1850–1914*, London, 1981.

Furniture Dealer and Cabinet Makers Guide, 1883.

Galton, F. W. (ed.), *Workers on Their Industries*, London, 1895.

Garenc, P., *L'Industrie du Meuble en France*, Paris, 1957.

Garvan A., 'Effect of technology on domestic life 1830–1880', in *Technology in Western Civilisation*, I, New York, 1967.

Gay, G., 'The furniture trade', in C. Depew (ed.), *One Hundred Years of American Commerce*, II, New York, 1895.

Giedion, S., *Mechanisation Takes Command*, New York, 1948; reprint 1969.

Gilbert, C., 'A windfall of Edwardian furniture catalogues', *Antique Finder*, XIV, No. 7, July 1975.

Gilbert, C., *Introduction to Victorian and Edwardian Furniture by Pratts of Bradford*, exhibition catalogue, Bradford City Art Gallery, November 1979–January 1980.

Gilbert, K., *The Portsmouth Block-making Machinery*, Science Museum, London, 1965.

Gill's Technical Repository, 1827–30.

Gill, T., 'On French varnish for cabinet work', in *Annals of Philosophy*, XI, London, 1818.

Gloag, J., *History of Cast Iron in Architecture*, London, 1948.

Gloag, J., *The English Tradition in Design*, London, 1959.

Gloag, J., *Victorian Comfort 1830–1900*, London, 1961.

Gloag, J., 'The nomenclature of mid-Victorian chairs', *Connoisseur*, August 1968.

Gloag, J., 'Ball, bobbin and ring turning', *Connoisseur*, August 1980.

Gloag, J., *A Dictionary of Furniture*, revised ed., London, 1990.

Goodman, R., *London Cabinet-makers Union Book of Prices*, 1831.

Gomme, A., *Patents of Invention. Origins and Growth of the Patent System in Britain*, London, 1946.

Gonzalez-Palacios, D., *Mosaici e Pitre Dure*, Milan, 1981.

Goodchild, W., 'Economic development of High Wycombe', typescript, High Wycombe Public Library, 1933.

Goodman, J. B. (ed.), *The Memoirs of a Victorian Cabinet-Maker* [the memoirs of James Hopkinson], 1968.

'Grand Rapids. History of a quality market', *Interiors*, November 1952.

Grant, I., 'The machine age; the nineteenth century', in *History of Furniture*, London, 1976.

Great Exhibition, Prospectuses, 1850–1.

Greeley, H., *The Great Industries of the United States*, Hartford and London, 1872.

Greenough, H., *Form and Function; Remarks on Art, Design and Architecture*, 1853; reprint, University of California, 1947.

Grier, K., *Culture and Comfort, People, Parlours and Upholstery, 1850–1930*, New York, 1988.

Guilmard, D., *Le Menuisier Moderne*, Paris, 1860.

Habakkuk, H., *American and British Technology in the 19th Century*, Cambridge, 1962.

Hackney Furnishing Co., *British Homes, Their Making and Furnishing*, 1911.

Hall, J., *The Cabinet-Maker's Assistant*, 1840.

Hall, P., *Industries of London Since 1861*, London, 1962.

Halphen, S., *Exposition Universal de 1867. Examen Detaille des Produits Exposes dans Classe 91*, 1867.

Hamilton Jackson, F., *Intarsia and Marquetry*, London, 1903.

Handbook of Turning, London, 1852.

Handley-Read, C., 'England 1803–1901', in H. Hayward (ed.), *World Furniture*, 1965.

Hanks, D., *Innovative Furniture in America from 1800 to the Present Day*, New York, 1981.

Harrie, C., *Industrialisation and Culture 1830–1914*, 1970.

Harris, R., 'Wycombe memories', *Cabinet Maker*, 1951.

Hasluck, P. N., *The Cabinet Worker's Handbook*, London, 1890.

Hasluck, P. N., *Bamboo Work Comprising The Construction Of Furniture, Household Fitments And Other Articles In Bamboo*, London, 1901.

Hawkins, D., *The Techniques of Wood Surface Decoration*, 1986.

Hawley, H., 'American furniture of the mid-nineteenth century', *Cleveland Museum of Art Bulletin*, No. 74, May 1987.

Hayward, C., 'The seamy side', *Working Wood*, 1981.

Hazen, E., *Popular Technology; or Professions and Trades*, I/II, New York, 1843–4.

Heal, A., 'The firm of Seddon, 1756–1868', *Country Life*, LXXV, 20 January 1934.

Heals Ltd., *Catalogues 1853–1934. Middle Class Furnishing*, 1972.

Heller, H., '*Michael Thonet. The inventor and founder of the bentwood furniture industry*', typescript at the Royal College of Art, London, 1926.

Herve, F., *French Polishers and Their Industry*, 1897.

Heskett, J., *Industrial Design*, London, 1980.

Bibliography

Hesse, E. von, *Machine Tools for Working Wood*, Leipzig, 1874.

Heywood Bros., *Heywood Bros. and Wakefield Company. Classic Wicker Furniture. The Complete 1898–99 Catalogue*, Dover, New York, 1982.

Heywood Co., *Heywood-Wakefield and Co. A Completed Century 1826–1926*, Boston, 1926.

Himmelheber, G., *Biedermeier Furniture*, translated and edited by S. Jervis, London, 1974.

Hjorth, H., *Machine Woodworking*, Milwaukee, 1937.

Hobsbawm, E., *Economic History of England; Industry and Empire*, London, 1968.

Hoffman, W., *British Industry 1700–1950*, Oxford, 1955.

Holley, D., 'Upholstery springs', *Furniture History*, XVII, 1981.

Holtzapffel, C., *Descriptive Catalogue of the Woods Commonly Employed in this Country for the Mechanical and Ornamental Arts*, 1843.

Holtzapffel, C., *Turning and Mechanical Manipulation*, London, 1843–84.

Hope, T., *Household Furniture and Interior Decoration*, London, 1807.

Hounshell, D., *From the American System to Mass Production, 1800–1932*, Johns Hopkins University Press, Baltimore, 1984.

Hughes, G. B., 'English furniture castors', *Country Life*, CIII, 23 April 1948.

Hughes, G. B., 'Mechanical carving machines', *Country Life*, CXVI, 23 September 1954.

Hughes, G., 'Day Gunby and patent furniture', *Country Life*, CXXI, 21 February 1957.

Hughes, G. B., 'The origins of house furnishers', *Country Life*, CXXII, 3 October 1957.

Hughes, G., 'Regency patent furniture', *Country Life*, CXXIII, 2 January 1958.

Hunter, G., *Home Furnishing*, New York, 1913.

Huth, H., *Laquer of the West. The History of a Craft and Industry, 1550–1950*, Chicago, 1971.

Illustrated Guide and Directory of Manufacturers, 1873.

'Improved woodworking machinery' *Scientific American*, XXXIII, 14 August 1875.

Ingerman, E. A., 'Personal experiences of an old New York cabinet maker', *Antiques*, LXXXIV, November 1963, pp. 576–80.

Ingold, T., 'Tools, minds and machines: An excursion in the philosophy of technology', *Techniques et Culture*, No. 12, Paris, 1988.

Janes, R., 'Wycombe memories', *Cabinet Maker*, 4 August 1951.

Jeffrys, J., *Retail Trading in Britain 1850–1950*, Cambridge, 1954.

Jenkins, J., *The Craft Industries*, London, 1972.

Jervis, S., *Victorian Furniture*, London, 1968.

Johnson, A. P., *Manual of the Furniture Arts and Crafts*, New York, 1928.

Johnson, W., *The Imperial Cyclopaedia of Machinery*, London, 1851–6.

Joiner and Cabinet Maker; His Work and its Principles, Houlston Industrial Library, No. 21, London, 1883.

Joy, E., 'Georgian patent furniture', *Connoisseur Yearbook*, 1962.
Joy, E., 'Pococks. The ingenious inventors', *Connoisseur*, CLXXIII, February 1970.
Joy, E., 'The overseas trade in furniture in the nineteenth century', *Furniture History*, VI, 1970.
Joy, E., 'Victorian and Edwardian furniture by Pratts of Bradford', *Antique Collector*, July 1972.
Joy, E., 'Early nineteenth century invalid furniture', *Furniture History*, X, 1974.
Joy, E., *English Furniture 1800–1851*, London, 1977.
Joy, E., 'Woodworking and carving machinery', *Antique Collecting*, XII, April 1978; XIII September 1978
Joyce, E., *The Techniques of Furniture Making*, London, 1970.
Kane, P., 'Samuel Gragg: his bentwood fancy chairs', *Yale University Art Gallery Bulletin*, XXXIII, autumn 1971.
Kirkham, P., 'Recollections of furniture-makers. Labour history, oral history and furniture studies', *Furniture History*, XIV, 1978.
Kirkham, P., 'Furniture-making and the industrial revolution, 1750–1870', *Design and Industry. The effects of industrialisation and technical change on design*, Design Council, 1980.
Kirkham, P., 'The London furniture trade 1700–1870', *Furniture History*, XXIV, 1988.
Knight, C., *A Description and History of Vegetable Substances used in the Arts and Domestic Economy; Timber Trees*, London, 1830.
Knight, C., *The Working Mans Companion*, 3rd edn, London, 1831.
Knight, C., *Knight's Encyclopaedia of Industries of all Nations*, London, 1851.
Knight, E. H., *New Mechanical Dictionary*, Boston, 1884.
Knight, E. V. and Wulpi, M., *Veneers and Plywood*, New York, 1927.
Kranzberg, M. and Pursell C. W. (eds), *Technology in Western Civilisation*, New York, 1967.
Landis, M., 'Henry Hermann', *Antiques*, CIXX, May 1981.
Lasdun, S., 'Victorian magazines and taste', *Country Life*, CLX, 9 September 1976.
Latham, B., *Timber. A Historical Survey*, London, 1957.
Lawford, H., *The Cabinet of Marquetry, Buhl and Inlaid Wood*, London, undated, (*c*. 1855).
Learoy, S., *English Furniture Construction and Decoration 1500–1910*, London, 1981.
Leiss, W., 'Icons of the market place', *Theory, Culture and Society*, I, No. 3, 1983.
Lindsey, G., 'Papier Mâché', in G. P. Bevan (ed.), *British Manufacturing Industries*, London, 1876.
Logie, G., *Furniture from Machines*, London, 1947.
Loudon, J. C., *An Encyclopaedia of Cottage, Farm and Villa Architecture and Furniture*, 1833; revised edn, London, 1839.

Bibliography

Lucie-Smith, E., 'Riches in little room', *Art and Antiques*, September 1984.

Luff, R., 'Chayres with iron work. An account of some late 17th century sleeping chairs', *Antique Collector*, L, April 1979.

McClaugherty, M., 'Household art; creating an artistic home, 1868–1893', *Winterthur Portfolio*, XVIII No. 1, 1983.

McIntyre, W., 'From workshop to factory; the furniture maker', *Material History Bulletin*, No. 19, National Museum, Ottawa, 1984.

McKendrick, N., Brewer, J. and Plumb, J. H., *The Birth of a Consumer Society*, London, 1982.

McNeill, I., *Joseph Bramah, A Century of Invention 1749–1851*, Newton Abbott, 1968.

Macquoid, P. and Edwards, R., *Dictionary of English Furniture*, revised edn, III, 1954.

'Machinery For Carving', Journal of the Franklin Institute, 3rd series, No. 6, June 1845.

Madder, L., *How to Find Out About the Victorian Period*, Oxford, 1970.

Madigan, M., *Nineteenth Century Furniture, Innovation, Revival and Reform*, New York, 1972.

Maiden, S., 'An officer's travelling furniture', *Connoisseur*, CXXXIX, April 1957.

Mang, K., *History of Modern Furniture*, New York, 1979.

Mansfield, H., 'Woodworking machinery. History of its development 1852–1951', *Mechanical Engineering*, No. 12, December 1952.

Marek, D., *Arts and Crafts Furniture Designs: the Grand Rapids Contribution 1895–1915*, Grand Rapids Art Museum, 1987.

Martin, T., *The New Circle of the Mechanical Arts containing Practical Treatises on the Various Manual Arts, Industries and Manufactures*, London, 1820.

Mateaux, C. L., *The Wonderland of Work*, London, 1883.

Mathys, H., 'Patents as a source of information', *ASLIB Proceedings*, IV, No. 2, 1952.

Mayes, L., *History of Chairmaking in High Wycombe*, London, 1960.

Mayhew, H., *London Labour and the London Poor*, London, 1861.

Merlin *John Joseph Merlin, The Ingenious Mechanick*, exhibition catalogue, Iveagh Bequest, Kenwood, London, 19 July–26 August 1985.

Miller, D., *Material Culture and Mass Consumption*, Oxford, 1987.

Molesworth, G. L., *On the Conversion of Wood by Machinery*, 1852.

Muthesius, S., 'Why do we buy old furniture? Aspects of the authentic antique in Britain 1870–1910', *Art History*, XI, No. 2, June 1988.

Neuberger R., 'History and development of the leathercloth industry', *Upholstery*, I, No. 4, July 1934.

Newark Museum, *Century of Revivals, Nineteenth Century American Furniture*, exhibition catalogue, Newark Museum, USA, 1980.

Newlands, J., *The Carpenter and Joiners Assistant*, reprint, 1882.

194

New York, *Nineteenth Century American Furniture and Other Decorative Arts*, exhibition catalogue, Metropolitan Museum of Art, New York, 16 April–7 September 1970.

Nicholson, P. and M., *The Practical Cabinet Maker and Upholsterer*, London, 1826.

North, B., *Autobiography of Benjamin North*, Aylesbury, 1882.

Nosban, M., *Nouveau Manuel Complet du Menuisier, l'Ébéniste et du Layetier*, Paris, 1843.

Novelties, Inventions and Curiosities in Arts and Manufactures, London, 1858.

Olive, G., 'Brass fittings (account of a contemporary catalogue)', *Antique Dealer and Collectors Guide*, April 1977.

Oliver, J., 'In and out of Curtain Road', *Furniture Record*, CLV, 18 December 1958.

Oliver, J., 'East London furniture industry', *East London Papers*, IV, No. 2, The University House, October 1961.

Oliver, J., *Development and Structure of the Furniture Industry*, Oxford, 1966.

Oliver, J., 'The location of furniture manufacture in England and elsewhere', *Tijdschrift voor Econ. en Soc. Geographie*, February 1974.

Orvell, M., *The Real Thing. Imitation and Authenticity in American Culture 1880–1940*, University of South Carolina Press, 1989.

Ostergard, D. (ed.), *Bentwood and Metal Furniture 1850–1946*, Washington, 1987.

Ottillinger, E., 'August Kitschelt's metal furniture factory and Viennese metal furniture in the nineteenth century', *Furniture History*, XXV, 1989.

Otto, C., *American Furniture of the Nineteenth Century*, New York, 1965.

Pain, F., 'Early days in the woodturning shop', *Woodworker*, August 1967.

Paris 1855, *Reports on the Paris Universal Exhibition of 1855*, London, 1856.

Paris 1867a, *Modern Industries; A series of reports on industry and manufactures as represented in the Paris Exhibition in 1867*, by twelve British workmen of the Paris excursion committee.

Paris 1867b, *Reports of Artisans Selected by a Committee Appointed by the Council of the Society of Arts to Visit the Paris Universal Exhibition of 1867*.

Paris 1867c, *Reports on the Paris Universal Exhibition of 1867*, London, 1868.

Paris 1878, *The Society of Arts. Artisans Reports on the Paris Universal Exhibition of 1878*.

Paris 1889, *Reports of Artisans Selected by the Mansion House Committee to Visit the Paris Universal Exhibition of 1889*.

Payne, P., *British Entrepreneurship in the Nineteenth Century*, London, 1974.

Perrin, R., *No Fear No Favour*, High Wycombe, 1986.

Perry, T. D., *Modern Plywood*, New York, 1948.

Pevsner, N., 'The first plywood furniture', *Architectural Review*, LXXXIV, August 1938.

Pevsner, N., 'The history of plywood up to 1914', *Architectural Review*, LXXXVI, September 1939.

Bibliography

Pevsner, N., 'Evolution of the easy chair', *Architectural Review*, XCI, March 1942.

Pevsner, N., *High Victorian Design*, London, 1951.

Peyton, E., *Manufacture of Iron and Brass bedsteads*, 1866.

Phillips, J., 'Patent metamorphic furniture', *Antique Collector*, February 1979.

Phillips, J., 'Travelling and campaign furniture 1790–1850', *Antique Collector*, June 1984.

Philp, P., 'Furniture fittings, locks handles etc.', *Antique Dealer and Collectors Guide*, September, October, November, 1971.

Philp, P., 'Charles Stewart. Furniture Inventor', *Antique Collector*, January 1975.

Pick, E., *Human Documents of the Victorian Age*, 1967.

Pierce, D., 'Mitchell and Rammelsberg', *Winterthur Portfolio*, XIII, Chicago, 1979.

Pinto, E., *Tunbridge Ware and Scottish Souvenir Woodware*, London, 1970.

Plas, S., *Les Meubles à Transformation et à Secret*, Paris, 1975.

'Plywood pioneers' (no author acknowledged), *Hardwood Record*, LXX, Chicago, May 1932.

Poe, E. A., 'Philosophy of furniture', *Burton's Gentlemans Magazine*, Philadelphia, May 1846.

Pollen, J. H., 'Furniture and woodwork', in G. P. Bevan (ed.), *British Manufacturing Industries*, London, 1876.

Portoghesi, P. and Massobrio, G., *La Seggliola di Vienna. Thonet and the History of Bentwood Technique*, Turin, 1975.

The Practical Cabinet-Maker, by A Working Man, London, 1878.

Practical Carpentry, Joinery and Cabinet-making, 1826.

Practical Upholstery, 1883.

Practical Upholstery, by a working upholsterer, Wyman, 1885.

Prosser, R., *Birmingham Inventors and Inventions*, Birmingham, 1881.

Pugin, A. W. N., *An Apology for the Revival of Christian Architecture in England*, London, 1843.

Pye, D., *The Nature and Art of Workmanship*, Cambridge, 1968.

Quimby, I. and Earl, P. A., *Technological Innovation and the Decorative Arts*, Charlottesville, 1974.

Ramond, P., *La Marqueterie*, Dourdan, 1981.

Ransom, F., *The City Built on Wood. A History of the Furniture Industry in Grand Rapids Michigan, 1550–1950*, Michigan, 1955.

Ransome, J. S., *How to Select Woodworking Machinery*, 1891.

Ransome, J. S., *Modern Woodworking Machinery*, London, 1896.

Ransome & Co., *Illustrated Catalogue of Patent and Improved Wood-Working machinery*, 1879.

Ransome, S., *Modern Woodworking Machinery*, London, 1924.

Rapport sur L'Exposition Publique des Produits de L'Industrie Française de 1844, Paris, 1845.

Redfern, P., *The Story of the CWS 1863–1913*, Manchester, 1913.

Redgrave, R., *Supplementary Report on Design at the Great Exhibition*, London, 1852.

Reid, H., *The Furniture Makers. History of the Trade Unions in the Furniture Trade, 1868–1972*, Oxford, 1986.

Richards, J., *A Treatise on the Construction and Operation of Wood-working Machines Including a History of the Origins and Processes of Woodworking Machinery*, London, 1872.

Richards, J., *On the Arrangement, Care and Operation of Woodworking Factories and Machinery Forming a Complete Operators Handbook*, London, 1885.

Roe, F., *English Cottage Furniture*, Phoenix House, 1949.

Roe, F., *Victorian Furniture*, London, 1952.

Rolt, L., *Tools for the Job*, 1965; reprint 1986.

Romaine, L., *Guide to American Trade Catalogues, 1744–1900*, New York, 1960.

Rosenberg, N. (ed.), *The American System of Manufactures: Report of George Wallis*, [on the US Exhibition, New York, 1854] Edinburgh, 1969.

Rosenberg, N., *Perspectives on Technology*, Cambridge, 1976.

Roth, R., 'The Colonial Revival and centennial furniture', *Art Quarterly*, XXVIII, No. I, 1964.

Roth, R., 'A patent model by J. H. Belter', *Antiques*, CXI, May 1977.

Routh, G., *Occupations of the People of Great Britain 1801–1981*, London, 1987.

Rybczynski, W., *Home. A Short History of an Idea*, New York, 1986.

Sable, C. and Zeitlin, J., 'Historical alternatives to mass production', *Past and Present*, CVIII, 1985.

Salaman, R., *Dictionary of Tools used in the Woodworking and Allied Trades 1000–1900*, London, 1975.

Samuel, R., 'Workshop of the world. Steam-power and hand technology in mid-Victorian Britain', *History Workshop*, No. 3, 1977.

Schaefer, H., *Nineteenth Century Modern; The Functional Tradition in Victorian Design*, New York, 1970.

Schmidt, C. H., *Technologisches Skizzenbuch*, Stuttgart, 1865.

Schmidt, R., *Machinery for woodworking*, Leipzig, 1861.

Schmiechen, J., 'Reconsidering the factory; Art labor and the Schools of Design in nineteenth century Britain', *Design Issues*, VI, No. 2, spring 1990.

Schnookler, J., *Patents Inventions and Economic Change*, 1966.

Scott, T., *Fine Wicker Furniture 1870–1930*, Schiffer Publishing, Pennsylvania, 1990.

Seidler, J., 'Transitions in New England's nineteenth century furniture industry: technology and style, 1820–1880', in Kebabian, P. and Lipke, L. (eds), *Tools and Technologies*, Burlington, Vermont, 1979.

Bibliography

Sheraton, T., *The Cabinet-maker and Upholsterers' Drawing Book*, London, 1793.

Sheraton, T., *The Cabinet Dictionary*, London, 1803.

Siddons, G., *The Cabinet-Makers Guide*, 5th edn, London, 1830.

Silliman, B. and Goodrich, C., *The World of Science, Art and Industry, Illustrated From Examples in the New York Exhibition 1853–4*, New York, 1854.

Simmonds, P., *Commercial Dictionary of Trade Products*, 1892.

Sims, W., *200 years of History and Evolution of Woodworking Machinery*, 1985.

Singer, C., *Technology and History*, Oxford, 1955.

Skemer, D., 'David Allings chair manufactory. Craft industrialisation in Newark N. J. 1801–1854', *Winterthur Portfolio*, XXII, spring 1987.

Skull, C., 'Fifty years in the furniture trade', *South Bucks Free Press*, 8 October 1915.

Sloane, S., *Sloane's Homestead Architecture*, Philadelphia, 1867.

Smith, C., *From Art to Science*, Cambridge, Massachusetts, 1979, pp. 324–30.

Smith, J., *The Panorama of Science and Art*, 2 vols, Liverpool, 1815.

Smith, J., *The Mechanic or Compendium of Practical Inventions*, 2 vols, Liverpool, 1816.

Smith, N. A., *Old Furniture; Understanding the Craftsmans Art*, Boston, 1975.

Snyder, E. M., 'Victory over nature, Victorian cast-iron seating', *Winterthur Portfolio*, XX, winter 1985.

Soden-Smith, R. H., in [Paris 1867] *Reports on the Paris Universal Exhibition of 1867*, London, 1868.

Sparkes, I., *The English Country Chair*, Bourne End, 1973.

Sparkes, I., *The Windsor Chair*, Bourne End, 1975.

Sparkes, I., *The Book of Wycombe*, 1979.

Sparkes, I., 'The furniture town', *Oxford Diocesan Magazine*, October 1980.

Sparrow, W. S., *Hints on House Furnishing*, London, 1909.

Spofford, H. F., *Art Decoration Applied to Furniture*, New York, 1878.

Staudenmaier, J. M., *Technology's Storytellers*, MIT Press, Cambridge, Massachusetts, 1985.

Stearns, J. M., *European Society in Upheaval (Social History Since 1750)*, New York, 1959.

Stickley, G., 'The uses and abuses of machinery and its relation to the Arts and Crafts', *The Craftsman*, XI, no. 2, November 1906.

Stokes, J., *The Complete Cabinet-Maker and Upholsterers Guide*, London, 1829 (and later editions).

Strassman, W., *Risk and Technological Innovation; American Manufacturing Methods in the Nineteenth Century*, New York, 1959.

Strattmann, R., 'Design and mechanisms in the furniture of J. F. Oeben', *Furniture History*, IX, 1973.

Sussman, H., *Victorians and the Machine*, Cambridge, Massachusetts, 1968.

Sutcliffe, G. L., *Modern Carpenter, Cabinet-Maker and Joiner*, London, 1911.

Sutherland, G., *An Encyclopedia of Arts, Manufactures and Commerce of the United Kingdom*, London, 1837–97.

Swedberg, R. and H., *Victorian Furniture*, Des Moines, 1976.

Symonds, R., 'English furniture – traditional and modern', *Journal of the Royal Society of Arts*, July 1948.

Symonds, R., 'From craft to industry', *Antiques*, LIV, October–November 1948.

Symonds, R. W. and Whineray, B. B., *Victorian Furniture*, London, 1962.

Talbert, B. J., *Gothic Forms Applied to Furniture and Decoration for Domestic Purposes*, Boston, 1873.

Taylor, Rev., *Scenes of Commerce by Land and Sea or 'Where does it come from?' Answered*, London, 1845.

Thompson, E., *The Unknown Mayhew (Selections from the Morning Chronicle 1849–50)*, 1971.

Thompson, F., *The Complete Wicker Book*, New York, 1979.

Thompson, P., *The Cabinet-Makers Sketch Book; a Series Of Original Details For Modern Furniture*, Glasgow, 1852–53.

Thornton, P., *Authentic Decor. The Domestic Interior 1620–1920*, London, 1984.

Tice, P. M., 'The Knapp dovetailing machine', *Antiques*, XXIII, May 1983.

Tilley, J., 'Industrial Evolution of High Wycombe', typescript, 1958.

Tilson, B., 'Stones of Banbury 1870–1978', *Furniture History*, XXIII, 1987.

Tingry, P., *The Varnishers Guide*, London, 1832.

Toller, J., *Papier Mâché in Great Britain and America*, London, 1972.

Tomlinson, C., *Encyclopedia of Useful Arts*, 2 vols, London, 1854; 3 vols, 1866.

Tomlinson, C., *Illustrations of Trades*, London, 1867.

Trant, J., 'The Krug Bros furniture factory, Chesley, Ontario: Industrialisation and furniture design in the late nineteenth century', *Material Culture Bulletin*, No. 30, Fall, 1989.

Turgan, J., *Les Grandes Usines*, Paris, 1867 and 1884.

Ure, A. *Dictionary of Arts, Manufactures and Mines; Containing a Clear Exposition of Their Principles and Practice*, London, 1839.

Vaughan, A., *The Vaughans, East End Furniture Makers*, ILEA, London, 1984.

Veblen, T., *Theory of the Leisure Class*, Unwin reprint, 1970.

Vegesack, A., *Das Thonet Buch*, Munich, 1987.

Victoriana; Exhibitions of Arts of the Victorian Era, Brooklyn Institute of Arts and Sciences, 1960.

Vincent, C., 'John Henry Belter. Patent parlour furniture', *Furniture History*, III, 1967.

Bibliography

Vincent, C., 'John Henry Belter. Manufacturer of all kinds of fine furniture', *19th Annual Winterthur Conference Report*, 1973.

Wainwright, S., *Modern Plywood*, Benn, 1928.

Walkling, G., 'For the comfort of invalids', *Connoisseur*, CCII, December 1979.

Walkling, G., *Antique Bamboo Furniture*, London, 1979.

Wallace, J. and M., 'From the master cabinet-makers to woodworking machinery', *Transactions of the American Society of Mechanical Engineers*, October 1929.

Walters, B., *The King of Desks. Wootons Patent Secretary*, Smithsonian Institute, 1969.

Ward, G. (ed.), *Perspectives on American Furniture*, New York, 1988.

Ward, J., *The World in Its Workshops, A Practical Examination of English and Foreign Processes of Manufacture*, London, 1851.

Weaver, L., 'Tradition and modernity in craftsmanship. Furnishing and shopkeeping', *Architectural Review*, LXIII, June 1928.

Weaver, L., 'Tradition and modernity in craftsmanship. Furniture at High Wycombe', *Architectural Review*, LXV, January 1929.

Weaver, L., *High Wycombe Furniture*, London, 1929.

Webster, T., *An Encyclopaedia of Domestic Economy*, New York, 1845.

Wells, P., *Furniture for Small Houses*, London, 1920.

Wells, P. and Hooper, C., *Modern Cabinet Work, Furniture and Fitments*, 1909.

Wheeler, G., *Rural Homes*, New York, 1851.

White, J., *A New Century of Inventions, being Designs and Descriptions of 100 Machines Relating to Arts, Manufactures and Domestic Life*, 1822.

Whitaker, H., *The Practical Cabinet-Maker and Upholsterers Treasury of Designs*, London, 1847.

White, W., *White's Directory of Birmingham, Wolverhampton etc and the Hardware District*, 1869.

Whittock, N., *The Complete Book of Trades*, London, 1837.

Whitworth, J. and Wallis, G., *The Industry of the United States,* in *Machines, Manufacture and Useful Arts. Compiled from the Official Reports of J. Whitworth and George Wallis.* 1854.

Wickersham, J. B., *Victorian Ironwork Catalogue*, Philadelphia, 1977.

Wilcoxon, A., *Wholesale Cabinet Makers Trade List*, 1856.

Wilk, C., *Thonet, 150 Years of Furniture*, New York, 1980.

Williams, H., *The Workers Industrial Index to London, Showing Where to go for Work in All Trades*, 1881.

Williams, H. S. and E. H., *Ingenuity and Luxury*, New York, 1912.

Williams, S., *Sophie in London*, London, 1933.

Wilson, C., 'Economy and society in later Victorian Britain', *Economic History Review*, 2nd series, XVIII, 1965.

Winstanley, M., *Shopkeepers World 1830–1914*, Manchester, 1983.

Wood, A. D. and Linn, T. G., *Plywoods, Their Development, Manufacture and Application*, 1942.
Wood, A. D. and Linn, T. G., *Plywoods of the World, Their Development and Manufacture*, Edinburgh, 1963.
Wood, H., *A Useful and Modern Work on Settees, Sofas, Ottomans and Easy Chairs*, London, c. 1830.
Woodcroft, B., *Patent and Inventions 1617–1853. Subject Matter Index*, London, 1854.
Worrsam, W. S., *History of the Bandsaw*, Manchester, 1892.
Wright, C. D., *Thirteenth Annual Report of the Commission of Labor*, Washington, 1898.
Wrigley, E., 'The process of modernisation and the Industrial Revolution in England', *Journal of Interdisciplinary History*, III, autumn 1972.
Wyatt, M. D., *Industrial Arts of the 19th Century at the Great Exhibition, 1851*, 2 vols, 1851–53.
Wyatt, M. D., *The Industrial Arts of the Nineteenth Century. A Series of Illustrations of the Choicest Specimens Produced by Every Nation at the Great Exhibition 1851*, London, 1851.
Wyatt, M. D., *On Furniture and Decoration; Reports on the Paris Universal Exhibition*, London, 1856.
Yapp, G. W., *Art, Furniture, Upholstery and House Decoration*, c. 1879 and 1885.

Parliamentary papers

Royal Commission on Technical Instruction. 2nd Report, Cabinet Making III (211) and iv (77), 1884.
Profiteering Acts 1919–1920. Report of the Sub-Committee on investigation into prices in the Furniture trade, 1919, Cmd 983.
Select Committee on Arts and Manufactures, IV, 1835, Cmd 598.
Select Committee on the Sweating System, 1888 (13), XX, Q. 2143.

Unpublished sources

Auslander, L., 'The creation of value and the production of good taste; The social life of furniture in Paris, 1860–1914', PhD thesis, Brown University, 1988.
Blankenhorn, D., 'Cabinet makers in Victorian Britain. A study of two trade unions', MA thesis, University of Warwick, 1978.
Cooper, C. C., 'The roles of Thomas Blanchard's woodworking inventions in nineteenth century American manufacturing technology', PhD thesis, Yale University, 1985.

Bibliography

De Falbe, S., 'James Schoolbred & Co. late victorian department store furniture', MA dissertation, Royal College of Art, April 1985.

Dennis, G. L., 'American factory-made parlour suites 1871–1901', MA dissertation, University of Delaware, 1982.

Ducoff-Barone, D., 'The early industrialisation of the Philadelphia furniture trade 1800–1840', PhD thesis, University of Pennsylvania, 1985.

Edwards, C., 'Stimulus and response. An investigation into changes in the furniture industry 1880–1920', MA dissertation, Royal College of Art, 1988.

Fillos, D-A., 'The American furniture trade in the 1890s. The evidence of the furniture trade journals', MA dissertation, George Washington University, 1982.

Hallock, J., 'Woodworking machinery in nineteenth century America', MA dissertation, University of Delaware, 1978.

Kirkham, P., 'Furniture making in London c. 1700–1870. Craft design, business, and labour', PhD thesis, University of London, 1982.

Kurzhals, R. D., 'Initial advantage and technological change in industrial location; the furniture industry of Grand Rapids Michigan', PhD thesis, Michigan State University, 1973.

Lowe, D., 'Furniture industry of High Wycombe since 1870', MPhil, London University.

Menz, K. B., 'Wicker in the American home', MA dissertation, University of Delaware, 1976.

Oliver, J., 'A study of the location and migration of the furniture industry in metropolitan England', PhD thesis, London University, 1963.

Roessel, E. H., 'The way we've always made it. The C. Dodge Furniture Co. and the cabinet making industry of Massachusetts', MA dissertation, University of Delaware, 1987.

Magazines and journals

Architectural Magazine
Artizan
Art Journal
Art Worker
Art Workman
Builder
Building News
Cabinet Maker
Cabinet and Upholstery Advertiser
Civil Engineer and Architect's Journal
Decorator
Decorator's Assistant
Engineering and Building Times

Expositor
Furnisher
Furnisher and Decorator
Furniture Dealers and Cabinet Makers Guide
Furniture and Decoration
Furniture Gazette
Furniture Manufacturer
Furniture Record
Gregorys Mechanics
House Decorator
House Furnisher
House Furnisher and Decorator
Illustrated Builders Journal
Illustrated Carpenter and Builder
Illustrated Inventor
Inventors Advocate and Patentees Recorder
Inventors Gazette
Journal of Design
Journal of the Franklin Institute
London Journal of Arts and Sciences
Mechanics Magazine
Mechanics Oracle and Artisans Laboratory
Practical Magazine
Practical Mechanics Journal
South Bucks Free Press
Technical Repository (1–16, 1822–7; *Gill's Technical Repository* 1827–30)
Timber Market and Sawmill Reporter and Furniture Trade News
Timber News
Timber and Plywood
Timber Trades' Journal and Sawmill Advertiser
Times
Universal Decorator
Woodworker
Working Wood
The Workshop

Index

Index

Index

Walker and Sons, 31
Wallis, G., 131–2, 164, 174
Watt, J., 65
Webb, W., 34
wicker, 138–9
Wilkie, J., 112
Winfield, R. W., 120–1
wood, 94–6
  artificial, 60

exotic, 94
second-hand, 44
substitutes, 134–5
Wood Carving Company, 72
Wyatt, M., 54

xylography, 78
xylotechnography, 79